SELECTED BOOKS BY THE AUTHOR

Adventures of a Quixotic Professor: How One Man's Lifelong Passions for Social Justice Bristles Bureaucracies and Sparks a Landmark Free Speech Ruling (Phoenix: Marquette Books, 2021).

The Ivory Tower of Babel: Why the Social Sciences Are Failing to Live up to Their Promises (New York: Algora Publishing, 2011).

History and Future of Mass Media: An Integrated Perspective (Cresskill, NJ: Hampton Press, 2007).

An Interpretive Introduction to Mass Communication (Boston: Allyn & Bacon and Pearson Custom Publishing, 2004).

Global Media: Menace or Messiah? (Cresskill, NJ: Hampton Press, 1999, 2002).

The Menace of the Corporate Newspaper: Fact or Fiction? (Ames: Iowa State University Press, 1996).

Precision Journalism: A Practical Guide (Newbury Park, CA: Sage, 1987, with Suzanne Nichols).

To My Teachers and Professors

Lee B. Becker

Donald Bird

Hazel Dicken-Garcia

Simon Dinitz

George A. Donohue

Sharon Dunwoody

Thomas Flemming

Donald Gillmor

Jerry Hennessy

Richard Lundman

Marco Marcet

Jeylan T. Mortimer

Suzanne Nichols

Edward Roth

Rudolph Schmidt

Henry Schulte

Joseph E. Scott

Phillip J. Tichenor

Roger Tompkins

Dan Wackman

Margaret Y. Willis

"Scholar, professor, author, former newspaper reporter, maverick, and an advocate of First Amendment rights David Demers has written a ... highly readable and thought-provoking book." *–Lucy Heckman, St. John's University Library, Jamaica, NY*

Sociologist "C. Wright Mills defined sociology as the study of intersections between biography and history. By Mills's definition, this book is sociology par excellence. ... By tracing and reflecting on his personal initiatives and activities ..., Demers powerfully illuminates the direction of American society." *–Dr. Kenneth Westhues, professor emeritus of sociology, University of Waterloo, Canada, and expert on workplace mobbing*

"This book is ... incredibly well researched and a very interesting, relevant story. ... Demers has a great voice and manages to tell his narrative without sounding holier-than-thou or just someone with a grudge match." *–Amanda Scott, librarian, Cambridge Springs Public Library, PA*

This book "probes the systemic forces of bureaucracy and patterns of faculty co-optation and complicity that undermine, violate, and fail to defend the Enlightenment ideal of free speech. ... Ultimately ... the basic freedoms of us all hinge on the willingness of individuals ... to stand up and speak out. And Demers's tale is of how the freedoms of us all in the academy, and limits thereof, hinge on those who are 'crazy' enough to call colleges and universities, and ourselves, to our publicly expressed ideals." *–Dr. Gary D. Rhoades, former general secretary of the American Association of University Professors and professor of educational policy studies and practice at the University of Arizona*

This "memoir ... is well paced and ... engaging and thoughtful ... you will find a large interested audience for such a memoir." *–K. W., reviewer, Kevin Anderson & Associates, New York*

"With an approachable and easy style, Dr. Demers uses his life as a means to examine the history of the various sociological theories and trends that have shaped our culture to this day." *–Nancy Barthelemy, archivist, Peabody Institute Library, Peabody, MA*

Demers's "passionate commitment to being a proponent of change emanates off every page as well as his zest for upholding First Amendment issues ... Well worth reading for those interested in journalism, mass communication, and academia. ... The greatest strength of the book is the passion and questioning Demers has. I believe this is an important and relevant look into academic institutions and the responsibilities they have." *–Anne M. Miskewitch, librarian, literature and world language department, Harold Washington Library Center, Chicago, IL*

"The author writes in an easy-to-understand style that makes it very readable." – *Ken Neubeck, Patchogue, NY*

"I loved every minute of this piece ... beautifully written and very interesting." *–Carolyn Walker, book reviewer, Writer's Digest*

"I admire [Demers's] ability to distill some difficult-to-grasp concepts without 'dumbing them down,' ... and [I] laugh at [his] jokes." *–Erin McKnight, senior editor, Kevin Anderson & Associates, New York*

In "some ways the most worthwhile manuscript I've ever read — one that should be published as an exposé on academic politics." *–Dr. Cherri Randall, book reviewer, Writer's Digest*

Demers "persisted as one or two in 100,000 will, and it's persons like him who make civil rights history. He did it not for personal gain, but for principle. ... It's good to see that the *Demers* case has already been cited for its ground-breaking impact on academic freedom. It may well lead to system-wide reconsideration of the faculty-administration relationship." *–Dr. Phillip J. Tichenor, professor emeritus of mass communication and rural sociology, University of Minnesota*

The 2 Gauntlets

A Memoir about Censorship, Workplace Mobbing and the 'Sin' of Doing Nothing

David Demers

Balios Books LLC
Phoenix, Arizona

Printed in the United States of America

Library of Congress Control Number:
2026935495

ISBN: 979-8-218-84576-6

Balios Books LLC
16421 North 31st Avenue
Phoenix, Arizona 85053
623-363-4668 (voice and text)
www.BaliosBooks.com
BaliosBooks@yahoo.com

CONTENTS

AUTHOR'S NOTE

As a young man fresh out of college in the 1970s, I assumed most Americans embraced democracy, free speech and other civil libertarian ideals generated or amplified during the Age of Enlightenment.*

In principle, they do. Millions will even protest in the streets, as the "No Kings Day" protests show.

But defending such ideals is far more difficult when people have something to lose or nothing to gain. Polls show that commitments to principles dissipate quickly when people are asked to defend the right of a communist or fascist to speak in their neighborhoods. The same applies when educators and journalists — those most entrusted with protecting freedom of speech — are asked to defend the speech of colleagues whom administrators have targeted for dismissal or discipline.

This memoir is the story of two such cases.**

The first occurred at the University of Wisconsin–River Falls, where I, a tenure-track journalism professor, helped students publish some controversial news stories. The second took place at Washington State University, where I, now a tenured communication and mass media sociology professor, created a controversial 7-Step Plan to

---

*See page xix for a comprehensive list of ideals.

**Since 2000, at least 1,700 other scholars have faced sanctions over their speech, three-hundred of whom were terminated or forced to resign, according to data collected by the Foundation for Individual Rights in Education. "Public defense of academic freedom is rare," FIRE reports. "While many scholars report receiving private support from peers and others, public backing — especially from administrators and unions — was much less common."

improve the quality of my academic unit.

Administrators at both universities adopted extreme measures to fire me, creating gauntlets of new allegations as I successfully defended against previous ones. At WSU, the president even withheld a state audit of a WSU internal audit which showed that a conflict of interest tainted the university's investigation of me.

What surprised and stunned me more, though, was the lack of response from the 2,300 faculty at those institutions. Not one, including journalism and law professors, publicly criticized administrators for deliberately violating the free speech rights of faculty and students. At WSU, a regional daily newspaper and the campus student newspaper also refused to cover key aspects of the story because of their fealties to that institution and its administrators. The journalists and professors were both complicit — guilty of the 'sin' of doing nothing.*

The consequences of complicity in my case meant I was forced to file two federal lawsuits to protect free speech. I prevailed in both cases, even garnering a landmark federal appeals court ruling (*Demers v. Austin,* 2014; Ninth Circuit) that, for the first time in history, extended constitutional protection for service-related faculty (or shared governance) speech on issues of public concern related to teaching and scholarship.

These free-speech battles play an outsized role in this memoir. But this book also contains many other stories of journalists, professors, administrators and public officials censoring citizens and employees, ignoring democratic processes, withholding public information, and violating the due process rights of citizens. As I look back, I realize that the overarching theme of this book isn't the free-speech lawsuits, per se, but a much bigger social problem: *A systemic lack of commit-*

---

*Before 1865, the term *complicity* typically referred to active participation in an illegal or immoral act. Philosopher and political theorist John Stuart Mill helped broaden its meaning when he wrote, "Bad men need nothing more to compass their ends, than that good men should look on and do nothing." The Holocaust is often cited as one of the most horrific examples of complicity.

ment to Age of Enlightenment ideals. Intellectual as well as political and economic elites are not doing enough to promote, advance, and enact those ideals.

This is especially true when it comes to leveling the economic playing field, which currently is tilted heavily in favor of the wealthy, who have been getting richer at an alarming pace since 1980.* In contrast, more than six in ten ordinary Americans struggle to pay their bills partly because of low wages and because elites have created tax breaks and other rules and laws to benefit themselves. Many ordinary Americans are angry, and my own research on this topic suggests that this disaffection, in turn, has driven many Americans to openly embrace authoritarian politics as well as censorship.* I address this "grand theory" at the end of this book.

This memoir was written for general and scholarly audiences and is an updated and condensed version of a more scholarly book I wrote five years ago (*Adventures of a Quixotic Professor: How One Man's Lifelong Passion for Social Justice Bristled Bureaucracies and Sparks a Landmark Free Speech Ruling*; Phoenix: Marquette Books, 2021). That edition contains detailed endnotes and citations supporting much of the material presented in this book.

In both books, real names are used for litigants, public figures and officials, and the deceased. Pseudonyms are sometimes used to protect the identity of others. Copies of this book have been sent to all named defendants and antagonists to give them a chance to respond without comment from me. Former Provost Warwick Bayly was the only one who responded. His comments are published verbatim in Appendix B.

David Demers
Phoenix, Arizona
July 2026

---

*See <https://www.DrDavidDemers.com/falling-behind.html>.

Foreword By
Joseph Russomanno*

By definition, memoirs are self-reflective. Not all, however, are self-analytic. This one is, and its analysis offers insights that foreshadow what lies ahead.

This includes the author's admission that he suffered from attention deficit disorder, which, he writes, "nourished in me a naivete that propelled me professionally when I became a reporter and a professor. It also enabled me to hyperfocus when I took an interest in a subject."

His self-analysis also includes his belief that he watched "too many" TV Westerns in his childhood, which instilled in him the idealistic notion that justice almost always prevails. "Bad guys raise hell; good guys (often one individual) save the day." Like the cowboy heroes he once watched, David Demers has repeatedly tried to wear the good-guy hat, though some journalists and administrators didn't see it that way.

David's "good guy-bad guy" story is a fascinating tale that begins

---

*Dr. Joseph Russomanno is professor emeritus in the Walter Cronkite School of Journalism and Mass Communication at Arizona State University. He is author or editor of six books, including *Speaking Our Minds: Conversations With the People Behind Landmark First Amendment Cases* (Mahwah, New Jersey: Lawrence Erlbaum Associates, 2002) and *Speech Freedom on Campus: Past, Present and Future* (Lanham, MD: Lexington Books, 2021). He also has written two dozen refereed journal articles, several book chapters, and forty published reviews and commentaries. The news media have interviewed Dr. Russomanno for his expertise on free speech and the First Amendment more than one-hundred times.

in his childhood, where he developed a healthy skepticism that drew him into journalism, which undoubtedly enriched and demanded even more of his skepticism. At its heart was a desire to hold officials accountable by asking tough questions. The inability of others to be held accountable would later become David's nemesis.

A recurring theme emerges in this compelling memoir: the search for truth and the struggle to share it. Some people welcome facts; others reject them; some simply do not want to know. When truth surfaces, they avoid or try to bury it. Heaven help those who bring to light what others would rather keep hidden. What once passed for truth is too often vilified, as are the truth-tellers.

David is a truth-teller. It hasn't been easy. Wherever truth is spoken, there are often those determined to evade or suppress it. David knows these struggles well. He has lived them — again and again. Such episodes often follow the most steadfast truth seekers, people who hold true to a principle many overlook: the public's right to know.

Some devote their lives to discovering and sharing truth. Journalists, writers, teachers, and scholars make their work of it. As a former journalist and college professor, David is among them. This memoir is a testament to that commitment.

Learning about David's stories may lead some readers to conclude that he looks for trouble. I suspect he may agree, but with an important caveat: In the mold of civil rights activist and Congressman John Lewis, he looks for *good* trouble. Lewis wrote, "If you see something that is not right, not fair, not just, do something. We cannot afford to be quiet." David saw things that were not right. He was not quiet. "Life is too short not to stand up for what you believe in," he writes. "Complacency breeds regrets."

One reality David encountered was that academic freedom and free speech on campus, while good in theory, don't always live up to the billing. "I had failed to consider the politics of a small university community," he writes. "Loyalty often trumps principles." As one who spent three decades on a university faculty, I can vouch for the fact that politics can surface and overwhelm issues, perhaps more strongly on the college campus than anywhere.

Many subscribe to the notion that American colleges and universities are glass houses whose inhabitants should refrain from throwing stones. It's ironic that learning on the college campus, often dependent on sharing information, is sometimes limited by the suppression of that very information, the lifeblood of knowledge. The irony is especially acute when it's a journalism school — where free expression rights are fundamental — that restrains a professor's speech. And while larger universities and departments might appear to have the resources to best safeguard the Enlightenment values that David and others value, the people in higher education units also have the larger patches of turf to protect. They sometimes relegate their values in favor of preserving privilege and power.

As much as "truth" permeates this memoir, so does another concept: *justice* — not merely the law-based brand of justice found in courtrooms, but also social justice. How fairly people are treated is a measure of a society and its institutions. Achieving justice invariably requires truth, not only its presence but a general awareness of it. Absent facts, achieving justice becomes less likely. It's therefore no coincidence that *The 2 Gauntlets* embraces both truth and justice, just as its author does.

While David's story culminates with a court case, his memoir is not principally a story of law. Instead, it's the story of what ultimately drove him to become the plaintiff in *Demers v. Austin*, a court ruling that importantly changed the face of public employee speech freedom. The journey is a fascinating and deeply personal story.

The 2 Gauntlets' narrative is sometimes passed through the lens of sociological analysis, not only unsurprising but perfectly appropriate given David's doctorate in mass communication and sociology. He carefully considers the roles of news media and higher education, explaining them by utilizing theories of sociology and economics. Ideas in these areas dominated his research and impressive publication record as a professor. He smartly applies them here.

Although there are scenes that play out afterward, this memoir largely reaches its summit with David's years at Washington State University's Murrow Edward R. Murrow College of Journalism. The

College is named after iconic CBS News journalist, whose brand of "enlightenment journalism" is celebrated here. Referring to Murrow, David writes, "He embraced democracy, free speech, due process, egalitarianism, transparent government, education, rule of law and civil liberties." Clearly, David identifies with Murrow's righteousness, morality and sense of justice.

David would find himself seeking justice repeatedly during his Murrow years. Though he sought reforms that would have benefitted many if adopted, he typically found himself on islands left alone to defend his positions. "No one wanted to be associated with a professor who challenged the power structure." He became a casualty of what in that environment was a common administrator error: conflating "conformist" with "quality professor." Conformity, he discovered, is often rewarded, while venturing "too far" outside accepted boundaries is punished, regardless of where the truth lies.

The WSU stories that David describes are the substance of nightmares for university faculty, past or present. These were situations that defied logic and belong to the world of demented dreams. But David lived them. "None of this made sense," he writes at one point. Agreed! For anyone who ever served on a faculty, this is the stuff of horror tales.

No matter how noble his causes, David became a pariah, a casualty of workplace politics when co-workers and administrators shunned him and his viewpoints. He was both witness to, and victim of, officials who violated policy and ethics: covert, back-channel coverups; communication controlled to hide truth and protect wrongdoers; and conspiratorial strategies hatched to deny fair hearings. In opposing them he notes, "Some administrators just can't stand it when their authority is challenged."

Ultimately, David challenged WSU's authority in court, concluding there was no other way to find justice. He articulately describes how this lengthy clash unfolded. At its core was a plan he developed that he believed would significantly improve the Murrow College's structure and operation, including parts to better serve its students. David and his attorney claimed that because of his plan, the university punished him

— e.g., baseless performance review scores, workplace "mobbing," denial of privileges, harassment and generally making work life difficult. Just as important, his claim included that WSU denied his ability to even talk about his plan. In short, this was a First Amendment case arguing that speaking about the plan should be regarded as constitutionally protected speech. Punishing the speech had the intent of silencing it, creating a chilling effect and violating the First Amendment.

Among the many obstacles David faced in his lawsuit against WSU was a U.S. Supreme Court precedent, *Garcetti v. Ceballos*. That 2006 5-4 ruling severely limited speech freedom by public employees, saying that official, job-duty speech has no First Amendment protection, no matter how important the speech is to society at large. The ruling also limited lower courts that heard subsequent public-employee speech cases like David's, confining their options in how to rule.

For those reasons and others, the *Garcetti* ruling and its rationale have been vigorously criticized by numerous scholars, including David Hudson. In a chapter of a book project that I spearheaded and edited (*Speech Freedom on Campus*), Hudson calls the ruling "awful" and "the Dred Scott decision for public employees" that sacrifices their free-speech rights. Importantly, Hudson also recognizes the significance of *Demers v. Austin*. That impact, the ruling and the story behind it unfold on these pages.

First Amendment rulings like *Demers v. Austin* are each a piece of the puzzle that help to create a portrait of a just society in which the discovery of truth is not merely honored but also encouraged. They allow us to live up to the U.S. Supreme Court-declared national commitment to uninhibited, robust and wide-open debate on issues of public importance. Understanding these cases is a pathway to understanding the nation's potential character as its people strive for the more perfect union inspired by the Framers.

When I taught First Amendment-based courses, I firmly believed that an essential component in understanding these cases is the human element — people. Oh sure, courts, documents and doctrines are important. But without people, those can be empty and meaningless.

People drive the process. They seek truth and justice. They see wrong and try to right it.

The stories of these people are essential in understanding our laws, our rights and our society. David Demers is one of those people. *The 2 Gauntlets* is one of those stories.

DEFINITIONS

Academic freedom is a scholar's freedom to express ideas without interference.

Age of Enlightenment is a broad philosophy of thought that embraces individualism, reason, logic, facts, civil liberties, decentralized power, science, social justice, due process, governmental accountability, economic equity, political equality, separation of church and state, democracy, progress, and the pursuit of happiness. Ideas hostile to the Enlightenment (also called the counter-Enlightenment) include collectivism, dogma, superstition, traditionalism, autocracy, conspiracy theories, political inequality, economic inequity, and asceticism.

Complicity is the act of assisting, participating or knowingly allowing an illegal or immoral act to happen.

Gauntlet (running the gauntlet) is a metaphor that refers to a difficult ordeal or a series of challenges or obstacles that one has to endure.

Workplace Mobbing is the act of using physical or emotional abuse to force someone out of the workplace through intimidation, humiliation, discrediting, isolation, and false accusations.

Part I

FREE-SPEECH DILEMMAS

Chapter 1
Grumpy Judges and Professors

Wednesday, November 7, 2012
Seattle, Washington

The morning of my appeals court hearing has arrived, and I feel like vomiting. I've got that god-awful acidic taste in my throat, which means I'm one step away from the painful involuntary stomach convulsions and the surge of clumpy porridge that brings on the sense of asphyxiation.

Normally I can manage a lot of stress.

But this morning isn't normal.

The hearing in Seattle before a three-judge panel of the Ninth Circuit Court of Appeals will determine whether the First Amendment protects a 7-Step Plan I created to improve the quality of the Edward R. Murrow College of Communication at Washington State University, where I teach. If the court denies protection, professors, and schoolteachers in nine Western states — like the other forty-one states — will have no constitutional protection for on-the-job speech that questions administrators' policies and decisions related to teaching and scholarship.

The hearing also will determine whether I, a tenured journalism professor and mass media sociologist, will be forced out of my job and into bankruptcy. I have accumulated more than $350,000 in legal fees, which is five times greater than my annual salary.

If I lose, how will I support my 12-year-old daughter and spouse?

I am so stressed I pop a beta blocker to block the flow of adrenaline and the emotional state commonly called "stage fright." A colleague once told me that blood-pressure medications are more popular than sex among artists, musicians, and actors. I find that hard to believe, because all of the performing artists I know are sex fiends.

I brush my teeth, shave, and shower.

The beta blocker is working. My heart rate is down. The butterflies are resting.

I'm more confident but not cocky enough to put on a multicolored progressive tie that could offend the three elderly white male judges who will be presiding over this hearing. I play it safe and don a conservative navy-and-red-striped tie and match it with a light blue oxford shirt, tan slacks, and a snappy dark blue sport coat.

Not too rich looking; not too poor.

J. C. Penney right.

It's raining and 43 degrees as I make the short drive from my hotel in downtown Seattle to a parking garage near the William K. Nakamura Courthouse. Court opens at nine, seventy-five minutes from now. I'm meeting my attorney, Judith (Judy) Endejan of Graham & Dunn, for breakfast at Tulio, an Italian restaurant located on Fifth Avenue, adjacent to the courthouse.

Judy arrives right on time in a dark blue pantsuit — garb that's sure to keep the judges' minds on the case and not her attire. We begin our conversation with complaints about the rainy weather because that's what people in Seattle do all winter long. Then she gives me a copy of her prepared notes, printed on a yellow legal pad.

"Is the organization of this presentation okay?" she asks, looking at me through radiant azure eyes that convey a gentle but sure-footed manner. Judy is about my age, 59, though she's smarter than me. I often feel that about other people, but it doesn't bother me. What bothers me are smart people who fail to use their intelligence. Judy's not one of them.

"You might want to reduce the background information a bit in case the judges cut you off," I suggest. I'm no expert on how to argue a case before an appeals court, but I have watched a lot of courtroom TV dramas.

"Good suggestion," she says, adjusting her reading glasses. "Did we miss anything?"

"I don't think so. Nice job."

"You nervous?" she asks.

"Of course. And you?"

"No," she declares.

But I suspect she's a little nervous, too. After all, it's not every day a First Amendment attorney has the privilege of appearing before the second-most powerful court system in the land, second only to the U.S. Supreme Court.

I can tell she's excited.

That calms me.

We walk half a block through the drizzle and enter the ten-story courthouse, which was built just before World War II. The floors are polished starburst-patterned terrazzo with shades of brown and beige. The walls are surfaced with turquoise, mustard and salmon terra cotta panels. Stepped coffers accent the ceilings. The architecture is Art Deco, a style that symbolically reflects an unwavering faith in social progress. My free-speech lawsuit is a form of social progress, too — a call for decentralization of political power, because it asserts faculty have the right to criticize administrators' policies, a process commonly known as "shared governance."

Judy and I ride the elevator to the second floor, and shortly after entering the courtroom, the defendants' state-appointed assistant attorney general, Kathryn M. Battuello, greets us with a professional smile and handshake. I smile, too, but am disingenuous. It's hard for me to respect attorneys who argue against free-speech rights, especially in the name of the state.

The legal brief she filed with the court maintains that I do not deserve First Amendment protection, because my 7-Step Plan does not deal with an issue of public concern. My plan recommended, among other things, that the Murrow College seek national accreditation for its mass media (print and broadcast journalism, advertising and public relations) programs and remove the communication studies (interpersonal and organizational communication) programs from the college. The latter suggestion angered some administrators and all half dozen faculty in that program. None talk to me anymore.

The university's brief also argues that the 7-Step Plan does not deserve protection because it was penned in my role as a public employee, not as a citizen. To support this argument, the brief cited *Garcetti v. Ceballos*, a 2006 U.S. Supreme Court decision in which the 5-4 conservative majority held that public employees have no free-speech rights on the job, even when they find corruption among supervisors. Although Battuello's legal strategy casts her clients as free-speech villains, a federal district court judge in Spokane agreed with her and threw my case out of court in June 2011. Today's hearing will determine whether that judge's decision was constitutional and whether I'm entitled to collect damages and attorney fees if I eventually win the case.

Promptly at nine, three black-robed judges enter the courtroom through a door that blends into the wall behind their seats. Three or four other court cases are scheduled before mine. Time drags, giving me another chance to perseverate on the wisdom of my decision to file the lawsuit three years ago.

"You're crazy," one colleague advised me at the time. "The university is too powerful. It will destroy you and your career."

"Even if you win, you may not even be able to recover your legal costs," another said. "How are you going to support your daughter?"

"Who really cares about your case?" said one government attorney. "Twenty years from now, no one will care."

I console myself with advice offered by Izzy Stone, an investigative reporter and champion of civil liberties who uncovered corruption and abuse of power in American political and business institutions from the 1940s to the early 1970s: "The only kinds of fights worth fighting are those you are going to lose, because somebody has to fight them and lose and lose and lose until someday, somebody who believes as you do wins. ... You mustn't feel like a martyr. You've got to enjoy it."

Very reassuring words, except that, to be honest, I wasn't having much fun. I'd rather win now than become a de facto member of the Joan of Arc club.

When my case is called, Judy leads me to the left side of the inner court area, where I sit in one of the chairs in front of a railing that separates the inner court area from the gallery. Battuello sits at a table on the right side. None of her four administrative-defendant clients show up. This surprises me. Did they feel confident they would win and thus their presence would do little to help their case? Or were they ashamed to show up at a hearing in which their lawyer takes a position opposed to free-speech rights for faculty?

The three judges avoid any eye contact with me. I wonder if they are ever haunted by the eyes of those they rule against.

Judy speaks first because I am appealing the lower-court ruling.

She gets off to a great start.

"This case is not about a petty personality conflict instigated by a lazy disgruntled professor, as the administration would have you believe. Rather, this case is about a professor with a deeply felt view that the First Amendment should protect a professor's speech." She adds that I deserve protection because I submitted the 7-Step Plan as a citizen, on my personal business stationery, not in my role as a government employee. But our legal brief argues that my speech is protected even if I submitted it as an employee.

Several minutes later, the lead judge, William A. Fletcher, interrupts Judy.

My heart skips a beat.

"I have trouble — speaking only for myself — treating that 7-Step Plan as clearly private speech," says Fletcher, who was appointed to the court by Bill Clinton in 1998. "[I]t originates when he is a member of a committee. It's clearly undertaken in tight relationship to his job and the things that he cares about in his job. He is suggesting an important restructuring of two departments. I mean, I have trouble seeing that as purely private speech."

Fletcher's demeanor is pleasant but out of step with what he just said.

"Your honor, might I address that?" Judy asks.

"Yes, please."

"Well, first of all, your honor, the question of whether it is part of his job duties, as this court has said in at least five cases, is a mixed question of fact and law that should be reserved for the trier of fact."

She argues that only one part of my 7-Step Plan — removing the communication studies program from the Murrow College — was connected to my work on a college committee. The other six suggestions were unrelated to the committee's work and, therefore, are private speech.

"You know, I disagree with that," Fletcher strikes back. "The 7-Step Plan ... is a thoughtful proposition for restructuring how journalism is taught, how the faculty is organized, how money is raised. All of that has to do with running of the institution in a very important way."

My heart skips a couple more beats.

Battuello then presents the university's side of the case, asserting that my 7-Step Plan does not deserve First Amendment protection because, among other things, it fails to address an issue of public concern. After all, she points out, I never accused the university of wrongdoing.

Does anyone have a defibrillator?

"Obviously he [Demers] is not accusing the university of stealing money," Fletcher responds, knocking down her argument and restarting my heart. "We're not talking financial malfeasance. But it [7-Step Plan] is very clear that it [Murrow program] is managed in a way that it shouldn't be managed, and he has an important suggestion for improvement."

I appreciate Fletcher's comments, of course. But they don't cheer me up much, because he implies at one point that even if the First Amendment protects my speech, I may not be able to recover damages from the university because of "qualified immunity" — a doctrine that shields government officials from monetary damages if the courts or the legislature do not clearly spell out in advance what kinds of actions violate the Constitution.

"But if victims are denied compensation when offenders violate the Constitution, where's the fairness in that?" I want to add, but don't, because even plaintiffs like me don't have a free-speech right to speak during such hearings.

After the hearing, Judy and I ride the elevator to the ground floor and sit on a bench in the hallway. I stare at the terrazzo floor. My mind flashes back to the many dreadful moments I encountered during the past six years: accusations that I had violated university rules and state law and that I was an incompetent professor. Colleagues who I considered friends now shunned me, including a classmate from graduate school who also had the same Ph.D. advisor as I. The WSU Faculty Senate even refused to allow me a chance to speak with the full Senate about the importance of free speech and my lawsuit. And a faculty grievance committee refused to hear my appeal.

But the biggest disappointment of all was the complicity.

None of the two thousand professors on campus — including three journalism professors, twenty-six communication faculty, and thirty faculty senators — publicly criticized the administration for trying to restrict the free speech rights of faculty. Their professional codes of ethics or professional norms morally obligated them to defend free speech and academic freedom on campus, but they chose to do nothing.

I raise my head and look at Judy. "I'm ninety-nine percent certain we will lose the case," I say, "because Fletcher clearly thought my 7-Step Plan was job-related speech."

I'm hoping she will dispute my prediction.

She doesn't.

She simply says: "You never know until the court issues its ruling."

She is trying to cheer me up, of course.

That's part of her $345-an-hour job.

Chapter 2
THE LONG DRIVE HOME

Wednesday, November 7, 2012
I-90, Between Seattle and Spokane

The drizzle feels colder as I lumber back to my seven-year-old Volvo XC-90 for the five-hour drive back to Spokane, where I live. Drivers who share the road with me on I-90 are oblivious to my anxiety, as I am to theirs.

To treat workplace stress, clinical psychologists often prescribe emotion-dampening drugs and cognitive therapy, which encourages sufferers to change their behaviors and thought patterns. This approach treats the symptoms, of course, but not the cause. The real culprit is the social structure in which they work: heavy workloads, abusive bosses, unfair job performance reviews, back-stabbing colleagues, low pay. Studies show that nearly half of Americans are ready to quit their jobs because of workplace stress.

People feel stressed because control and power in most societies and organizations flow down, not up. Americans love to think of themselves as rugged individualists, but the reality is that the organizations in their lives — work, governmental, educational, religious — exert a lot of control over them. The "collective" is always there, like the hellhound in Robert Johnson's 1937 blues tune, which is now playing on my SUV's Sirius radio channel.

I got to keep movin' ... blues fallin' down like hail ...
Umm-mm-mm-mm, blues fallin' down like hail,
... And the day keeps on worryin' me;
there's a hellhound on my trail ...

My hellhounds don't have glowing red eyes, mangled fur, or even a foul smell. But they, as administrators of a public university with a half-billion-dollar annual budget, are no less lethal. With the stroke of a pen or a tap on a keyboard, these administrative demons can take away raises, promotions, prestigious appointments, preferred teaching assignments and even careers.

I know these things, because this isn't the first time my passion for free speech and civil liberties has gotten me into trouble.

In the late 1970s, when I was a newspaper reporter, I interviewed a hockey coach after he was charged with molesting boys on his team. He confessed to the crime, but my editor removed his comments from my story after the county sheriff, worried that my story might damage the prosecutor's case, threatened to withhold police reports from our newspaper. Three years later, another editor killed a story I was researching about cancer rates in Midland, Michigan, after representatives of Dow Chemical Company, the largest employer in town, complained.

In 1989, the Minneapolis Police Department refused to give my journalism students access to routine reports about crimes committed by police officers, so I filed an open records lawsuit. The case wound its way up to the Minnesota Supreme Court, which released some of the data — enough to show that evidence of racism existed in the police department nearly three decades before the death of George Floyd.

In the mid-1990s, I helped journalism students publish some controversial stories and file an open records lawsuit to obtain access to student evaluations of faculty at the University of Wisconsin–River Falls. Administrators were furious and tried to fire me. They called me lots of names, including troublemaker, rabble-rouser, a professor with a hidden agenda, and, my favorite, sociopath.

Me? A sociopath?

Okay, I confess that when I was about eight years old, I threw stones at a small window in the back of a semitrailer parked in a field composed of knee-high beige-dry grass. I thought the trailer was abandoned. I had no guilt or remorse — until a sheriff's deputy yelled, "We've got your bike."

I knew then that I had committed a crime, so I raised my hands and turned myself in. The deputy was eight feet tall, or so he seemed to me. He threatened to throw me in jail but decided he'd rather talk to my parents.

"They're working," I said, providing a half-truth. My mother was at home.

Fortunately, he didn't lock me up. "I'll be keeping my eye on you, Dave," the peace officer said. "Now be careful on your ride home."

I learned an important lesson that day.

Never throw stones at trucks unless my bike is at my side.

But in hindsight, perhaps the real lesson was "never throw stones at powerful institutions." No one understood this proposition better than Voltaire, the eighteenth-century French philosopher who spent much of his life on the run from the French authorities and the Catholic Church. He extolled the virtues of free speech but also warned of the folly of thinking that science and progress can eliminate injustice and wickedness. His timeless novel, *Candide*, chronicles the adventures of a young man whose optimism and idealism are swept away by the harsh realities of the real world. At the end of the book, Candide concludes that the best course of action is to "tend one's own garden" — to stop trying to make the world a better place because humans are too flawed. In other words, one should become complicit.

Was I a Candide who had not yet learned that fighting city hall is a losing proposition? Would my experiences turn me into a complicit person?

These questions and others swirl in my stress-weary mind as my SUV meanders through the Cascade Mountains east of Seattle, across the mighty Columbia River, and through central Washington's dry rolling hills called the Palouse (rhymes with "caboose") just west and south of Spokane. Geologists believe the Palouse was created when loess, a sedimentary deposit composed largely of silt-size grains that are loosely cemented by calcium carbonate, was carried by winds from glacial outwash plains before and after the Pleistocene ice age. Loess is a nutrient-rich soil. The Palouse only gets about twenty inches of rain a year, so deciduous trees survive only near creeks or riverbeds or from yard watering. Conifers, which need less water, survive best on shady slopes or in low-lying areas.

When I arrive home, my spouse, Theresa, and my daughter, Lee Ann, tame my angst with hugs and kisses.

"I missed you, Dada," Lee Ann says.

"I missed you more, honey," I respond, hugging her, holding back tears of joy and dread.

Family and relationships are the real wealth in life.

They are my garden.

Yet even familial wealth is not untethered by the political, economic and social institutions that rule this land. When universities, government or corporations fire workers or deny opportunities or aid to disadvantaged groups, familial relationships are often harmed and sometimes unravel. In an interdependent world, we all depend upon each other to achieve our goals.

That evening, after tucking my daughter into bed, I headed to my office in the basement to write and distribute via email a news release to several hundred colleagues and news organizations across the country. I've been distributing updates on the free-speech battle at WSU since it began six long years ago, partly because one cannot depend upon the news media.

Although local newspapers in Lewiston and Moscow, Idaho, and the *Chronicle of Higher Education* covered the story intermittently, the two newspapers that I thought would have most thoroughly covered the story — the Spokane *Spokesman-Review* and the WSU campus student newspaper, the *Daily Evergreen* — devoted little space to the lawsuit, despite its obvious man-bites-dog newsworthiness: a journalism professor suing a journalism administrator and three others for violations of the First Amendment.

My goal in writing the news release is to soften what I perceive to be the coming disaster. In the world of politics, losing often leads to the delegitimation of good principles and ideas — at least in the minds of outsiders or the public. And delegitimation, in turn, makes it more difficult to overcome injustices. Don't take my word for it, just ask any civil rights leader.

Although my news release cannot stop an adverse appeals court ruling, it might blunt delegitimation and prepare other free-speech advocates for future battles, as journalist Izzy Stone no doubt would have agreed.

J-PROFESSOR PREDICTS U.S. APPEALS COURT WILL DENY FACULTY RIGHT TO CRITICIZE ADMINISTRATORS

> A journalism professor who filed a free-speech lawsuit against four administrators at Washington State University is predicting the Ninth Circuit Court of Appeals will rule that university professors, as employees, do not have the right to criticize administrators and their policies.
>
> "If I am right, it means the balance of power at universities in Washington State and eight other Western states will be radically altered," said David Demers, an associate professor of communication in The Edward R. Murrow College of Communication at WSU. "The decision will undermine shared governance, a centuries-old principle in which professors share power with administrators when it comes to making decisions that affect university budgets and programs."

When I returned to the university the following day, things were pretty much the same.

Most faculty refused to make eye contact with me in the hallways, especially those from the communication studies sequence — the program that I suggested should be removed from the Murrow College. I felt like Gary Cooper in that classic scene in the movie "High Noon," where the camera pans back and shows Cooper standing alone in the street as the bad guys arrive in town. The townsfolk were too afraid to back him up.

"Colleagues, let's get the rope," I imagined faculty were saying at lunch.

Fortunately, the semester ended with my neck intact.

None of the faculty asked about the court hearing. I wasn't surprised. The university had framed me as an incompetent professor.

Subordinates easily accept the social constructions of their administrators, especially when those subordinates are not the targets.

In another month, I will resign from my position. I was fifty-nine and soon would have access to my retirement funds. I would move back to Phoenix, where I lived for four years during the 1980s. I missed the sunshine and year-round warmth. The timing was also good, because my daughter was graduating from eighth grade in the spring and could start high school in Phoenix in the fall. My wife had completed thirty years of work as a security attendant at a mental institution near Spokane, and so she was fully vested in her pension.

The Appeals Court panel didn't say when it would hand down its decision in my case. Judy estimated three months to two years. I wished for three months. It took ten.

By then, I was teaching a mass media law class in the Walter Cronkite School of Journalism and Mass Communication at Arizona State University.

Judy calls me about twenty minutes before class.

"Dave," she says in a tone of voice that does not give away the outcome, "I've got good news and bad."

My heart skips a beat.

Part II

GAUNTLET ONE

Chapter 3
A Flag Burning and Cockroaches

Twenty Years Earlier
University of Wisconsin–River Falls

Political science professor Jeffrey Gerson just told his students that flag burning was legal and now he's leading them outside to burn one.

It's March 11, 1991.

Forty-two degrees.

Chilly.

But Gerson's mind is on the day's lesson, not the weather.

He's hoping the demonstration will "put a fire under the students and get them thinking." That was not an easy thing to do at the University of Wisconsin–River Falls. A survey of full-time students showed that half of them spent fewer than six hours studying per week. That's about 24 hours less than professors usually recommend.

Poor study habits bothered Gerson. This was his first year at UW–RF, and he was determined to make education a meaningful experience for his students.

So, to set the stage for a vibrant class discussion, he divides the students into two groups. One will take a position in opposition to the 1990-91 Persian Gulf War and the other in support.

Gerson gives a short lecture on the U.S. Supreme Court decision in *Texas v. Johnson* (1989), which held the First Amendment protects flag burning. He escorts his class outside of South Hall, strikes a match, and ignites a four-by-six-inch American flag, which swiftly burns.

"All of a sudden I hear banging," Gerson tells me eighteen years later. "Two or three people in the basement of the building banged on the window. They were angry that I burned the flag, and they opened the window and yelled, 'You could have set the building on fire. We have chemicals down here.' Then one of them went to the telephone. When we got back to the classroom, campus security came to the door and said, 'Are you the one who burned the flag?' I told him I was, and then he went on to comment that 'you created a dangerous situation.'"

The accusations are absurd, of course.

"They were just angry about me burning a flag," Gerson says. "This was their way of expressing it."

A brief time after the flag burning, Gerson tells a newspaper reporter at the *St. Paul Pioneer Dispatch*: "It was a good class. I think people really got into the discussion on both sides. I think it was an effective teaching tool."

Some of his students agree.

"Once he burned the flag, people started talking about it," one student tells the reporter. "I think it was a very effective teaching method. It did spark discussion."

But at least one student thought the flag burning was wrong. She calls her father, a county government official, who complains to UW–RF's top administrator, Chancellor Gary A. Thibodeau.

"If this guy wants to go burn a flag someplace, that's certainly his right," the official tells a reporter after contacting Thibodeau. "But, in his role as a professor, to force students to witness this kind of thing is an abuse of his position."

Thibodeau, a biology professor with a flattop haircut, issues a written statement condemning Gerson for using "extraordinarily bad judgment in his choice of illustrations" and "offensive and insensitive" teaching methods.

Gerson disagrees.

Administrators "should be encouraging faculty to take chances and not try to stifle them." A nonscientific telephone survey of two-hundred faculty by the UW–RF student newspaper seems to agree: Six of ten support Gerson's right to burn the flag.

Gerson had planned to burn another flag in a separate class three days later but changed his mind after more than two-hundred students showed up to protest outside of his classroom. They recite the Pledge of Allegiance, sing the national anthem, and chant "U-S-A."

"Everyone was just out showing their true colors," one student protester says. "There was a lot of patriotism today."

In a letter to UW System President Kenneth Shaw, state Senator Marvin Roshell, a conservative Democrat, says four of his constituents complained about the flag burning. Roshell suggests that "Gerson be returned to wherever he came from and not be invited back." He later questions "whether academic freedom is the best thing we have" and describes Gerson as "inept at his profession."

Gerson is stunned.

He — a presumed expert in politics — had misjudged the politics of some of his students and their parents. Many were from rural areas or small towns in Wisconsin and Minnesota, where conservative values ran deep.

The law is on Gerson's side, of course.

But that didn't matter.

A month later, Gerson is informed that his one-year teaching contract would not be renewed and that he was no longer a finalist for a permanent position in the department.

The head of the political science department later said the decision not to renew Gerson's contract was unrelated to the flag-burning incident. But he conceded that he could "probably not convince a lot of people of this."

I would become one of them.

* * * * *

"Hey, Dave, what do cockroaches and professors have in common?"

I was waiting to make copies of an exam when my new academic colleague and friend, Jimmy, a UW–RF business professor, asked me that question in October 1991.

"They are both disgusting?"

"No, but nice try," Jimmy replies as he collects copies from the machine's tray. "They are the only two species that consume their own kind."

I laugh, of course.

Self-deprecating jokes, whether applied to a person or profession, are always funny. They are a way of telling others that "we're not too big for our britches," even if we know we are.

I was thirty-eight and into my second month of teaching in the journalism department at UW–RF. I was ABD — All But Dissertation, which meant I had completed all the requirements for a doctorate in mass communication at the University of Minnesota except for the dissertation. I would finish that in a year.

Like most scholars starting their first jobs in academia, I was flush with energy, hope and pride. I was going to change the world, or at least part of it.

I was also scared.

To obtain tenure, I would have to publish refereed journal articles and get good teaching evaluations over the next six years. We newly minted professors had heard stories of faculty who had been terminated before the end of that time. We pitied them, of course, but not as much as we pitied ourselves.

My commute from Shoreview, a St. Paul suburb near the University of Minnesota, to River Falls — a city of 10,000 residents located six miles east of the St. Croix River — took about forty-five minutes. During that time, I listened to rock 'n' roll, blues and jazz, especially Ray Charles, Queen, Stevie Ray Vaughan, and Steely Dan. One of my favorite songs was Charles's "If It Wasn't for Bad Luck," which tells the story of a man whose woman has left him and who is kicked out of his house and wrongly accused of committing a crime.

That's why if it wasn't for bad luck, sugar
Oh, I tell everybody if it wasn't for bad luck now, now
I believe, I believe I would have no luck at all
I just wouldn't have no luck at all

I loved that song even though I didn't believe in bad luck. Bad luck is a euphemism for "I screwed up, but I don't want to blame myself."

I know there's no such thing as bad luck because there's no such thing as good luck. People always praise themselves, not luck, when they do something right.

When I started teaching at UW–RF, I was unaware of the Gerson flag-burning controversy, which had occurred about six months earlier. I learned about it from Frank, another UW-RF professor, shortly after I heard the cockroach joke. He said no faculty publicly supported Gerson or his right to burn the flag.

"So, they were complicitous," I respond, shaking my head.

"I suppose so," Frank says. "Are you saying Chancellor Thibodeau was wrong?"

"Depends. He certainly had the right as a citizen to disagree with Gerson's decision to burn the flag. But free-speech advocates could point out that Thibodeau, as an administrator, had a duty to defend Gerson's right to burn the flag. UW–RF even has a rule specifically protecting professors' rights to free speech. Why didn't faculty criticize Thibodeau?"

"Don't know," Frank says, shrugging his lean shoulders. "Fear, maybe. Why should faculty risk their careers and the well-being of their families for an abstract principle like free speech? It doesn't pay the bills, nor does it advance your career."

"But what if all faculty were complicitous? Who would defend free-speech rights on campus?"

"Hey, Dave, as a media sociologist, you know there's no such thing as absolute free speech on campus or anywhere else. Information and knowledge are highly controlled in all societies. There's no protection for people who shout 'fire' in a theater that isn't burning. And what parent wants his or her children to cuss like a sailor?"

Frank had a point. No constitutional right is absolute.

"But too much regulation can deny society access to new ideas," I passionately counter. "Gerson's teaching method might have been unorthodox, but it appears to have succeeded in stimulating a good intellectual discussion among his students. Isn't that a goal of education?"

Frank rolls his earth-brown eyes.

"Should a criminologist shoot someone to teach students that murder needs to be outlawed? All faculty must make choices about what kind of content is appropriate in their classes. You know that."

Frank pauses and shakes his head. "You sound like a hopeless idealist."

He was half right.

I was an idealist, but hopeful, not hopeless. A bit naive and temerarious, too.

I acquired some of these traits while working as a newspaper reporter in the late 1970s. Questioning and challenging government authorities was part of the job. I was never afraid to ask tough questions because my job was to get the news.

In fact, when I took the job at UW–RF, the thought never crossed my mind that it might have been inappropriate for professors to criticize university administrators. After all, the principle of shared governance required professors to speak up when administrators made bad decisions or violated rules or laws. Administrators are supposed to share power with faculty. It's even in the Faculty Handbook.

Journalism professors like me also have an extra responsibility to safeguard free-speech rights, both in and out of the university community. Many people have a poor understanding of the First Amendment. They say they support free speech, but many are not willing to defend the right of communists, fascists, racists, and anarchists to speak out on issues in their communities. The corrective for bad speech isn't censorship, but more speech, as Nadine Strossen, president of the American Civil Liberties Union, was forcefully arguing at the time.

Idealistic?

You bet I was.

As the weeks passed, though, I quickly forgot about the flag-burning incident. Like other professors, I saw it as an outlier, not as an indicator of a systemic problem.

I should have known better.

* * * * *

My first three years at UW–RF were glorious.

I taught courses in reporting, editing, media law, public opinion, and media history — four per semester. This was a heavy teaching load for faculty who were also expected to conduct research. But I didn't mind. I loved both teaching and research.

Although teaching was the No. 1 priority at UW–RF, as it is at most non-doctorate granting institutions, I was hired to help meet the scholarship and research criteria needed for national accreditation of the journalism program. The other three faculty members in the journalism program did not have doctorates and, hence, were not expected to conduct research. Without a scholar in its ranks, the UW–RF journalism program would lose its national accreditation.

The UW–RF students were very likable. They were polite, honest, guileless, and unworldly. They reminded me of myself at their age, except that I studied a lot in college. As Gerson pointed out, most were lazy when it came to their studies.

I attributed this shortcoming to lax enrollment requirements at UW–RF. Although the admissions office looked at a variety of criteria when reviewing applications, the only formal requirement was a high school diploma and a C average. In the early 1990s, this meant the university accepted more than 85 percent of the students who applied.

Although UW–RF faculty often griped about students who did not take their studies seriously, there were some bright, talented students among the five thousand enrolled.

In terms of teaching evaluations, my students rated me slightly above departmental and college-wide averages. I thought I deserved better. I attributed the ratings to my difficult tests, but I had no evidence to back this up and no one has ever told me that I am a charismatic teacher.

Although I had a heavy teaching load, I was a productive researcher. By my third year, I had published one scholarly refereed book and eight refereed journal articles.

The director of our program, J. Michael Norman, was pleased. He gave me high ratings in my annual reviews during my first three years. At the beginning of my third year, he suggested I go up early for promotion to associate professor, which would be effective in my fifth year. Normally faculty are promoted in their seventh year, at which time they also receive tenure. I appreciated his support.

Mike was an amiable man and well-liked by students and faculty, including me. He had worked in broadcasting briefly before earning his master's degree and becoming a professor. He wasn't a social scientist, but he was a good writer. He had authored some books on paranormal phenomena that sold more than 200,000 copies.

Mike had been at UW–RF for nearly two decades and played the lead role in securing national accreditation for the journalism program. This was not easy to do. The standards for accreditation were, and continue to be, high. The UW–RF program had the distinction at that time of being the smallest accredited journalism program in the United States.

The program served about one hundred fifty majors in print journalism and radio broadcasting. The other two full-time faculty included Rebecca, who taught mostly print journalism courses, and Paul, who taught broadcasting courses.

Although my long-term goal was to teach at a research university and work with graduate students, I was grateful for the job at UW–RF. My spouse, Mona, had secured a wonderful job as a market researcher at a major financial institution in Minneapolis. She had earned a master's degree in psychology and we met in Phoenix, where we both worked for a national market research company.

We and our one-year-old fluffy white Bichon Frisé, named Pouché (poo-shay), lived in a middle-class house in Shoreview, a suburb north of St. Paul. The house was built on the side of a hill, so the lower level was a walkout. The sloping backyard was peppered with smooth sumac bushes, whose root system stabilizes hillsides. Their long, thin, fern-like leaves turn crimson in the fall.

The upstairs living room had large windows with a view of a massive sugar maple tree in the backyard. I installed a bird house on the tree. A pair of red-headed house finches moved in, and soon thereafter, the number of occupants grew to five. I planted a garden, which produced big, juicy, sweet Big Boy tomatoes. We had dinner parties at the house. I loved to cook.

I made friends with a divorced mother and her 11-year-old son who lived next door. He and I played basketball in our driveways. I was looking forward to having a child of my own with Mona.

Life was good.

For a while.

Chapter 4
DAMNED LIES AND STUDENT EVALUATIONS

Friday, March 25, 1994
University of Wisconsin–River Falls

I'm grading papers when journalism chair Mike Norman stomps into my office and before I can say "good morning" bellows, "Dave, English chair Bill Turnball wants a written apology from you."

Mike's eyeglasses are cockeyed and his face is flushed.

I've never seen this Mike before. The pudgy man known for his jocular personality is now stern and strident. His baritone radio voice adds authority to his demand for an apology.

I'm blindsided because the whole thing is much ado about nothing.

I had been helping some of my students file a lawsuit to obtain access to student evaluations of faculty. Bill told me at a meeting that his department gives students access to the evaluation records when they ask for them. I passed that information along to the students' attorney, Peter Seguin of River Falls, who was looking for evidence of capriciousness in the handling of student evaluations. Seguin called Bill, who denied that he gave students access to the evaluations.

"Mike, Bill is lying," I say with a composed demeanor, even though I feel my pulse rate jump. I slowly rise from my chair. "He told me in front of other faculty at a meeting that his department gave the evaluations to students who asked for them. I cannot apologize because that's what he told me."

I expect Mike to back me up, not only because I work for him, but also because journalism faculty are supposed to embrace openness and accountability in government.

But Mike isn't on my front page.

"Bill is my friend, Dave," he roars. "You will apologize, or he can destroy your career."

I'm offended that Mike thinks I'm lying. Journalistic blood is supposed to be thicker than water. There's no room for lies in a newsroom or in a journalism college office.

Like flag-burning professor Jeffrey Gerson, though, I had failed to consider the politics of a small university community. Loyalty often trumps principles. Mike's loyalty to his friend was more important than journalistic truth.

Now I have a difficult decision to make.

If I apologized, the controversy would blow over, but the scarlet letter "L" (liar) would be branded to my chest. If I stood by my principles, I could lose my job. But does Bill have enough power to get me fired?

* * * * *

The seeds of this controversy were planted six months ago, when I began my second year as advisor to the campus student chapter of the Society of Professional Journalists — a professional organization that promotes the interests of journalists and the ideals of free speech, open records, and government accountability. At that time, many campuses had student chapters. Most of the SPJ students were juniors and seniors who also worked for the UW–RF campus newspaper, the *Student Voice*.

"Okay, what project would you like to take on this year?" I ask the dozen or so students early September 1993, at the first meeting of the year.

They stare at me and each other for a few seconds before one of them blurts out, "I'd like to see us go after student evaluations of faculty. There are a lot of terrible professors on campus. Why doesn't the university do something about that?

Everyone in the room nods.

For a moment, I wonder if I'm on their shitty teacher list.

At UW–RF, like most universities across the country, students evaluate their instructors and courses at the end of a semester or quarter. The evaluation process is anonymous and most departments on campus treat the evaluations as confidential personnel records. The results are used to evaluate faculty for contract renewal, tenure, and promotion.

"You know," I say, "university officials will argue that those records are confidential, because they're part of a faculty member's personnel file. They'll fight attempts to release them."

"We know that," says the student who raised the issue. "But we still feel they should be public. Students deserve to know how faculty are rated."

Although I was an advocate of government accountability, I hadn't formed an opinion on whether the teaching evaluations should be available to the public. But my opinion was irrelevant. My role as advisor was to help students achieve their goals, not dictate their projects.

I agree to help, even though I'm certain the university will reject the students' request. But this could be a great learning experience, especially if the case goes to court.

To start the process, I suggest that the students contact Wisconsin Attorney General James Edward Doyle, Jr. One of his assistant attorneys general, John Tallman, responds several weeks later, saying Doyle believed the student evaluation records are public data. But Doyle doesn't have the authority to release them. Tallman doesn't elaborate.

On November 17, 1993, the students write to Chancellor Thibodeau, requesting the records, citing Wisconsin's Open Records Law to justify the request.

Meanwhile, I informally canvass faculty opinions on campus.

"Those evaluations contain a lot of false statements and damned lies," one mathematics professor tells me during lunch. "Some are even defamatory. Students don't have to put their names on the evaluations, so they aren't accountable. The records should never be released to the public."

"Students are not competent to evaluate faculty," says another professor. "Those ratings are biased. Faculty who give high grades get high evaluations."

All of the two-dozen faculty and administrators I spoke with oppose release of the records, except one. "Our department allows students to see those evaluations if they ask," says Bill Turnball, chair of the English department, after a college-level committee meeting I am attending ended.

"Really?" I ask.

"Yes," he says with confidence. "If a student wants to see the evaluations of a faculty member, we show them. We've never prohibited access to the evaluations when students request them."

"Do a lot of students ask for them?"

"Not many. We get a couple of requests every year."

Turnball points out that there is no formal university policy prohibiting the release of student evaluations, so his department isn't violating any rules. But most departments, like journalism, still treat them as confidential personnel records and, thus, refuse to release them to students and the public.

On December 2, Chancellor Thibodeau turns down the SPJ students' request to see the evaluations. "There is a need to protect the integrity of the evaluation process ... Further, disclosure of this information could expose the reputations of individuals to damage."

* * * * *

Several days later, Mike appointed me advisor to the campus newspaper, *Student Voice*. The job wasn't too demanding. But it could be controversial.

For example, several months before I took the position, the newspaper published a display advertisement stating the Holocaust never occurred. The ad came from a man who for many years sent the camera-ready print advertisement to college newspapers across the country, hoping some would publish it. Almost none did. But the *Voice* advertising student staffers and the faculty advisor didn't read the content of the ad. The students just pasted it onto the page and accepted the $60 payment check from the author.

Naturally, controversy erupted after it was published. Local newspapers covered the story. Many administrators, faculty, and Jewish and Christian leaders around the area condemned the ad, its creator, and the student journalists. Chancellor Thibodeau also criticized the *Voice* editors, saying they showed poor judgment. Everyone was demanding an apology.

"So, what do you intend to do?" I ask one of the student editors.

"We're going to apologize."

"For what? For not censoring someone? You know, a U.S. Supreme Court justice once said that prior restraint or censorship isn't the solution for evil or bad speech. More speech is. And this is exactly what happened. The local community responded with 'good speech,' and the 'hateful speech' has been drowned out. The system worked. You don't need to apologize. You helped remind the community that this is a society that respects free-speech rights, even for those who hold controversial, false ideas."

A day later the student editors apologized.

I wasn't surprised. The students were scared. Administrators can be intimidating.

Once again, it appeared to me that Thibodeau had failed in his role as administrator to support free speech on campus. He had the right to personally disagree, but he should have defended the students' right to publish the ad.

No disciplinary action was taken against the students or their faculty advisor, to the best of my knowledge. But nationwide, many advisors have lost their jobs over similar kinds of controversies.

To prevent such firings, conventional wisdom holds that the faculty advisor should be a tenured faculty member. Tenure is a guarantee of due process, not a "job for life," as many people assume. The targeted professor has an administrative right to a formal hearing of one's peers and the right to challenge accusers and the evidence. I wasn't tenured, so I was a bit nervous about the appointment. But I had an undying faith that the First Amendment would protect me should any controversy erupt.

My philosophy of advising was simple: Students control the editorial process, even to the extent that they be allowed to publish content that would be offensive or libelous. Of course, as advisor, I would strongly recommend against doing that. But the final decision on publication rests with the students, not me.

* * * * *

In January 1994, I began teaching an advanced reporting course. Several students were interested in looking at faculty salaries. I had coauthored a book on the use of quantitative social science research methods in journalism, and the project was perfect for illustrating what has come to be called "precision journalism." University officials gave us a file containing information on salaries. I employed regression analysis and showed the students how to interpret the results. Then they wrote up the stories.

The findings revealed great disparity in faculty salaries between various departments on campus. Salaries are not based on the principle of equal pay for equal work. For example, business professors who taught research methods were paid about fifty percent more than social science professors who taught similar courses. English professors and librarians made less than journalism and social science professors.

University officials attributed these differences to "market factors." Business professors are paid more, they argued, because comparable jobs in the real world pay more. English professors are paid less, because the pool of candidates for those jobs is far greater than the number of positions available.

In March, I helped the students publish a three-part series for the *Student Voice*, the last of which presented the salaries of all university faculty and administrators. I wrote up the results from the statistical analysis. The students conducted the interviews and wrote the rest of the series. The series was informative and not very controversial.

But some faculty and administrators were angry about their salaries being published in the newspaper. This surprised me because everyone knows salaries for public officials are public data.

“What’s the big deal?” I ask one faculty member who is upset about the release of the salary data.

“This is a small town,” she responds. “People are upset that others know what they make. Faculty are also angry, because it shows who is and who is not being favored by the administration.”

To me, that comment about favoritism justified publishing the salaries — to make government accountable for its decisions. Faculty have a right to know their colleagues’ salaries, if for no other reason than to reduce cronyism. Taxpayers also have a right to know how their tax dollars are being spent.

My democratically driven free-speech journalistic philosophy was appreciated by some students but not by many faculty and administrators, as I would soon learn.

* * * * *

In mid-January 1994, the SPJ students contacted SPJ regional director Terry Rindfleisch, a working journalist himself, who was delighted to help with the students’ attempt to get access to the student evaluations. The regional chapter committed three hundred dollars to hire an attorney.

The freedom of information lawsuit was filed March 23, 1994.

“We’re the reason professors are here,” Tiffany Thibideau, one of the SPJ students, told the *Milwaukee Sentinel*, which published a story about the lawsuit. “We do the evaluating, and we should be able to see them. A student should be able to know what other students thought of a professor.” Two other students also agreed to be named as plaintiffs in the case.

One day after the story appeared, Peter Seguin, a River Falls attorney representing the SPJ students, calls me.

“Dave, do you have any evidence that might help our case?” he asks.

“Yes. An English professor told me several months ago that his department gives the results of the evaluations to students when they ask for them.”

"Great. That shows capriciousness in the handling of the evaluations. Who is the professor?"

"Bill Turnball — chair of the English Department."

"I'll give him a call."

A day later Seguin calls back.

"Turnball denies ever telling you the English Department gave the evaluations to the students."

"That's false, Pete. We talked openly about it at a meeting, and several other faculty were there."

The next day Mike storms into my office, telling me I need to write a letter of apology to Bill. I doubt Bill has that kind of power, so I refuse to apologize.

* * * * *

About two weeks after the SPJ lawsuit was filed, the UW–RF Faculty Senate suspended the student evaluation process. The resolution also contained language supporting Chancellor Thibodeau's earlier decision not to release the records.

In contrast, UW–RF students, in a campus-wide referendum conducted just before the resolution, voted 7-to-1 in favor of the SPJ students' attempts to get access to the records. The Student Senate ignored the referendum, however, and approved a resolution supporting the Faculty Senate and Chancellor Thibodeau. This was a textbook example of co-optation: subordinates often identify more with the power structure than with their own constituents.

"Traitors," one journalism student labeled the student senators.

Yet, ignoring the wishes of the governed is a common feature of America's political landscape. Polls show that a majority of voters want universal health care, increased social security benefits, medical debt forgiveness, and the right to control their bodies. They also want to eliminate super PACs and the electoral college, reduce global warming, and make the wealthy pay more taxes. But, as of this writing, these desires have not been translated into public policy.

In early April 1994, after the UW-RF faculty and student senate votes on access to the student evaluation data, a political science professor whom I had befriended confronted me in a stairwell in North Hall.

"You've done a great disservice to this university, Dave," she says, referring to the lawsuit to make public the student evaluations.

"I am just helping students achieve their goals," I say, shrugging. "Besides, the courts will probably rule against the students. This is a good lesson in how politics works."

I thought she would understand, because she was a political scientist and we had a cordial relationship. I was wrong again. I wondered if she received poor evaluations from her students.

* * * * *

On April 13, 1994, Patrice Peterson, one of the SPJ students who was working at the student newspaper, called me. I was in my office preparing a lecture. I could hear students laughing and shouting in the background.

"Dave, the attorney general's office has ruled that the student evaluations of faculty are public data," she says. "We won the lawsuit. Isn't that incredible?"

I was floored. I never thought it would happen. "Wow, that's incredible, Patrice. Congratulations."

What a wonderful lesson for the students. They made government more accountable to the people.

UW–RF political science chair Jan Hillard told a reporter for the *Student Voice* that "no one was against the evaluations. Faculty were upset that promises stated in department chair manuals about what was public or private were changed."

SPJ Regional Director Terry Rindfleisch told the newspaper that he was surprised and pleased the records were made public so quickly. He said he was proud of the students for pursuing their ideals.

Me too.

* * * * *

In May 1994, the Midwest Region 7 Society of Professional Journalists Board of Directors named the UW–RF chapter the Top Regional Student Chapter, because of its efforts to make public student evaluations.

At the awards banquet, I was surprised when Rindfleisch also announced that the regional chapter had given me a Director's Award for Outstanding Service as faculty advisor. As I got up from the table, my students were smiling and clapping. They all knew about the award but had kept it a secret. I blushed, of course.

Later, the national SPJ Board of Directors presented the UW–RF student chapter with a national First Amendment Award, one of the most prestigious national awards offered to a student chapter.

The student evaluations of faculty were eventually released. The *Student Voice* published them in one issue. No faculty were fired as a result. It was probably the most-read issue in the history of the newspaper. I received a few stern looks from professors as I passed them in the halls and on the sidewalks in the days that followed.

It was a glorious time for the students.

But not for me.

* * * * *

In late May, several faculty and staff tell me privately that my role in helping students sue the university and publishing the faculty salary stories might have an adverse impact on my chances of being retained or tenured. I dismiss the comments at first, because I believe academic freedom protects me. But I had trouble sleeping.

So I wrote to College of Liberal Arts and Sciences Dean Cal Stricter, Mike Norman's superior and friend, asking whether my involvement in the SPJ lawsuit and faculty salary project could "be used to deny me tenure, or are tenure decisions based solely on one's performance in teaching, research and community service?"

Stricter didn't pull any punches.

"Yes, they can."

Holy shit!

Meanwhile, tensions were building in the journalism office.

Rebecca stopped interacting with me. Paul empathized but would not publicly defend the free-speech issues underlying my case. To be fair, I had no right to expect either of those two faculty members to take my side in the dispute. However, I did believe they had a professional obligation to defend free speech on campus.

As the days passed, the number of complaints about me grew. Paul told me that faculty from various departments across the campus complained often about me over lunch. I used to be invited to those lunches.

Mike told me that one of them even asked, "What's Demers's hidden agenda?" Another faculty member told a journalism student, "Demers is a sociopath."

The whole thing was surreal.

And it was taking a mental and physical toll on me.

I was only getting about four or five hours of sleep a night. I was short-tempered. I wasn't just worried about losing a job — I was worried about losing my career.

What university would hire a professor who has been fired from his job?

Yet, part of me was still in denial.

I kept telling myself that the university couldn't fire me. After all, SPJ, the nation's leading professional journalism organization, had just given the students and me awards for our work. I had better-than-average student evaluations and an outstanding publication record; in fact, I had more publications than most of the full professors on campus. I had published one book, ten refereed articles and one refereed seventy-five page monograph, and my conference papers had won four national research awards. Mike even supported my decision to go up early for promotion to associate professor.

Surely the principle of academic freedom would also protect me. The American Association of University Professors, which American philosopher John Dewey helped to create, defined academic freedom as encompassing "the right of faculty to full freedom in research and in the publication of results, freedom in the classroom in discussing their subject."

Yes, I am on solid ground, I tried to reassure myself.

But as Johann Wolfgang von Goethe once said, "With wisdom grows doubt."

I called an attorney.

Chapter 5
'YOU'VE GOT NO CASE'

July 1994
Attorney's Office, Madison

The middle-aged attorney with black-rimmed eyeglasses leans forward in his chair and clasps his hands. "If they decide to fire you, you'll lose."

"You're kidding," I moan. "What about academic freedom?"

My spouse, Mona, and I are sitting in the office of Jay Willardson, an employment attorney in Madison, Wisconsin, which is a five-hour drive from our home in Shoreview, Minnesota. A framed diploma on the wall says he earned his Juris Doctor degree from the University of Wisconsin–Madison. I got Jay's name from a colleague at the University of Minnesota, where I had earned my Ph.D.

The meeting came shortly after I had learned that I could be fired for my role in helping students file a lawsuit to obtain access to student evaluations and to publish stories about faculty salaries. I gave Jay a ten-minute summary of my free-speech case, and he didn't mince words.

"Listen, no one wins those cases. The only cases that win are those arising from the protected categories. If you're a woman, a minority, over age fifty, or have a unique set of religious beliefs, you might have a chance. But none of those apply to you, and even if they did, the university will create a host of other reasons to fire you."

I feel light-headed.

"Right now, university officials are probably developing a long list of things to hang you on," he continues, "and your boss and other faculty and administrators are actively helping to develop that list.

Academic freedom and the First Amendment are noble ideals, but it is virtually impossible to win a lawsuit using them as a defense. I'm sorry. I wish I could be more positive, but the legal system doesn't really provide much protection for faculty who speak their minds."

How can that be?

Although I taught courses in mass media law and knew a fair amount about the First Amendment, I was no expert on free speech in the academy. I knew the courts had generally held that the First Amendment protects controversial speech uttered in the classroom and in scholarship. But what about my service-related efforts to help SPJ students obtain access to student evaluations and publish controversial stories? Aren't they protected, too?

What I didn't realize at the time is that the federal appeals courts had never extended constitutional protection for on-the-job service-related faculty speech. In fact, in 2006, the U.S. Supreme Court ruled that government employees have no free-speech rights on the job *(Garcetti v. Cabellos*). Faculty across the country could be fired for the things they said in committee meetings or in the hallways. Some were. In practice, though, most administrators at most institutions tolerate criticism from faculty, because administrators hold most of the power. Bullies on the playground don't really care about their victims. Open-minded administrators also appreciate faculty feedback and criticism.

To combat the cognitive dissonance building in me, I convinced myself that Jay was speaking beyond his realm of knowledge. After all, he was an employment attorney, not an expert on the First Amendment. Yes, he could be wrong. But for the moment he was the only hope I had. I gave him a thousand-dollar retainer, and he gave me advice on navigating the bureaucratic backwaters.

"Do your job, keep copies of everything, keep communicating with your boss, and keep contributing to departmental goals."

I am crestfallen on the drive back home.

Mona could feel my angst and conjures up an antidote. "I've got a book that I think you'll find inspirational, Dave. You've got a lot in common with the main character."

The book was Ayn Rand's *The Fountainhead,* which chronicles the adventures of an architect who refuses to compromise his principles. In the end, he defeats his enemies and gets the woman of his dreams. I read the book in the days that followed.

Mona was right — the story lifted my spirits, even though I found Rand's extremist form of individualism difficult to swallow. Her theory provides no room for compassion, as this quote from Howard Roark, the book's protagonist, shows: "Independence is the only gauge of human virtue and value. What a man is and makes of himself; not what he has or hasn't done for others. There is no substitute for personal dignity."

I disagreed.

The fight for free speech and civil liberties isn't a fight for any one individual.

It's a fight for everyone, and its purpose is to check power.

* * * * *

I had hoped the summer of 1994 would cool things down at the university.

It didn't.

When school resumed in fall, Mike and the journalism faculty continued to shun me. I was excluded from some of the decisions affecting the department.

The stress was getting to me, but I didn't realize how much until Patrice, one of my students who previously let me know that SPJ had won access to student evaluations, told me that I was "no fun anymore." She was one of the top students in our program. She was about my age, around forty-two, and we eventually became lifelong friends. "What's happened to you?"

She was right.

I didn't laugh or joke anymore. I was always serious and obsessed with the details of the dispute. It was difficult to put it out of my mind.

"My apologies, Patrice. You're right. I'm worried about losing my career."

Patrice sympathized but there was nothing she could do, nor should she get involved. She was a student and had good relations with Mike and Rebecca. This was not a matter for a student. It was between the administration and me.

But I deeply appreciated her support and friendship.

The next day I scheduled an appointment with a psychiatrist. After fifteen minutes he rendered his diagnosis: "You're suffering from clinical depression."

I was stunned and relieved at the same time. Stunned because I thought I was tough enough to manage this ordeal. Relieved because now there was hope I could get more sleep. The shrink put me on an anti-depressant and a non-narcotic sleeping aid. Five weeks later I was a new man. Joy and purpose were back in my life. I would need that to deal with the events to come.

* * * * *

As the weeks passed, things at the university didn't improve.

So, I followed the advice of George Washington and other military experts, "The best defense is a good offense." I informed a staff member and Jimmy, my business department colleague, that I had hired an attorney. My goal was to get administrators off my back — to let them know that I was prepared to fight this out.

But my plan backfired.

When Mike heard the news, he reduced his interactions with me even more.

I became persona non grata.

Now I understood why my high school English teacher forced me and my fellow students to write essays about the Titan Prometheus, who defied Zeus and gave humans fire, knowledge, and culture. In response, Zeus chained him to a rock, and a buzzard would pluck out his liver every day. Prometheus declared:

Behold me bound, a God to evil doomed
The foe of Zeus, and held in hatred by all Gods
Who tread the courts of Zeus: And this for my great love,

Too great, for mortal men.

In other words, Prometheus loved humans so much that he sacrificed himself.

To be honest, I had no intention of sacrificing myself. I loved my liver and my career.

Protecting free speech was my passion, though. If university administrators can punish faculty who help student journalists cover controversial issues on campus, then what's to stop them from punishing faculty who question ill-conceived administrative policies or decisions? Although I didn't want to sacrifice my career, I wouldn't sacrifice my principles to keep it.

God, I was naive.

* * * * *

University administrators and professors did not understand my passion for free speech. I was simply refusing to accept the "social ethic" that former *Fortune* editor-turned-sociology professor William H. Whyte Jr. perceptively identified in his famous 1956 book, *The Organization Man*. To succeed in corporate or bureaucratic America, he argued, individuals must embrace the collective and give up much of their individuality and creativity.

Whyte defined the social ethic as that "contemporary body of thought which makes morally legitimate the pressures of society against the individual." In plain English, the social ethic justifies the repressive power of the collective over individuals and fuels complicity.

The social ethic encompassed three beliefs: (1) The group, not the individual, is the primary source of creativity; (2) Belongingness is the ultimate need of the individual; and (3) Scientific methods should be used to achieve belongingness.

The opposite of the social ethic is the Protestant ethic, which Whyte defined as the "pursuit of individual salvation through hard work, thrift, and competitive struggle."

Modern complex bureaucratic organizations cannot function

effectively if their workers or participants embrace the Protestant ethic. That's because cooperation and teamwork, not competition and individualism, are necessary to get things done. The social ethic assumes that group decision-making is superior to individual decision-making.

Whyte disputed that idea. He studied top executives at major corporations and found that they were risk-averse because they wanted to keep their high-paying jobs.

In modern organizations, workers give their loyalty to the organization. In return, they get "belongingness," or acceptance and respect from others, and the organization rewards them with long-term employment, raises, promotions, and homes in the suburbs.

The social ethic also contends there is no inherent conflict between the individual and society. Conflicts are just misunderstandings. And when they occur, the social sciences — organizational and management theories and research — can be used to solve them and restore harmony to the organization.

"Essentially, it is a utopian faith," Whyte wrote. "It is the long-range promise that animates its followers, for it relates techniques to the vision of a finite, achievable harmony."

But Whyte argued that modern bureaucratic corporations were robbing the "organization man" of his individuality — of control over his life and thoughts. And, ironically, the organization man didn't even realize it was happening. In fact, he believed he was still pursuing the Protestant ethic, despite working in a collectivist environment.

He also argued that most people in organizations never escape the tyranny.

"There are only a few times in organization life when he [an organizational man] can wrench his destiny into his own hands — and if he does not fight then, he will make a surrender that will later mock him. But when is that time? ... By what standards is he to judge? ... If he goes against the group, is he being courageous — or just stubborn? Helpful — or selfish? Is he, as he so often wonders, right after all? It is in the resolution of a multitude of such dilemmas, I submit, that the real issue of individualism lies today."

So how does Whyte's theory affect me?

Administrators viewed me as a non-team player, as a naive idealist and rule-breaker. In fact, when I left my university office for the drive home one day, I found a black-and-white line drawing of Don Quixote and his sidekick Sancho Panza pinned beneath my windshield wiper. Quixote was the fictional character in Miguel de Cervantes's famous seventeenth-century novel who goes insane after reading many chivalric romances and embarks on a ludicrous mission with Sancho to revive chivalry for the betterment of Spain. They endure many indignities and humiliations. In the end, Quixote regains his sanity and denounces chivalric truths. Then he dies from a fever, which brings an end to the knights errant.

Well, that flier on my car pierced me like the dull tip of Quixote's spear.

Was I naive?

Yes, at least a bit.

Was I idealistic?

Of course.

But even naive, idealistic people can achieve goals.

So, I responded like any good follower of Quixote would: I tore the flier up and vowed to press on, which meant I needed to develop a plan if I were going to defeat my enemies, real or imagined.

I knew I would be denied early promotion and perhaps renewal of my contract. What I didn't know, though, was how administrators would justify the decision. My performance on all three criteria for tenure and promotion — teaching, research, and service — was satisfactory for three straight years. So how could they justify a firing?

The answer came several days later, in mid-September, when I was making copies of tests.

Chapter 6
COLLEGIALITY AND SECRET RECORDINGS

Fall 1994
University of Wisconsin–River Falls

"Collegiality," says Jimmy, my business professor friend. "They can fire you if they think you're not nice enough or if you don't play well with others on the playground."

"What?"

"Go look at university rules."

Sure enough, there it was, in Chapter 4 of the UW–RF Faculty Handbook, under "Promotional Criteria," under subsection "Contribution to the University," paragraph (b). I could feel the chains tightening on my wrists and ankles as I read the paragraph:

> Ability and willingness to maintain such working relations with colleagues as are essential to effective accomplishment of the mission of the academic unit, the college and the university.

My career is over. Send me to the underworld.

I didn't sleep well that night. I couldn't stop perseverating on the issue of collegiality. In the unwritten norms of academic life, there's an expectation that faculty and administrators respect each other and work together to solve social problems.

Nothing wrong with that.

Yet collegiality has a dark side.

Sociologist Max Weber warned that elites — university administrators in my case — sometimes use collegiality as a mechanism to control individuals, to prevent experts and professionals from challenging their authority. The American Association of University Professors and other organizations drew upon this theme in the twentieth century, arguing that punishing professors for not being nice tramples on their free-speech rights. They urged universities to cut collegiality clauses from their handbooks. Many did. Could the University of Wisconsin system be one of them?

I called the UW System office in Madison, where I spoke with an attorney who dealt with university policies and rules.

"Several years ago," she says, "we [the system-wide administration] informed all satellite campuses to strike collegiality clauses from their faculty handbooks and administrative rules. When it comes to evaluating an employee, the key criterion is job performance — not attitude or whether others like you." The collegiality clause at UW–RF was still on the books, she adds, because someone had failed to do their job and remove it.

Unchain me.

For the first time in months, I felt hopeful.

But how was I going to prove that collegiality would be the cause of my expected dismissal? No administrator would admit to it.

I needed to find someone who has inside knowledge.

Someone like an accreditation official.

* * * * *

The journalism program was up for national re-accreditation this semester, and the site visit team for the Accrediting Council on Education in Journalism and Mass Communications would be here in a week or two.

So, on September 21, 1994, I snail-mailed team chair Sue Talberson informing her about the controversy in the department. My hope was that she and the team might serve as independent moderators and help resolve the conflict.

Wishful thinking on my part.

A brief in-person meeting with Sue after she arrived revealed that she already had been co-opted into the administrative point of view.

She had spent much of her professional life managing newspapers, working as a publisher and executive editor. She identified with management, not rank-and-file.

So how could I obtain evidence of collegiality?

Sue would never publicly declare that the university was violating the collegiality clause and the First Amendment. So, I had only one other option: to secretly tape-record her. I got the idea from the *Lexington Herald-Leader.*

In 1986, the newspaper won a Pulitzer Prize for publishing a series of stories that exposed cash payoffs to University of Kentucky basketball players in violation of National Collegiate Athletic Association rules. Early in the investigation, reporters and editors decided to secretly tape-record conversations with players and others from whom they were receiving incriminating evidence.

Second-party tape recording, as this is called in legal circles, was not illegal. At the time, Kentucky and thirty-nine other states, including Wisconsin, allowed one party to a conversation to record conversations without the knowledge of the other party. Attorneys and police are devotees of second-party tape recording. Some attorneys secretly record conversations with clients to protect themselves from malpractice lawsuits. Police use second-party tape recording to collect evidence against lawbreakers.

Although the practice is still legal in most states, some people and professionals think it's unethical. In 1974, the American Bar Association ruled that it was unethical for attorneys but not for police. In 2001, the ABA reversed itself and said it was not unethical, at least in areas where it was not outlawed.

Journalists have never reached consensus on the issue. But one thing is certain: The secret tape recording saved the *Herald-Leader* from libel lawsuits. After the stories were published, some of the sources who gave incriminating evidence tried to recant their statements.

My case was a bit different.

I wasn't acting as a journalist. I wasn't going to publish the results of the recording in a news story. I was an employee trying to save his job and career. I was trying to prevent the university from violating the First Amendment. You might call me a "free-speech cop." I would use the recording as evidence in a hearing or a lawsuit, much like police use evidence to convict the bad guys.

I purchased a small tape recorder and put it in my desk drawer just before my meeting with Sue, whose job was to interview all faculty and some of the students. I was nervous. I don't like the idea of deceiving people, but I had no other choice.

Sue arrives at my office dressed in a dark blue pantsuit.

We chat for a while about various issues, including the dispute over the controversial student newspaper articles and the SPJ lawsuit. She tells me university administrators are angry because I had hired an attorney.

"Why did you hire the attorney?"

I tell her I hired the attorney to protect my due process rights.

"I can tell you the impact of hiring the attorney has basically been to shut the university out of the process," she says. "You shut it down. In hiring that lawyer and making it a civil action, now there is a fear that everything that is said to you is going to wind up as documentation and so on. I know they have a great sense of respect for you as a teacher and I know they would not say this, but I picked up a strong sense of sorrow. And they really want to resolve this, but now that the lawyers are involved they feel that their hands are totally tied."

Wow!

Sue had drunk the administrative Kool-Aid. Not only did she not appear to understand the importance of free speech in the academy, but she was also suggesting that university officials had the right to punish me for hiring an attorney. I wanted to ask more questions about that, but I was worried a digression could derail my goal of obtaining evidence about collegiality.

I take a deep breath and sit back in my chair.

"Do you think I'll be fired?" I calmly ask.

"That is likely if you don't sit down and talk with administrators."

"My attorney had tried to do that, but university officials thus far have refused to negotiate."

"For any teacher to get tenure there has to be a good productive working relationship," she says confidently. "So that's the thing that has to be established. So that you can all move ahead together."

Her condescending arrogance was annoying, but I didn't let it deter me from my plan.

"A good working relationship certainly is a great asset," I say, preparing to bait her. "What you're suggesting to me is that they feel that collegiality is still an important part of being able to be part of the university community."

"Well, it always has been and probably always will be, and that's the nature of tenure."

BINGO.

Sue went on for a couple more minutes, talking about how much she dislikes tenure and how she believes employers, including universities, should have the power to fire workers or faculty whenever they wish. She also talks about trust and good working relationships.

Good working relationships are useful, I respond. But protecting free-speech rights of faculty takes precedence. "The rules of the university say that faculty are evaluated for teaching, research, and service. The UW System eliminated the collegiality clause several years ago."

My comment startles her. "Oh, I didn't realize it was eliminated. But the thing is, you know, that hiring of legal counsel usually comes after you go through the process, not before."

In other words, she's saying that I could still be punished for hiring an attorney.

Did she, a journalism professor, really understand the function of tenure and free speech in a university setting? She told me she was an absolutist in terms of the First Amendment, but she failed to see the contradictions in her statements.

She was complicit, as were the WSU faculty. I didn't expect anyone to support me. But I did expect them to defend free speech on campus.

I secretly recorded conversations with two other university employees, both of whom would become members of my promotion and retention committee. They, too, confirmed that university officials were upset with me because I helped students file the lawsuit and author stories about faculty salaries and because I hired the attorney.

Now I had all the evidence I needed to defend myself.

My next step was to inform university officials to shut this down before it really turns ugly. My departmental promotion and retention hearing would be a good place to do that.

Chapter 7
'Nothin' but a Troublemaker'

Early November 1994
University of Wisconsin–River Falls

Rebecca's hands shake and her voice crackles as she shouts, "I can't believe you secretly recorded Sue. That's offensive, Dave. Unethical. Did you ever secretly tape me? I feel violated. This is shameful. What you did was wrong. Wrong!"

I had just informed her and two other members of the journalism faculty that I had audio-taped evidence showing that the university was violating the First Amendment and University of Wisconsin system rules. To reveal these facts at a promotion and tenure meeting was a bit unorthodox, I concede. But my purpose was to put that evidence into the official record.

"I never tape-recorded conversations with you," I say calmly, looking at Rebecca, who is still shaking. "I only taped conversations with Sue and two of the people on my promotion and annual review committee. It was the only way to show that the university was violating the First Amendment. If there was any other way to produce the evidence, I would have done it. But there was no other way."

Rebecca's performance was Oscar-worthy, I must admit. Even if she were wrong, the emotional intensity of her voice could have convinced any unknowledgeable bystander that the law and God were on her side. Fortunately, only the four of us in the journalism faculty and one student were in the room.

I didn't expect empathy from the journalism faculty. There was no question that all three of them would oppose my request for promotion and contract renewal.

But Patrice Peterson, the student who pointed out that I was no fun anymore, was about to say some nice things about my teaching. She informed me before the hearing that she was going to show up. I tried to dissuade her, because her testimony would have no effect other than to possibly hurt her standing with the other professors in the department.

But she insisted.

I don't remember what she said, but she was exceedingly kind.

Patrice was one of those rare students who was never afraid to speak her mind, including criticizing me on occasion. She was a fan of the Protestant ethic, not the social ethic.

* * * * *

I slept better that evening.

But evenings like this would be an exception rather than the rule for the next six months. I was getting about three to six hours a night. When I woke, often from a nightmare, I went to my office in the lower level of my house and worked on my research and book projects. That took my mind off the controversy, at least temporarily, and it also increased my productivity as a scholar.

By this time — my fourth year at UW–RF — I had published twelve refereed journal articles and two peer-reviewed academic books. I was close to finishing a third scholarly book.

Meanwhile, Sue's accreditation team noted in its report that there was no evidence that the free-speech dispute was interfering with the education of students at the university. The team did this in part to protect the department's chances for accreditation, but it also protected me. It showed that I had not created a major disturbance in the program, a condition that can be grounds for dismissing faculty. Sue never told me what she thought about my tape recording of her.

On November 29, 1994, Jay, my employment attorney, offered a compromise to resolve the conflict: expunge the records, including letters or materials that Mike and others had put together about the dispute, and then move on. I thought the university would accept it. It was an inexpensive and effortless way to solve the dispute.

But a week later, John Tallman, the same assistant attorney general who told my students that student evaluations were public data, notified Jay that the university would not accept the offer.

The university was digging in its heels.

And my status was changing from pariah to demon.

* * * * *

On December 16, 1994, Mike and three faculty members from other campus departments met in closed session to consider my request for promotion to associate professor as well as to issue an advisory vote on progress toward tenure. As expected, this formal Journalism Department Retention Committee rejected my request and issued an adverse vote on progress toward tenure.

"Professor Demers' inability to maintain productive communication channels within his department has inhibited his ability to contribute to department goals," the committee wrote.

That comment surprised me. Sue pointed out that it was university officials, not I, who had stopped communicating, because they didn't like the fact that I had hired an attorney.

The retention committee vote also revealed the rationale that administrators would use to fire me: "failure to maintain productive communication channels." That statement reminded me of a line delivered in the movie *Cool Hand Luke*, which I watched in high school. Paul Newman, who played Luke, was punished for violating jailers' rules.

One could easily argue that a failure to communicate is an element of collegiality. That's because faculty in general are notoriously famous for not getting along with each other and with administrators. Hell, if a failure to communicate was used as a criterion to pink slip faculty, half the faculty in America would be out of a job.

But I knew now that no matter how elaborate or careful I was in developing rational arguments to support my case, administrators would never listen. When you hold power, you don't have to listen, or respond, or be nice.

The administration's failure-to-communicate allegation was a clever strategy, though, because it meant I would have to prove that it was an indicator of collegiality to remove it as one of the reasons for firing me. I could spend hours writing more letters to defend myself. Or, alternatively, I could just ask the administrators whether they were using collegiality as the grounds for dismissal. My guess was that they were not well-informed about the collegiality clause problem. I could even bait them during my appeals in spring.

* * * * *

The next three months were difficult.

I was the most despised faculty member on campus — a male version of Hester Prynne, the protagonist of Nathaniel Hawthorne's 1850 novel *The Scarlet Letter*.

Faculty would avoid walking near me and avert their eyes when I looked at them. "But I'm fighting for your free-speech rights," I wanted to yell. But it was futile. They would never understand. The administration had framed me as a troublemaker, and there was little I could do to alter that social construction.

The only friendly colleague I had left on campus was Jimmy, the business professor. He and I chatted occasionally about my dilemma as the months passed. He was supportive, at least for a while. But I could tell he was increasingly uneasy with our meetings, so I stopped confiding in him.

I had plenty of colleagues at other universities who sympathized with my plight. But they didn't really understand what was going on, either. Email was awkward to use in those days, and the telephone was too time-consuming.

The worst part of the controversy was the toll it was taking on my personal life. Mona was always supportive, and I appreciated that. But the dispute stole time away from our relationship, and that was something that cannot be recovered. I still feel bad about that to this day. She put up with a lot but never complained.

On March 6, 1995, the Journalism Department Retention Committee issued its final decision about my request for promotion and contract renewal. I lost again.

Two reasons were given this time.

The first was that I allegedly had failed to establish a working relationship with faculty because I had closed off communication. The second reason given was my secret audio taping of Sue and two members of the retention committee.

"Tenure is based on some assurance that a good, productive working relationship over the long term is likely," the committee wrote. "Without evidence of that, an institution is playing loose with the best interests of students in the long run."

I responded in writing that this statement violates the prohibition against collegiality. I added that taping the officials did not violate university policy or the law, and that it was the only way to prove university officials were violating the First Amendment.

The committee and university officials ignored my comments. Bureaucracies are like that. They only respond when they want to because they have the power.

On March 15, I got a bit of good news.

The College of Arts and Sciences Promotion Committee voted in favor of my request for promotion. This committee was composed of faculty from other departments — faculty who were not personally involved in or affected by the dispute. The committee concluded that my teaching, service and research met or exceeded university standards.

But support from this committee wouldn't matter. In university systems, administrators hold final power when it comes to tenure and promotion decisions. The final decision rested with the dean, vice chancellor, and chancellor. I would meet one-to-one with all three.

Dean Stricter and the vice chancellor both allowed me to tape record the meetings.

Stricter tells me he is going to vote against retention because a "faculty member must have good working relations with colleagues." To ensure collegiality is the basis of his decision, I bait him with the actual "outlawed" wording directly from the unrevised UW–RF Faculty

Handbook.

"Do you think 'ability and willingness to maintain good working relations with colleagues is essential to accomplishing the mission of the department and university' and should this policy be used to assess whether I should be granted tenure and promotion here?"

"Of course," he says.

BAZINGA.

The vice chancellor also confirmed that collegiality is the reason he would vote against me.

The chancellor of the university, Gary Thibodeau, refused to allow me to tape-record our meeting, so I left his office without an interview. But that meeting would not have affected the outcome. Thibodeau had already made up his mind. He voted against my promotion and contract extension.

My subsequent appeals were ignored as the school year ended. The university gave me one year to pack my bags.

The extra year didn't give me much solace.

My thoughts were filled with trepidation that my academic career was ending.

But I can't say I didn't know this could happen. I knew the risks.

Principles can be a real pain in the ass sometimes.

* * * * *

"Demers deserved this," I overheard one professor telling another as I was leaving North Hall on the last day of class in spring 1995. "He's nothin' but a troublemaker."

Was I a troublemaker?

That question tormented me as I drove home that evening on I-94, which crosses Lake Saint Croix, an upper tributary of the Mississippi River. It reminded me of Willie Nelson's song, "The Troublemaker."

I could tell the moment that I saw Him
He was nothing but the trouble-making kind
His hair was much too long and His motley group of friends

Had nothing but rebellion on their minds

As the lyrics suggest, a troublemaker is often defined as a person who habitually causes difficulty or problems and incites others to defy those in authority. Jesus is the troublemaker in Nelson's song.

Jesus and I never incited others to defy those in authority.

But he and I are vastly different in all other respects. He is the "son of God." I am the son of a printer. He could walk on water and convert it to wine. I am not a good swimmer, but I am an excellent wine drinker.

"You're going to need a miracle to get out of this one," one of my graduate school colleagues tells me. "You're an activist without a social movement — a lonely activist."

He was right.

I learned this role decades earlier from my Lutheran elementary schoolteachers, from bullies in high school, and from my undergraduate journalism and social science professors.

Part III

ANATOMY OF A FREE-SPEECH ACTIVIST

Chapter 8
The Morality-Building Years

Sixty-Six Years Earlier, Spring 1960
Carrollton Township, Michigan, near Saginaw

I was in second grade when I showed the world, for the first time, that I could be a troublemaker.

I wrote "Shawn is dumb" on the blackboard during class recess.

Shawn was one of my classmates, and for reasons I no longer remember, I perceived her as being less intelligent than me and other students in the class.

I was wrong about that.

I was dumber. Not just for writing that contemptuous comment about her, but for allowing myself to be caught. When our teacher, Ms. Anton, enters the room after calling students back from a short recess, I'm standing at the blackboard, holding a piece of white chalk.

I knew from the frown lines on my teacher's forehead that I was about to get a well-deserved scolding. "Dave, that was not a nice thing to do. How would you like it if someone called you dumb?"

I hang my head.

"I want you to apologize to Shawn," she adds. "Then, after that, go back to the blackboard and write 'Dave is dumb' one hundred times."

Shame consumes me even though I didn't possess *mens rea* — a guilty state of mind — when I committed the "crime." Under the law, children under nine normally cannot commit crimes, because most haven't fully learned the difference between right and wrong. Psychologists say most children begin to develop an acute sense of morality at age seven or eight. I had barely turned seven, but that was no excuse.

I shuffle past several neat rows of Munkegård school desks and into the aisle where Shawn is sitting, about four desks from the front of the class. Twenty or so pairs of eyes are watching my walk of shame. When I arrive at her desk, I avoid looking into her eyes. The only thing I remember about her was that she was a blonde.

"I'm sorry," I meekly say, staring at the linoleum-tiled floor.

From the corner of my eye, I see her nod.

I pivot and quicken my pace to the blackboard, where I begin writing "Dave is dumb" as the teacher begins a new lesson. For the next fifteen minutes or so, I am in a state of banishment.

The chalk incident had a profound impact on me. I never wrote another hurtful comment about anyone unless they deserved it.

* * * * *

I grew up in an apolitical family.

Both of my parents, who were high school graduates, worked hard to make ends meet. My dad was a printer and my mother an insurance underwriter. They didn't have time for politics or protest. They had four kids to support: me and my younger brother and two sisters. All four of us were born over a five-year span.

Many years later, when I was a graduate student, I stumbled upon a book that provided a structural explanation for my parents' lack of political involvement. The authors, who were British sociologists, called it the "dull compulsion of economic relationships." In plain English, my parents, like most working people, didn't have time to get involved in politics, because they were too busy trying to pay the bills.

Aside from the time I threw rocks at a semi-truck trailer about a year later, the rest of my early childhood was uneventful. I enjoyed catching polliwogs in glass jars from a creek about a block away from our house. Those cute little black swimmers had the power to transform themselves from a gill-breathing fish to an air-breathing frog. I never thought I would share much in common with them. But I was about to undergo a big transformation, too — one with both physical and emotional consequences.

* * * * *

The physical part involved moving in June 1963 to Frankenmuth, Michigan, a small city of three thousand residents about twenty minutes from Carrollton and ninety minutes northwest of Detroit. That happened after my dad landed a new job as the printer for Frankenmuth Mutual Insurance Company.

"Franken what?" people would say through the years when I told them where I was from. "Franken" refers to the province and "mut" means "courage," so "courage of the Franconians," I would elaborate.

"Franken what?" they would respond.

Lutheran missionaries from Franconia (now part of Bavaria), Germany, founded the town in 1845. Their initial goal was to convert the Chippewa Indians living in the area. That mission didn't last long. The Indians left as more white people took charge of everything.

In the early years, Frankenmuth was a logging and farming community. One of the hotels in town developed a reputation for serving savory chicken dinners and homemade beer and wine. In the 1920s, William Zehnder Sr. purchased the hotel and renovated it, further cementing the town's reputation as a destination for good food and spirits.

During the Prohibition era, Zehnder's Restaurant and the Fischer Hotel across the street quietly continued to serve beer and wine. On July 30, 1930, federal agents from Detroit raided the establishments. Zehnder was fined $3,800 and Herman Fischer, owner of the hotel, was fined $8,800. The latter fine was the highest paid during the Prohibition era.

Zehnder was a member of St. Lorenz Lutheran Church in Frankenmuth. He told the congregation that he would apologize if other members of the congregation who violated the law did the same thing. The pastor saved everyone the embarrassment, pointing out that the law was "crazy."

Those Germans loved their beer and wine.

To the best of my knowledge, the decision to violate Prohibition laws was the most radical organized act of defiance mainstream

Frankenmuthers ever committed against the U.S. political system.

During the 1950s, another Frankenmuther named Wallace "Wally" Bronner created a sign-making business and began painting Christmas bulbs for his employees. Twenty years later his business was the largest Christmas store in the world, and Frankenmuth was now the third most popular tourist destination in Michigan, right behind Henry Ford Museum/Greenfield Village in Dearborn to the south and Mackinac Island to the north.

The two restaurants and Bronner's Christmas Wonderland kept growing through the years, in part because the families running them had nowhere else to invest the profits. In those days, Lutherans didn't tolerate "conspicuous consumption," a term introduced by Norwegian American economist and sociologist Thorstein Veblen in his 1899 book *The Theory of the Leisure Class.*

Veblen applied the term to the nouveau riche, an economic class that emerged in the nineteenth century because of the accumulation of wealth in modern capitalism. In F. Scott Fitzgerald's novel, *The Great Gatsby*, the nouveau riche were those who lived in West Egg on Long Island Sound, which included Gatsby himself. East Egg was populated with "old money."

The term "conspicuous consumption"— more popularly referred to in the 1960s as "keeping up with the Joneses" — is now broadly applied to people who spend money on goods and services to show off their status as opposed to just using them for their intrinsic value.

More than one million tourists were visiting Frankenmuth every year in the 1960s to gorge themselves on all-you-can-eat chicken dinners at Zehnder's or the Bavarian Inn (the former Fischer Hotel) and to shop at Bronner's or one of the scores of little specialty stores in town that sold wood carvings, cheese, fudge, t-shirts, ice cream, woolen blankets and clothes, and souvenirs. Most of the shops were housed in buildings adorned with Bavarian architecture — a gingerbread-like aesthetic with multiple peaks on roofs and intricate woodwork and detailing on windows and doorways.

The Bavarian Inn even built a large Glockenspiel with sound and life-size wood characters that told the story of the Pied Piper of

Hamelin, who lured the town's children away after its residents refused to pay the Piper for ridding the town of rats. Tourists loved standing in the parking lot and listening to Glockenspiel's bells and watching the Piper lure the rats into a watery grave. The lesson in this story is to "keep your promises."

I never saw any rats in Frankenmuth. Nor were there any homeless or poor people. The city had no poverty. Every street was curbed. And everyone was white.

Some people, then as now, think of Frankenmuth as Bavarian Disneyland. Later, others preferred to characterize the city as the nonfiction version of the fictional Stepford, Connecticut, which was the setting for the 1972 movie "Stepford Wives"—a place brimming with patriarchy, conservatism, dogma, and traditionalism.

As a kid, I was in the Disneyland crowd.

* * * * *

I was nine and initially unhappy about moving to Frankenmuth, because it meant leaving my best friend, Timmy, who had a "very cool" ERECTOR Set containing small metal beams and nuts and bolts to construct toy bridges, buildings and cranes.

But I adapted quickly.

More than a dozen kids lived in our new neighborhood. We played kickball and Ante Over. We also played "World War II" in Pine Woods, a small, wooded area with numerous paths for engaging in playtime warfare. Although Frankenmuth was a German town, even the kids who had one-hundred-percent German parents wanted to play the role of the American soldier. Kids in modern societies identify more with the social constructions of the culture they grow up in than with their family heritage.

I made a new best friend very quickly.

Fritz lived next door. He was my age, nine, and we bonded quickly, so much so that we would walk around the neighborhood with our arms on each other's shoulders. Best buddies. But that ended abruptly when Fritz's mother told us arm-locking was inappropriate. She didn't explain why. Years later I figured it out. She feared her son would be perceived as being a gay person.

Like me, Fritz was awkward, physically. Neither of us were good at sports, although that shortcoming wouldn't turn into emotional baggage for me until I entered high school, when jocks held a much higher social ranking than sports-challenged weaklings like me.

For now, though, I was happy.

I had a good self-concept.

Life was fun, even after my parents enrolled us four kids in St. Lorenz Lutheran Elementary School in Frankenmuth. At the time, it was the largest Lutheran elementary school in the country with more than six-hundred students enrolled in grades K-8. For a while I wondered if my past crimes against Shawn and the tractor trailer contributed to the decision to enroll me in a parochial school instead of a public school. If so, my parents never mentioned it, and I was too cowardly then to rat on myself.

But it didn't matter.

I had no intention of returning to a life of troublemaking, and attending a Lutheran school could help keep me straight. After all, religious organizations are powerful institutions of social control. Take the Fourth Amendment — "Honor Thy Father and Mother" — for instance. We kids were expected to respect not just our parents but pastors and other authorities, too, including the police and politicians. As the Missouri Lutheran Synod explains: "Through them, God richly blesses us, and our world, with orderly authority, as opposed to the chaos that sin brings."

I didn't want to sin.

But what if authorities were the ones creating chaos?

Do we subordinates have a right to challenge them?

Absolutely, according to Lutherans, because Jesus and Martin Luther, the founder of Lutheranism, were some of the biggest troublemakers of all time. Jesus had the guts to proclaim, "Blessed are the meek, for they shall inherit the earth," and fifteen centuries later Luther had the gall to nail to a Catholic Church door the Ninety-Five Theses, which jump-started the Protestant Reformation.

Of course, I wasn't pondering these moral questions in 1963. I was more concerned with bigger things, like how to have as much fun as possible. Subtly, though, I was acquiring a set of principles that would turn me into a troublemaker.

The first principle was empathy.

* * * * *

I am sitting at my desk in fifth grade at St. Lorenz school watching my friend Fritz, who is sitting next to me, fidget. Then he thrusts his arm into the air, trying to get the teacher's attention.

But Mr. Brookman doesn't notice. He is writing something on the blackboard and talking at the same time. About twenty seconds pass and Fritz is now frantically shaking his hand to get the teacher's attention. Mr. Brookman can see him now but continues to lecture, presumably because he doesn't want to lose his train of thought.

When Brookman finally acknowledges Fritz, it's too late.

A yellow-tinged ammonia-smelling liquid splatters on the beige linoleum tiled floor from Fritz's wooden seat. Time stood still for a moment, enough to allow my heart to sink like an anchor through the wet floor next to me.

Poor Fritz.

His full face is now a deep red.

I feel helpless.

I also feel anger at Mr. Brookman for failing to call on Fritz sooner.

Fritz rises from his chair and Mr. Brookman helps him out of the room. A custodian arrives a few minutes later and cleans up the mess. Class continues. Fritz never returns to his seat that day.

After school, I went to Fritz's house to see how he was doing. I pretend the event never happened. No use rehashing an embarrassing moment like that. I am there to show him that he is still my best friend.

When I leave to go home, Fritz's mother gives me a short lecture in the kitchen about not making fun of Fritz. It can happen to anyone, she says. Of course, I think to myself. What ticked me off, though, is that she apparently didn't think I could experience empathy.

Some politicians today also think empathy is a sign of weakness.

They are dumb, of course.

Empathy is necessary if one is going to raise hell and change the world.

Just ask Jesus or Luther.

* * * * *

My elementary school years at St. Lorenz were heavenly, for the most part.

Everyone was nice. No drama. I even forgave Mr. Brookman, as any good Lutheran would.

There was also no social hierarchy among the students, or at least none that I could see. No one acted like they were superior to anyone else. We were all equal in the eyes of God and the Constitution. Perhaps things would have been different if minorities were attending our school. Everyone was white.

Over the next four years, the teachers taught me and other students the importance of individual responsibility, hard work, frugality, honesty and deferred gratification. They taught us the Golden Rule — "Treat others as you would have them treat you" — and to apologize when we wronged or hurt someone. Apologizing was particularly important, because it was a sign of humility — a sign that the person committing the wrong respected the dignity and worth of the person who was wronged. People or organizations that never apologize are arrogant, self-absorbed and disrespectful.

Our Lutheran teachers also taught us to tell the truth, respect our parents and elders, help others whenever we can, practice thriftiness, work hard and confront social injustice. The latter did not mean Lutherans should challenge the military-industrial establishment. For the most part, Lutherans accepted the established political order, including America's involvement in the Vietnam War, which was raging during the time I attended St. Lorenz.

But Lutherans in those days did have at least one "enemy": The Catholics, who, we were told, distorted the Bible and had a history of persecuting Lutherans and other Protestants. The Catholics could be going to hell. I say "could be" because the Lutheran teachers never told us outright that Catholics were destined for eternal damnation, but we kids were smart enough to connect the dots.

Fortunately, times have changed.

Lutheran teachers today are far less judgmental. No one is going to hell except a lot of crooked and mean-spirited politicians. But I wouldn't be here had one of my two parents been a Catholic.

"Are you Catholic or do you smoke?" my dad asks my mother when they meet for the first time in 1949 at a roller-skating rink.

"No," my mother responds.

Thanks, Mom.

Unlike my earlier days, I now was a well-behaved kid.

Quiet. Shy. Very religious. Honest to a fault. I would have ratted on my brother and even on myself now.

But I wasn't immaculate, as the Catholics were fond of saying.

My biggest sin was watching too much television. I loved Westerns and adventure movies and the stars who dominated them, including Jimmy Stewart, Gregory Peck, Henry Fonda, Glenn Ford, Robert Mitchum, John Wayne, Cary Grant and Gary Cooper. The story line in the movies was almost always the same: Bad guys raise hell; good guys (often one individual) save the day. These movies instilled in me the idealistic notion that justice almost always prevails.

In hindsight, I should have spent more time reading novels like George Orwell's *1984,* John Steinbeck's *The Grapes of Wrath,* and Fitzgerald's *The Great Gatsby*, where the bad guys win or the good guys lose in the end. In real life, injustice often rules.

I can see now that I also watched a lot of television because I had trouble focusing. My mind often wandered. I daydreamed a lot. It was difficult to stay focused when reading. Television, though, was very passive and fast-paced. Easy to stay focused.

I likely was suffering from "hyperkinetic reaction of childhood," which was first listed in the Diagnostic and Statistical Manual of Mental Disorders in 1952, a year before I was born. In 1980, it was renamed: "Attention Deficit Disorder," or ADD for short. I wasn't formally diagnosed with ADD until I was sixty-nine. Had I been diagnosed earlier, it's quite possible I would never have become an activist. ADD nourished in me a naivete that propelled me professionally when I became a reporter and a professor. It also enabled me to hyperfocus when I took an interest in a subject. That paid off in college when I discovered the joy of book-learning.

But first I had to survive high school.

Chapter 9
THE HEATHEN AND BULLY YEARS

Fall 1967
Frankenmuth High School

My Lutheran school education ended in eighth grade, at which time I joined the so-called heathens in public high school. They didn't respect the Ten Commandments like we Lutheran kids did.

Take the Sixth Commandment, for example. "Thou shalt not kill."

We Lutheran kids interpreted that to mean you also should not hurt other people. But some football players at Frankenmuth High School had other ideas. They enjoyed using their lineman-sized hands to lift and pin me — at eight-six pounds, the third smallest boy in the entire school of six-hundred-twenty-four — by my neck against the hallway walls.

Another senior bully slugged me in the stomach or back during gym roll call when the coach turned his back. When my parents complained, the gym coach suggested I put on boxing gloves and duke it out with Ted, who was six feet tall and weighed at least one-hundred-seventy pounds. Before I had a chance to decline this brattish offer, slugger-boy did me a favor: He dropped out of school. I facetiously tell people today that "I coulda been a rich man" had I been born forty years later, when parents decided the courts were better than boxing rings for taking down bullies and complicit school systems.

But, as we Lutherans are fond of saying, there's always a silver lining. Being bullied in high school nourished in me an even deeper empathy for the underdog, which is, of course, a highly desired trait for journalists, professors and social activists.

Although I never bullied anyone in high school, I would be lying if I said I never strayed from the path of the righteous. I was a fringe member of the male-only faux-hippie clique during my junior and senior years. We had long hair and thought we were cool. We drove around in our muscle cars, listening to loud rock music while drinking beer and smoking cigarettes. Some of us were experimenting with marijuana and other drugs, and with love, too.

I dated a cheerleader from another high school for nearly a year. That puppy love was wonderful until she asked me to marry her and have children. Hell, I was only 16. I had a tough time taking care of myself.

Of course, during these times my friends and I were in a desperate search for identity in an increasingly complex world — a world in which young people were questioning the power of traditional paternalistic authorities to control their lives, especially the war in Vietnam.

That anti-establishment theme got a boost from a number of 1960s-era Hollywood films, including *Cool Hand Luke*, as I mentioned earlier. Paul Newman starred as Lucas Jackson, a decorated war veteran who is sent to a southern chain-gang prison for cutting off the tops of parking meters in a drunken stupor. Luke tells the prisoners he cut them off to settle an "old score," but he doesn't explain what he means by that. Some viewers assumed stress from his war experiences in either World War II or the Korean War (not specified in the movie) played some role.

In prison, Luke refuses to submit not only to the prison camp's repressive authority system but to the inmates' authority system as well. He earns the respect of the prisoners after fighting a more powerful inmate, eating fifty boiled eggs, and trying to escape on several occasions. The escapes earn him severe beatings from prison guards, who throw him in the "box" to break him.

The captain of the guards, while beating Luke with a stick, delivers the most famous line in the movie: "What we've got here is failure to communicate." At the end of the movie, Luke mocks the guards with that phrase (adding the article "a" before the word "failure"), just before a rifle shot rings out.

The movie was shown to the entire FHS student body in the school's gymnasium during my junior year.

One of my best high school friends, Scott, recalled years later that the purpose of the movie was "to help motivate us [students] to be good people." Another friend, Rod, concurred and jestingly added that "if we students failed to get a good education, we would end up talking like — chewing and spitting tobacco like — the people in the movie."

But if the purpose of the movie was to scare us into conforming, I'm not sure it was effective. To me, Luke wasn't the bad guy. He was the hero. And he was a victim of a corrupt correctional system and a naive military bureaucracy, which expected that young soldiers would be unaffected by combat and killing.

Of course, the film never said the stress of war made Luke cut off the parking meter heads. But the screenwriters could not have expected that viewers would fail to make the connection, given the many psychological and emotional problems that soldiers returning from the Vietnam War brought with them.

A poignant real-life example was Ted the bully — the senior who slugged me in gym class. Shortly after he dropped out of school, he was arrested for stealing a car and armed robbery. The judge gave him a choice: jail or Vietnam. He chose poorly.

Through the years, Ted tried to suppress memories of the horrors he saw in Vietnam, according to one relative. His wife eventually kicked him out. Doctors tried to treat his mental illness. But in 2007, at the age of fifty-seven, he shot himself in the kitchen while his daughter was taking a shower.

"The storm is stilled and he is at rest," his obituary stated.

Some might say "just deserts."

I had no love for Ted, of course.

But no one, not even Ted the bully, deserves to suffer the mental torture that war unleashes upon people — especially a war built on lies, as the Pentagon Papers showed.

That would become my state of mind after I enrolled in college.

* * * * *

Although I strongly identified with Cool Hand Luke's character, in real life I was more like the inmates in the movie, who didn't have enough courage to challenge the system like Luke did.

The biggest act of defiance I committed during high school was helping a fellow friend and classmate skip classes. I crossed out his name on attendance slips I collected when I worked for the assistant principal's office. Fortunately, the school did not have a "box." The assistant principal punished me with several after-school detention hours.

But Luke and I did share one thing in common: Neither of us had a clear vision of what we wanted to do with our lives.

Looking back, it's fair to say that I was suffering from clinical depression in high school. I wasn't handsome, athletic, popular, or even a good student. I suffered from a big inferiority complex. I was timid and unsure of myself, like a piece of driftwood in the Cass River, which wound its way through the center of Frankenmuth.

My high school counselor didn't know much about me, but she was well aware of my lackluster school performance. I was a C+ student because I didn't study much. She discouraged me from enrolling in a four-year college program. A trade would be better, she said. Community college would be a good choice.

Like a good Lutheran, I complied.

In hindsight, I realized that I had never learned the importance of getting a good education until it was almost too late. My parents never encouraged me to do well in school or to go to college. But I don't blame them. They were too busy trying to survive in a social system that was making it more difficult for people to achieve the American Dream.

Thus, when I started community college in the fall of 1971, I was, without question, more of a conformist than an activist.

But the Vietnam War and my professors were about to change me.

I became more politically active, partly because my life depended upon it and partly because my professors were teaching me about the substantive ideals that really made America great.

Chapter 10
Enlightenment for Everyone

Fall Semester 1971
Delta College, Saginaw, Michigan

Political science professor Roger Taggard leans on the lectern and takes a big drag from his Marlboro, blowing smoke into the air, moments before beginning the day's lecture.

"Picture yourself in eighteenth-century England," he tells his class of fifty students, which includes me. "You're watching a mob of Englishmen surround a Frenchman as he's walking back to the inn where he was staying. Then the mob shouts, 'Hang him! Hang the Frenchman!'"

For a moment, our classroom becomes so quiet that we could hear a dropped cigarette butt hit the floor.

"But the mob was no match for this man," Taggard adds, taking another puff. "'Men of England,' the man said to the mob, 'you wish to kill me because I am a Frenchman. Am I not punished enough in not being born an Englishman?'"

Grins appear on the faces of my colleagues and me.

"That clever remark quickly disarmed the mob," Taggard says. "In fact, the crowd even cheered and escorted the Frenchman safely to his lodge. The year was 1726. And the charmer was Voltaire, who would go down in history as one of the most important philosophers of the Age of Enlightenment. Some scholars also call him the father of the French Revolution."

Taggard drops his burning cigarette butt onto the tiled floor and extinguishes it with a twist of his leather-soled shoe.

In 1971, professors and students could smoke in class. It was up to the professor. Nearly forty percent of college students smoked then. Cigarettes were cheap, twenty-five to thirty cents a pack, and the powerful tobacco lobby was still able to suppress or counter information about the dangers of smoking. Classrooms were often filled with a haze, especially during the winter, when the windows were closed. The floors were filled with butts at the end of the day.

Disgusting, I know.

But nonsmokers rarely complained.

Smokers ruled back then.

It was my first semester at Delta College, which was located north of Saginaw near I-75, about a twenty-minute drive from Frankenmuth. Most of the students were commuters who worked jobs. I was enrolled full time and worked as a short-order cook in a small Frankenmuth restaurant managed by one of my former high school classmates.

I was grateful to be in college.

My driftwood had reached the shore.

* * * * *

Taggard was a Socratic professor. He stimulated a class discussion through questions. Today's session was no exception.

"What is the most central idea of the Enlightenment?" he asks.

Twenty seconds of awkward silence elapses.

Some students avert their eyes from the professor, hoping this will diminish the chances of them being called upon to answer the question.

"To enlighten?" cracks a male student wearing a Detroit Tigers baseball cap in the back row.

Several students near him chuckle.

"That response is less than enlightening," the professor responds playfully, triggering a few more chuckles. "From what or from whom were they being enlightened?"

The students reply.

"From paternalism."

"The church."

"Despotic rulers."

"Narrow-minded professors."

"Precisely—with present company excluded, of course," Taggard says, drawing a few chortles. "The central idea of the Enlightenment is that human reason — not supernatural forces, tradition, superstition or dogma — should guide human affairs. This was a big deal. It legitimized the idea of separating the church from the state and reduced the political power of religious institutions in Europe and Great Britain."

Taggard explains that Voltaire and other Enlightenment philosophers — including fellow French thinkers Jean-Jacques Rousseau and Baron de Montesquieu; Isaac Newton and John Locke of England; and Scots David Hume and Adam Smith — wrote books and articles that embraced reason, scientific knowledge and the worth of the individual. The emphasis was on achieving happiness on earth, not after one dies and reaches heaven. Hence, that's likely one of the reasons Thomas Jefferson included the phrase "life, liberty and the *pursuit of happiness*" in the Declaration of Independence.

The Founding Fathers opposed tyranny and argued that ordinary people should play a bigger role in governing their communities and the state, Taggard explains, lighting another cigarette. "Most believed humans could, through scientific research and free-market economics, solve social problems and make the world a better place."

"But," one student interjects, "haven't people always thought that science could help make the world a better place?"

"Good question, and the answer is no. In fact, prior to the sixteenth century, many university scholars subscribed to the idea that all knowledge came from the church and the works of Aristotle. In contrast, Voltaire and others argued that knowledge of the real world came through observation and reason. The world was one big lab experiment — out there to be discovered. Doubt everything, philosopher René Descartes declared. Then use logic and observation to rediscover and understand the world."

Although Taggard was clearly an advocate of the Enlightenment, he did point out that implementation of its ideals didn't always produce a utopia. Industrialization and urbanization, two social structural consequences of the Enlightenment, generated many social problems, including crime, discrimination, poverty, and moral decay. Many conservatives are critical of Enlightenment ideals because they see them as challenging centralized power. Many liberals are critical because they see them as supporting centralized power.

Lectures like this were changing the way I looked at the world.

I began to see that the anti-Vietnam War movement was not an isolated historical event but part of a larger social movement already several hundred years old — one that had introduced the world to the importance of individualism, democracy, free speech, and self-governance.

Voltaire became my favorite philosopher. He criticized despotic authority and its penchant for suppressing free speech. In his *Treatise on Toleration*, he wrote, "We cannot cure the powerful of ambition, but we can cure the people of superstition. We can, by speech and pen, make men more enlightened and better."

Voltaire's masterpiece was *Candide*, a short book written in 1758 that attacked religious fanaticism and the injustices of war and class status. Candide is a young, innocent, naive disciple of Doctor Pangloss, who preaches that "in the best of possible worlds ... all is for the best." Pangloss means "windbag," and he symbolizes the philosophy of established religion, which holds that people should accept all forms of suffering and evil without complaint and always look for the silver lining.

Candide suffers many indignities and becomes disillusioned with the world. In the end, he concludes that "we must cultivate our gardens" — in other words, one must reject idealistic dreams and live within one's limitations.

I loved this book because its "best of possible worlds" maxim characterized the way many Christians saw the world. No matter how bad things get, they always look for the silver lining.

Nothing wrong with this.

But, as Voltaire pointed out, embracing the silver lining often discourages people from trying to fix real-world problems. Later Karl Marx even argued that "religion was the opiate of the masses." It makes them focus more on the afterlife than real life.

Enlightenment ideals permeate every mainstream institution in America, Taggard explains. The Constitution and Bill of Rights draw heavily from them. The legal system shouldn't convict people without "due process of law," which includes the right of presumed innocence until proven guilty and the rights to an attorney, public trial, and impartial jury. The government also is not supposed to punish people for their speech or religious preference or deny freedom of the press to journalists.

Taggard also pointed out that the debate over the U.S. military draft is simply part of the larger debate over whether society should respect the rights of the individual. Enlightenment philosophers argued that individuals have the right to self-determination, to control their own destiny, and to fight for social justice.

"You can see this ideal," Taggard adds, "in Hollywood movies, which show the lone cowboy or sheriff standing up to the bad guys; the superhero who defends society; and the individual who bucks the collective in a future dystopian world characterized by almost complete social control. Of course, these enlightened individuals almost always triumph in the end, and the message is clear: One individual can make a difference. But is this message realistic? Can one individual really make a difference today?"

"I don't think so," says one long-haired bearded student. "The military-industrial complex is very powerful in America. Ordinary people have little power. Polls show that nearly three-fourths of Americans are opposed to the Vietnam War, but the war goes on nevertheless. Power flows from the top down, not from the bottom up."

"I disagree," counters a woman with short, auburn hair. "People have the right to vote in America, and if they don't like the leadership, they can throw it out. The war goes on because the public has not demanded an end to it."

"That's not true," replies the bearded student. "We students and the public have been demanding an end to the war, but Nixon ignores the public. He's an ass."

Several students gasp and private conversations break out across the room.

"Okay, okay," Taggard says, exerting his power to control the class. "Let's get back to the question of making a difference. Let me ask it in another way. Are political, economic and judicial institutions in America as democratic as people are taught to believe? Are they egalitarian, tolerant of free speech, just and fair? Do those institutions encourage their members to practice and defend Enlightenment ideals?"

The discussion lasts another fifteen minutes.

About two-thirds of the students are skeptical of the idea that America embraces Enlightenment ideals. They point out that society has failed to provide equal pay and rights to women and minorities and that the public never had a voice in whether the United States should go to war in Vietnam. Politicians and bureaucrats called the shots.

I was in the skeptical camp, but I still believed that one individual could make a difference. The hopeful idealist, I was.

* * * * *

I loved college.

For the first time in my life, I felt a strong sense of purpose. I was becoming more interested in politics. I loved studying and was getting good grades.

But I wanted to attend a university with more prestige and move away from home. In January 1972, after one semester at Delta, I transferred to Central Michigan University, where my best friend from high school, Jerry, was attending.

My transition to CMU was seamless. The university known for training teachers was located in Mount Pleasant, a city of 20,000 in central lower Michigan, about a three-hour drive northwest of Detroit and seventy-five minutes from Frankenmuth.

I was assigned to Merrill Hall, an all-male dormitory where I shared a room with three other young men. Jerry lived in the room across the hall. A decade or so later Merrill would gain fame as the place where actor and director Jeff Daniels lived for a time before dropping out to pursue an acting career.

Unlike me, Jerry was easy-going. He flowed with the river. I was intense, like water backed up at a dam. His heritage was Eastern European. He had big brown eyes, bushy dark brown eyebrows, and a smile that disarmed everyone in the room. He was well-liked. He loved music and played guitar. When I was studying, he was jamming. He was kicked back and relaxed, and I was always kicking. I had to make something of my life, to regain my sense of self.

I studied for three to five hours every day and didn't party at the bars until later. The drinking age in those days was eighteen, which had been lowered from twenty-one in the 1960s, because, as many people argued, "if you can die for your country in Vietnam, you should have the right to drink a beer in a bar."

I wanted to learn more about the Vietnam War and politics.

So, I took my first class in sociology.

* * * * *

My first sociology professor had dark brown hair, parted in the middle, down to his shoulders. Although the phrase "Get a damn haircut, hippie!" had passed into history by 1972, long-haired male professors were still the exception to the rule. I thought the class was going to be cool simply because the professor looked like us students.

Professor Roman Brown didn't disappoint.

"The goal of sociology," he tells our class of a hundred students, "is to solve social problems. As societies become more complex, so do their problems. Crime, economic and political inequality, overpopulation, urban decay, divorce, and war are topics that sociologists study and hope to solve or manage."

These subjects were of great interest to me. I was not alone. From 1966 to 1972, enrollments in sociology programs in the United States soared, going from about fifteen thousand to thirty-six thousand. No one doubted that the Vietnam War and the civil rights and women's movements were the prime causes.

Many students were less concerned about getting a high-paying job than with finding a meaningful career that could help make the world a better place. I was one of them.

Our textbook, titled simply *Introduction to Sociology*, pointed out that industrialization was threatening the environment, producing cycles of prosperity and depression, creating huge disparities in wealth and income between people, and breaking down traditional values and norms that previously had kept crime and vice in check. "How do societies perpetuate themselves, teaching their children to believe most of what they are taught until they think of the attitudes as their own? What are the functions of nonconformity?"

Most of the early sociologists believed that sociologists should play an active role in solving social problems. Edward A. Ross of Stanford University, for example, argued that "we suppress smallpox, typhus, diphtheria, the bubonic plague — why should we not endeavor to banish such social maladies as prostitution, juvenile delinquency, child exploitation, trampery, mob violence, family disintegration, religious rancor, and race antagonism?"

As a professor in the 1890s, Ross criticized the Stanford family for using Chinese immigrants to build the rail lines for Southern Pacific. In response to his criticism, Jane Eliza Lathrop Stanford forced the university president in 1900 to ask for Ross's resignation. The university also dismissed another professor who defended Ross, which in turn prompted a half-dozen other professors to resign in protest.

These actions motivated philosopher John Dewey and other professors to develop the tenure system at American universities to protect the free-speech rights of faculty. Tenure does not guarantee professors and teachers a job for life. It merely grants them administrative due process should administrators try to fire them.

Although most nineteenth-century sociologists believed social science should try to eradicate or control societal problems, not all were fully behind the idea. William Graham Sumner vigorously opposed the idea of "social planning" and promoted English sociologist Herbert Spencer's idea of evolution, which emphasized that social change occurred naturally rather than through direct intervention from humans.

The authors of my textbook took what might be called a moderate position on the debate over whether social science should try to change the world: "Although the modern sociologist hopes his findings will help the human race, he sees his task as primarily the intellectual quest for knowledge and explanation. ... [T]he sociologist must study and learn; society, hopefully can put his knowledge to use."

Hopefully? What a strange qualification. If this knowledge is not used, then what use is it?

It didn't take me long to conclude that Ross had the better approach. But in later years I would learn that even though most social scientists agree that knowledge gained in research should guide public policy, many are reluctant to become politically active.

In principle, I didn't have a problem with this.

But what if policymakers ignore or refuse to use that knowledge when making decisions? Do social scientists have a moral obligation to prevent policymakers from making decisions that might harm people or society?

Chapter 11
THE LOTTERY AND ANTI-WAR MARCH

Wednesday, February 2, 1972
Central Michigan University

"Hey, Dave, how much money you got?" asks Johnny, one of my dorm friends, who is holding a wad of cash in his left hand.

I pull out my skinny wallet. "Two bucks. Why?"

"I'm takin' up a collection for the Selective Service draft lottery tomorrow. The unlucky bastard who comes closest to No. 1 wins the pot."

"Small consolation for getting sent to Vietnam, eh?" I sarcastically respond, handing him the two bills.

"Yeah, man. This is one lottery I don't want to win."

Johnny was canvassing dorm rooms on the third floor of Merrill Hall on the Central Michigan University campus that evening, asking for donations from all those who were born in 1953.

By the end of the evening, he had collected $44.37 from about two dozen potential draftees. Not much money in absolute terms, but in those days a small fortune for a first-year college male student, who typically carried less than $5 in his wallet.

On the following day about a dozen of us eighteen-year-olds gathered in Bob's room down the hall to listen to the results of the lottery on the radio.

A week earlier President Richard Nixon had proposed an eight-point peace plan for Vietnam. Secretary of State Henry Kissinger had been secretly negotiating with the North Vietnamese. But that wouldn't stop today's lottery. Hanoi would reject Nixon's plan. The war would go on.

The process of selecting the draft numbers in those days was what we now call "low-tech." Three-hundred-sixty-five blue balls — each imprinted with one date out of the year — were placed in a bin that was spun before selecting one of the balls and associating it with a birth date.

The first lottery was conducted in 1969. Prior to that, college students could obtain deferments. They wouldn't have to go into the military until they graduated from college. But Nixon ended the deferments in 1971, partly because of complaints that they discriminated against men who were Black or poor, as they were less likely to attend college.

In 1969, 162,746 young men who drew numbers of one-hundred-ninety-five or lower were inducted into the military the following year. The inductions dropped to 94,092 in 1971 and to 49,514 in 1972. The rumor we heard was that in 1973 Selective Service would induct all of us with numbers up to about ninety.

We were nervous.

To the best of my knowledge, none of the young men in that dorm room that day supported U.S. involvement in the Vietnam War. We believed the war was being fought for the wrong reasons — to serve the interests of the "military-industrial complex," a popular pejorative in those days for corporations that made the bombs and the military generals who dropped them.

Even worse, we felt it was immoral that young men who opposed the war were being sent there against their will. A democracy political system should not force men to fight a war unless it could convince them that it was a just war, we argued. Of course, it couldn't do that with respect to Vietnam. Politicians and government bureaucrats had repeatedly lied about our role over there, so the government had to conscript. If you refused to fight, you were jailed.

The only other options for single men were to become a conscientious objector, join the National Guard before you were drafted (like George W. Bush), stay in college to get a deferment and then hire a doctor who will fabricate an illness (like Donald Trump), join the Reserve Officers' Training Corps (R.O.T.C.) and later refuse to serve (like Bill Clinton), or go underground in America or flee the country.

The only sure way to avoid military service was to flee the country. By 1972, 70,000 young men had done just that. Most went to Canada.

What if I draw a low number? Should I run to Canada? How would I survive? What would my family think? Or should I just go into the military? If I don't go, then someone else may die in my place. Isn't that immoral?

The young men in the dorm room were quiet as the results of the lottery got underway. When a man in the room received a high number, the silence was broken with cheers and slaps on the back. When the number was low, the men cussed and moaned.

Jerry drew No. 292. He sighed. We cheered and shook his hand.

Johnny, the jackpot-raiser, was lucky, too, drawing No. 317.

Bob wasn't so lucky. He drew No. 1.

"Shit," he screamed, as a half-dozen friends joined him in feigned agony and tried to console him. Bob tried to "take it like a man" and laughed as he took possession of the $44.37 jackpot, but I could see the terror in his eyes.

Then came my number — 128. *Was that good? Would Selective Service change its mind and go above ninety?*

As the lottery ended, the young potential draftees returned to being young college students — joking, wrestling, bantering, shouting. Someone down the hallway put Crosby, Stills, Nash & Young's "Ohio" on the stereo and turned up the volume. The song was written about the four student protesters at Kent State University who were shot and killed by National Guardsmen on May 4, 1970, during an anti-war demonstration — an event that stunned America and solidified public opposition to the war.

Tin soldiers and Nixon's comin'
We're finally on our own
This summer I hear the drummin'
Four dead in O-hi-o ...

Seconds later the door to the room closed, muffling the music. The edge of a dark blue towel appeared from under the door. The room's occupants were lighting a joint. The towel helped block the smell of the weed from making its way into the hallway.

Were they celebrating or crying in that room?

I didn't know, but for months afterward I kept thinking about Bob and whether he would have to go to 'Nam.

Should young men be forced to die for a cause they didn't believe in? How can a country that enshrined the phrase "life, liberty and the pursuit of happiness" deprive its own citizens of these cherished values? How much does America embrace liberty?

These questions and others motivated me to action several months later, when I joined a thousand CMU students who marched to protest the Vietnam War.

* * * * *

"Okay, people, we've reached downtown — now you have to decide," a long-haired male college student with patches on his blue jeans yelled out to a thousand students or so who had just marched from campus to the center of downtown Mount Pleasant, Michigan. "Are you going with me and others to Mission Street to stop traffic — to really send a strong message to the establishment — or are you going to march back to campus?"

The "agitator," as the "establishment" would have called him in those days, and the students he was trying to persuade had just walked from CMU's campus to the downtown in an organized protest of the war in Vietnam.

It was Friday, April 21, 1972, about 7 p.m. Spring jacket weather. The march was a coordinated effort. Hundreds of other campuses across America were also the site of protests that day.

A police cruiser had been leading the procession through the streets as protesters sang and chanted slogans and carried placards displaying the peace sign. Many homeowners along the route stood on their front porches, clapped, flashed the peace sign on one hand, and cheered.

As one of those protesters, I couldn't help but think how times had changed.

Four years earlier, in 1968, anti-war protesters involved in violent confrontations with police and National Guard soldiers outside of the Democratic National Convention in Chicago were framed in news reports as "snotty-nosed brats who needed a little discipline," as my Ph.D. advisor Phillip J. Tichenor would later say. News reports maligned the protesters even though the Walker Commission concluded that police, not protesters, had started the riot and used excessive force on protesters as well as on more than sixty news media personnel.

In February 1967, fewer than half of U.S. adults believed the United States had made a mistake sending troops to fight in Vietnam. But four years later, in 1972, seven of ten adults believed the United States had made a mistake. The older generation — the so-called "squares" — now were praising student protesters. Protesting had gone mainstream.

In fact, the "agitator" in downtown Mount Pleasant was having trouble convincing students to march to Mission Street, which was the busiest thoroughfare in Mount Pleasant, because most students there were opposed to the idea of using violence or unlawful conduct to protest the war.

"Hey, man, this is supposed to be a peaceful protest," responded one woman with long red hair and beads around her neck. "If we break the law, we hurt our cause. We should continue with the original plan and march back peaceably to campus, as we promised."

Several other students spoke for and against the plan to march to Mission Street. Most of the students, including me, agreed with the woman.

"A promise is a promise," I said, drawing on my sober, small-town Lutheran values.

About ten minutes later, the gathering broke into two, with several dozen students trekking to Mission and the vast majority, including me, heading back to campus.

The students who went to Mission fulfilled their promise and disrupted traffic for several hours. They returned to campus and threw rocks and paint at the Reserve Officers' Training Corps building, breaking some windows. Police arrested two students who sat on the hood of a police car.

The event was the last major anti-war march at CMU as well as at many other colleges across the country. The Vietnam War was winding down. Soon many activist students would turn inward. Making money and getting rich would be fashionable again.

But it would be wrong to say the anti-Vietnam War movement had no impact on America. More American lives might have been lost in Vietnam had students across America not engaged in public protest. For a brief time, we students wielded a disproportionate amount of power. We embraced the ideals of the Enlightenment more than any cohort before or after us.

We were children of the Enlightenment.

* * * * *

I worked in a factory in the summer of 1972 and returned to CMU in the fall but had to drop out because I contracted a heinous cough that would not go away. Decades later pulmonologists would give it a name, "Reactive Airway Disease," sometimes thought to be a precursor to asthma. Since I was a child, I would contract RAD every year or two and would often cough for two to three months. In 1986, however, a pulmonologist cured me in less than week with a dose of steroids and hydrocodone.

After recovering from my cough several weeks later, I took a job as a clothing salesperson at Merry-Go-Round, the first unisex clothing store in the United States. I was good at my job, possibly because I was never pushy. Within seven months I was managing my own store in Indianapolis at age nineteen. I was the youngest manager in the chain of forty-two stores.

I enjoyed the job at first. But I had to work six days a week, about ten hours a day. After a year or so, I quit because the salary was so low that I had a tough time paying the bills. When I returned to CMU in January 1974, my attitude about the benefits of education was even more resolute.

I majored in sociology but eventually found my niche in journalism, because I had no interest in becoming a police officer, or a parole or probation officer. As a newspaper reporter, I reasoned that I could cover stories that had the potential to change the world and get paid for it.

Enrollments in journalism were soaring at that time. News coverage of the Watergate scandal had an enormous impact. More than 60,000 students were majoring in journalism. Everyone, it seemed, wanted to be Bob Woodward and Carl Bernstein, the two *Washington Post* reporters who helped the newspaper win a Pulitzer Prize for its reporting on Watergate.

I took an "introduction to mass media" course from Donald Bird, a dynamic professor whose class covered the role of media as an agent of change, promoting democratic ideals, free speech and openness in government.

These ideals were reinforced in my reporting class, which was taught by Suzanne Nichols, a former journalist whose effervescent personality drew many admiring students. She often affectionately called me "deadline Demers," because I wasn't a very fast writer. But I persevered and it got easier. She was the first teacher to take a personal interest in me. We became lifelong friends.

During the spring of 1974, I befriended a student who ran for and was elected to the office of student body president. Robert Bixon asked me whether I would manage a media center to monitor and promote student involvement in government when he took office in fall 1974.

I accepted with enthusiasm.

If there was any doubt about journalism as a career, it was quickly erased the following year, when I uncovered a mini-Watergate-like scandal at CMU. Coincidentally, at the time I was reading Woodward and Bernstein's *All the President's Men.*

Chapter 12
CMU GATE

Friday, April 21, 1975
Central Michigan University

"Where's the promissory note?" I ask Robert, president of the student government at Central Michigan University.

"It's back in my room," he replies. "I'll bring it tomorrow."

Robert was my friend, or so I thought. He was politically savvy and wanted to be a labor attorney. After being elected president in the spring of 1974, he appointed me to head a new office called Media Information Services. Student government funded the office. Part of my job involved publishing an eight-page newsletter called *3rd Faction*. I had a staff of about a half dozen student volunteers.

The lead story in the second issue, published November 13, 1975, attacked conservative-backed U.S. Senate bill S.1, formally called the Federal Criminal Justice Act of 1975, but more popularly known as the U.S. Official Secrets Act. In an editorial, I pretentiously wrote:

> In an attempt to codify the Federal Criminal Code, supporters of Senate Bill No. 1 (S.1) have done no less than to place our Constitutionally guaranteed freedoms on the butcher's chopping block. If S.1 is allowed to become law, freedoms of the press, speech and assembly will be hacked to pieces. S.1 goes beyond revising the Federal Criminal Code and is destroying our civil liberties and the Bill of Rights. ...

The bill, which was dubbed "Nixon's Revenge" — he supported the bill but was forced to resign on August 9, 1974, because of

Watergate — was never enacted.

As editor of *3rd Faction*, my job was to report student government news fairly and objectively, Robert told me.

"But if you ever find corruption," he says, "you must report it."

Robert would regret making that statement.

* * * * *

Three months later I heard a rumor that his running mate, Barry Chevy, the student government vice president, had been making personal long-distance phone calls using university phones. In those days, callers had to pay a fee for each long-distance call.

I confronted Barry with the allegations, and, to my surprise, he confessed to the "crime." But he said he would give me a better story if I didn't report that one.

I consulted Sue, my journalism professor, and then agreed to Barry's terms, with the proviso that the new story would have to be more newsworthy. Through the years, some colleagues have questioned whether my actions were ethical. I still have mixed feelings about it. But I did get a better story.

Barry told me that Robert and the student government treasurer both had withdrawn money from a little-known student government bank account to pay their tuition. The bank account had been set up several years earlier after an insurance company donated several thousand dollars to student government for rights to promote its products and services to students.

I confronted Robert with the allegations.

"Yes, I took the money, and so did the student body treasurer," he confesses. "But we only borrowed it. We signed a promissory note a year ago when we took the money. We will pay it back."

The next day Barry gives me the promissory note. Robert didn't know that Barry had "ratted" on him to save himself.

I am at once suspicious. First, why would he have Barry deliver the note? Second, the note was crisp and clean — too crispy clean to have been a year old. Could it have been just typed?

I leave Barry's office and go into an outer office area equipped with three IBM Selectric typewriters, all of which used one-strike ribbons. *Could they have been careless enough to type the promissory note on one of those machines?*

"What are you doing?" Barry says, worriedly.

I ignored him.

The first two typewriters had new ribbons, and I didn't want to remove them for fear of ruining them. The ribbon was nearly used up on the third typewriter. I pulled it and transcribed the impressions, which were upside down and backwards. Sure enough, the promissory note had been typed up the night before — not a year earlier, as Robert had told me.

My story was Central Michigan Gate.

No, CMU Gate. That was better.

A day later Robert obtains a vote of confidence from the Student Senate.

What the heck?

The Senators didn't seem to care that one of their own had secretly borrowed money from a student government fund and lied about when the promissory note had been created.

Because I didn't have the resources to publish the story right away, I went to the editor of *Central Michigan Life*, the student newspaper, and gave them the story. Robert and the treasurer resigned from their student government jobs. The university forced both to repay the loans. Barry also resigned from his position.

Journalism could change the world.

And I had found my professional calling — at least for a few years.

Chapter 13
JOURNALISM DAZE

November 1977
Rochester, Michigan

Anthropologist Margaret Mead pushes her eyeglasses up and utters a phrase that evokes cheers and thunderous applause from the audience of several hundred students, faculty and citizens.

"Men have more physical strength than women, but women have more stamina, because they bear the children and perpetuate the species."

It was November 14, 1977. She was speaking at Oakland University in Rochester, Michigan, a suburb north of Detroit.

At the time, Mead was the world's most famous living social scientist — so famous that many ordinary Americans, not just students or scholars, recognized her. Her popularity shot up when she advocated that women in America should have the freedom to choose casual sex. She became a central figure in the women's movement of the 1960s, but she detested the label "women's libber."

The topic of her lecture today was supposed to be "The World Food Crisis," but I can't remember a thing she said about that. I was there to write a story for the *Rochester Clarion*, a small-town newspaper in a suburb north of Detroit. I also had a personal interest in her lecture, because I had taken an anthropology course at Central Michigan University two years before.

The foundation of her reputation was her 1928 book *Coming of Age in Samoa.* She wanted to know whether female adolescents in a traditional culture have a difficult time making the adjustment from childhood to adulthood, as did many American female youths. The book created a firestorm of controversy, however, when she reported that Samoan women engaged in casual sex before marriage.

Mead died a year and a day after her appearance at Oakland University. Five years later, in 1983, another anthropologist, Derek Freeman, challenged Mead's findings. Freeman said the women told him that they did not have casual sex as young women.

Despite the controversy, scholars widely agree that one of Mead's greatest contributions was her observation that culture influences people more than biology or genetics. In fact, she once said, "Never doubt that a small group of thoughtful, committed citizens can change the world; indeed, it's the only thing that ever has."

One could add that one citizen can change the world.

She certainly did.

* * * * *

I had been working at the *Clarion* for more than a year when I covered Mead's speech.

I was one semester short of graduation but left Central Michigan University early, because I was worried about getting a job. The market was flooded with journalism graduates, and the national unemployment rate was nearly eight percent. I reasoned it was better to get a job now and finish school later.

My boss was Ridge Anderson, who was about seven years older than I and much more worldly. He understood politics in a small town. Although he wasn't a great writer, he was enthusiastic about journalism and enjoyed his work. I liked that about him.

Both of us spent many hours talking about local politics over beer and cigarettes. Ridge's wife, Lynn, worked in public relations, and was a former student of and good friends with my journalism mentor, Sue Nichols.

Our weekly newspaper covered all the news that the big newspapers ignored — school events, community functions and activities, library events, church functions, and city and township government meetings.

Few things I wrote about ever made news outside of Rochester. But the Mead story and a story about a hockey coach charged with molestation were exceptions.

* * * * *

When I saw the Oakland County Sheriff's incident report that deputies had arrested a hockey coach for child molestation, I was horrified but not too shocked. Even my little hometown of Frankenmuth had its share of problems. A postal employee there had been accused of molesting young girls some years earlier, but he was never formally charged. Small towns often hide their warts.

The hockey coach was charged and arrested. I didn't question the veracity of the incident report, but my journalism teachers had taught me that there are at least two sides to a story. The report said the coach was out on bail. The incident report included his address, so I drove to his apartment complex and knocked on the door.

I was nervous.

I expected a monster to open the door.

But it was a man.

I identified myself and told him I was there to get his side of the story. He confessed to the crime and said he needed psychological counseling.

"I'm a sick man," he said. "I need help."

Not what I was expecting to hear. I thought he would refuse to talk or declare his innocence.

In that moment, I pitied the monster.

I drove back to the newsroom and wrote up the story, which included the direct quotes mentioned above. The story wouldn't be published for another day because the *Clarion* only published once a week, on Wednesdays. Ridge called me into his cubicle.

"Dave, the sheriff's office and the hockey coach's attorney are very upset," he says. "The sheriff said that if we publish comments from the conversation you had with the hockey coach, it could jeopardize the state's case against the accused. The defendant's attorney also said the comments could adversely affect the defendant's Sixth Amendment right to a fair trial."

"So, what," I respond. "Journalists are paid to report the news fairly and objectively. I had every right to interview the coach. He didn't have to talk to me. But he did, and the right thing to do is to publish his comments."

"Well, we can't. The sheriff said if we publish the defendant's comments, he will refuse our newspaper access to all incident reports in the future."

"That would be an abuse of his power," I counter.

Ridge shrugs.

He knew I was right, but he also knew our publisher would be upset if we lost access to the sheriff's reports, because a competing newspaper in town would have exclusive access to the incident reports. Ridge was very loyal to the publisher.

I didn't lose too much sleep over it.

Small-town newspapers tend to shy away from controversy and conflict. I understood that because of my courses in sociology. The people who live in small towns tend to share common values and are less tolerant of new ideas and outsiders. Big cities are more culturally, racially and socially diverse. Social conflict is higher in big cities, which is reflected in news stories.

I filed the censorship incident away in my mind as a good example of how even newspapers, whose Enlightenment mission is to tell the truth, can allow the bottom line and powerful sources to trump principle.

Despite this incident, I enjoyed my time at the *Clarion.* People treated me well wherever I went. Life as a big fish in a small pond wasn't disagreeable.

The only downside was the salary: only $105 a week. After one year, I was making $125, but that still was never enough to cover all the bills.

Was I being exploited?

I sure felt like it sometimes.

But I convinced myself that I was getting "paid in bylines," and this job would be a stepping-stone to a better position.

I was right.

In January 1978, I took a job at the *Huron Daily Tribune* in Bad Axe, Michigan—a city of 3,100 located in the middle of the thumbnail of the mitten-shaped state.

About six months later, we learned the Michigan Department of Social Services was investigating administrators at an adult foster care home in Bad Axe for allegedly using a cattle prod to punish a resident who would not cooperate.

* * * * *

I wasn't familiar with cattle prods, so I drove to the local Ace Hardware store.

"Got any cattle prods?" I ask the clerk.

He grins, revealing a couple of missing front teeth.

"Sure do," he replies, walking me to the aisle where they're found. He picks one up and gives it to me. The end of the prod has two blunt metal prongs on it. When the user pushes a button, he says, it sends an electric shock to anything touching the prongs.

"Does it hurt much?"

"No, when we was kids, we use to poke each other for fun all the time," he says with a broad grin. "Cattle don't even hardly feel it."

I believe him.

I position the prongs on my left index finger, hold my breath, and push the button. A jolt of electricity shoots through my fingers and hand, and up my arm up to the back of my head.

"Shit!" I scream.

He sadistically laughs.

At the beginning of the cattle prod investigation, I was convinced a crime had been committed. After all, bureaucratic governmental officials tend to be credible. Social science research provides a lot of evidence to back this up, even though confidence in institutions has been declining.

However, the alleged perpetrators were always cooperative when

I asked questions, and the alleged tool of abuse — the cattle prod — was never found. State investigators speculated the prod had been thrown away and was at the bottom of a landfill somewhere. Most of their case was built on the allegations of the alleged victim, however, which were never corroborated.

The investigators were not law enforcement officers, so the accused caregivers were never charged with a crime or given due process. The DSS could pull their license for any infraction — and they did. The caregivers were forced to close their facility, which was their main source of income.

I wrote several in-depth stories about the incident.

In the end, I believe the DSS officials knew they had conducted a flawed investigation. But embarrassment and fear of retribution from higher-ups and the public kept them from admitting their screw-ups.

My series of articles on the alleged abuse won a first-place investigative reporting award from the Michigan Press Association. More important, though, was the lesson I took from this incident: Public bureaucracies have a great deal of power and can insulate themselves easily from public accountability. As the years passed, I would see this happen many times.

* * * * *

I loved my job at the *Daily Tribune*.

Bad Axe was a small city surrounded by farmland and dozens of small towns. Lake Huron and its hundreds of miles of sandy shoreline and endless cottages and cabins were a twenty-minute drive due north. I rented a small house up there. At one point, I thought I could live here for the rest of my life.

My editor was Richard (Dick) W. Carson, who was about a decade older than me and a consummate storyteller. Dick was a reporter's editor. He could have a good argument with a reporter and still go out later and have a beer and a friendly conversation. Now that was professionalism — the ability to separate one's personal feelings from one's professional judgment. Some lawyers and professors are blessed with that trait. At the time I thought many editors were like that. On my next job, I would be proved wrong.

Dick gave me and other reporters at the paper a great deal of latitude to cover stories, including some critical of powerful people in Huron County, population 36,000.

One memorable story I wrote involved the president of the most powerful bank in the county. I spent six months researching the bank and its president, who had been sued over a business deal gone bad. The bank, which was the second-biggest advertiser at our newspaper, threatened to pull its advertising if we published the stories.

Dick refused to back down.

The *Tribune* published my two-part series, and the bank never pulled its advertising. It needed us more than we needed them.

Dick had guts. He proved to me that even small-town editors can do their jobs without compromising their principles. He and I remain good friends to this day.

In May 1979, I finally graduated from CMU after taking a semester of courses at Oakland University and one correspondence course. After the graduation ceremony, my journalism mentor Sue Nichols wished me "an interesting and happy life."

In terms of my future jobs, the former would dominate the latter.

* * * * *

I loved working for Dick and the *Daily Tribune*. But I wanted to work someday as an investigative reporter for a large daily. To do that, I needed to work my way up the journalism food chain.

Dick was supportive.

In January 1979, I accepted a reporting position with the *Midland Daily News* in Midland, Michigan, home to Dow Chemical, the world's largest chemical manufacturing facility at that time. The *Daily Tribune* and *Daily News* had just been acquired by the Hearst Corporation, one of the oldest newspaper chains in America.

Throughout the Vietnam War and for many years afterward, anti-war protesters and environmentalists criticized Dow because it was one of the companies that made Agent Orange, the powerful and deadly herbicide that was used to defoliate jungles in Vietnam in a matter of days after a spraying. The purpose was to deprive the enemy of hiding places. It worked.

However, many Vietnam vets who were exposed to Agent Orange claimed years later that it gave them illnesses and even cancer. Vietnamese authorities also estimated that the defoliant killed 400,000 civilians and troops and led to 500,000 birth defects.

Dow didn't like being in the news.

* * * * *

I had only been on the job for a couple of months or so when, one day in September 1979, a disgruntled citizen called the *Daily News* and said workers at the Midland landfill were illegally selling topsoil.

"Would you look into this?" my editor, Mark, asks.

I covered city hall.

If the allegation were true, asking the landfill operators if they were illegally selling soil wasn't likely to elicit the truth. So, I called the landfill office and asked whether I could have a tour of the facility. Even if there was no wrongdoing, I could still write a story about how the landfill worked.

The representative there was delighted to help me.

The tour took about 45 minutes.

There wasn't much to it. Dig a hole and fill it with garbage. Earth digging machines filled the dirt into large dump trucks that left the site. I asked where the trucks were going, and the tour guide said he didn't know.

That made me suspicious.

After the tour, I waited along the roadside in my new 1979 blue Plymouth Arrow. I followed one of the trucks. Fortunately, the drive was only about 15 minutes on rural dirt roads outside of Midland.

The truck pulled onto an open field containing a lot of heavy earth-moving equipment, which was digging and dumping dirt from the landfill into the ground. The site displayed "No Trespassing" signs and was surrounded by barbed-wire fencing. That seemed odd because there was no livestock in the area.

I drove past the site and stopped to interview a woman walking down the dirt road. She said she didn't know what was going on.

I returned to the office and called officials in Williams Township and Bay County, who told me the property was owned by Dow, but they, too, didn't know what was going on there.

I eventually spoke with a state Department of Natural Resources official, who said Dow had used the site as a landfill in the 1950s. He added that the carcinogen ethylbenzene tar and other chemicals were leaking into underground aquifers. The problem came to the attention of the authorities after a dog drank standing water on the site and lost its fur.

Dow also began construction on the pit without obtaining the proper county and state permits. They were using dirt and clay from the landfill to contain the carcinogenic chemicals.

I wrote my story.

The headline soft-peddled the news. Instead of "Carcinogenic Chemicals at Dow Landfill Leaking into Groundwater," it stated:

CLAY LINING PLANNED AT ETHYLBENZENE SITE
By David Demers

An abandoned landfill near Midland — identified as the source of a leaking cancer-producing chemical — is the target of a massive cleanup effort by its owner, the Dow Chemical Co.

Construction of a clay-lined dike to isolate and hold the contaminants began Monday.

But local officials said they were unaware of the $500,000 project and its purpose.

When told of the work, a Bay County planning official said he would investigate to determine if the construction began before a permit required under state law had been issued.

A Dow official confirmed the project began without obtaining any permits. Another said the permit would be sought if needed.

...

The next day a Dow spokesperson told me the company started construction without the permits because it wanted to build the dyke before it rained. I wondered, however, if the company was trying to move quickly before it became a public relations problem.

One Dow executive chastised me in a letter to the editor for using the adjective "abandoned" when referring to the landfill. He was right. I should have used the word "inactive."

Dow allegedly sealed the leaking landfill and was never fined for not obtaining the necessary permits. The lesson I learned is that powerful corporations are less accountable than the rest of us. Three months later I also learned that my newspaper was not insulated from community politics.

* * * * *

It was sometime in February 1980. Mary, the police reporter at the *Midland Daily News*, informed me that she was working on a story about a Michigan State Police investigation of the Midland Police Department.

"Officers are accused of gambling and prostitution," she whispers to me from her desk, which was adjoined next to mine. "But the state police won't release the results of the investigation. You cover city hall. Have you heard anything?"

"No, but I'll check and get back to you."

I call the city manager, William Castle, who is a man I have learned to trust. "Yes, the state police are investigating, but you already know that," he says. "Your editor and publisher have already seen the state police report."

"What?"

"Your editor, Mark, has already seen the report," Castle says, contradicting what Mary told me.

I call the city attorney's office, but he's not in.

I inform Mary.

"That's strange," she says. "I just spoke with Mark, and he said nothing about that. I'll ask him again."

When Mary emerges from Mark's office a few minutes later, Mark motions for me to come in. Mary has a puzzled look on her face. I enter his office. He closes the door.

"Where did you hear that the publisher and I have seen the state police report?" he asks.

"The city manager," I say. "Have you seen the report?"

"No," he says, angrily. "I want you to stop investigating this story, Dave. This is not your story. It's Mary's. She's the police reporter."

I am dumbfounded. I never gave any hint that I was taking the lead on this story. I was just helping Mary.

"I'm not trying to take Mary's story, Mark."

He shakes his head. I leave his office.

Someone is lying.

Whom do I believe?

There's a sacred trust between reporter and editor in the newsroom, or at least that's the way I have always viewed it. But the city manager has never lied to me.

A brief time later the city attorney returns my call and confirms what the city manager told me — that the publisher and Mark have seen the State Police report.

I tell Mary but ask her not to tell Mark. She agrees.

The next day Mark calls me back into his office, where he confesses that he had seen the confidential police report. He says he had to lie to Mary and me, because he had promised the police confidentiality. Apparently, someone forgot to tell the city manager and city attorney.

I felt betrayed.

Mark deserved a good verbal lashing, but I've never been very good at calling people liars. Instead of lying to me, why didn't Mark just say, "I can't talk about it."

The state police never charged any Midland officers with a crime. But why lie about a report that never found evidence of a crime?

I never obtained an answer to that question.

This wasn't the only time that Mark failed to live up to my professional expectations.

I interviewed an attorney from a local bank who bad-mouthed another bank that was planning to open a branch in Midland. At the end of the interview, the attorney told me I couldn't use the information he gave me. But I pointed out we had never agreed to go off-the-record. I told Mark and he approved my story but then withdrew support when an attorney threatened to sue the newspaper. Our newspaper published a retraction the next day.

I was angry because the retraction implied that I had written a false news account.

I contacted a local attorney to see what I could do to restore my good name. He said the issue wasn't big enough to fight. Instead, he suggested I write a letter to the bank attorney and give him a piece of my mind. The attorney advised, "Put the words 'personal and confidential' on the envelope and the letter. That'll protect you from a defamation lawsuit should others read the letter."

I followed his advice.

Of course, the bank attorney was furious. He complained to Mark and the publisher.

Mark admonished me.

I finally suppressed the good Lutheran boy in me.

"You have no grounds to criticize me, Mark. You approved the original story and then caved in when things got tough."

He walked away. He knew he was wrong.

A third event that shook my confidence in Mark as an editor came after I started investigating cancer rates in Midland, where a large proportion of people work for Dow. I had been dating an attorney who was a social activist, and she wondered why no one had ever investigated cancer rates in Midland.

I went to the local hospital to get statistics on cancer rates. The public relations person there relayed my request to hospital administrators, who then informed the board of directors of the hospital, who in turn contacted the publisher and editor of the *Daily News*.

Mark called me into his office.

"You need to drop this investigation," he says.

"Why?"

"Because you don't have the expertise to investigate cancer rates. It's very complex."

Mark's argument was weak. Journalists often cover complex issues. It wasn't my goal to determine whether the Dow facility was causing cancer, but to see if cancer rates differed in Midland compared with other communities.

But the incident demonstrated how naive I was about local politics. I should have realized that the local hospital board was populated with Dow employees, since they were the biggest employer in town.

The stories about the state police investigation, Chemical Bank and cancer rates raised questions in my mind about the ability of some journalism organizations to promote the Enlightenment project. They also shook my confidence in Mark as an editor.

Two decades later pollsters would discover that my experiences with Mark were not unique in the news business. About four in ten local and national journalists reported that they had purposely avoided covering newsworthy stories or softened the tone of stories to benefit the interests of their editors or news organizations.

But I didn't dwell on these matters for long, because my short, yet intense, four-year-long career as a reporter was coming to an end.

Although I enjoyed news reporting and felt my stories often had a meaningful impact on public policy, the daily grind of cranking out two or more stories a day was losing its appeal. I wanted something more challenging. An investigative-reporting position.

So, I applied for the Kiplinger Program in Public Affairs Reporting at The Ohio State University, hoping a master's degree would open doors for me.

I left the *Midland Daily News* in August 1980.

Ten years later I bumped into Mark at an academic conference in Minneapolis. He apologized for the way he treated me and told me I was the best reporter he ever had.

I thanked him.

Few people I know have that kind of courage.

He would have made a good Lutheran.

Chapter 14
KIPPY FEVER AND JOURNALISM'S DECLINE

August 1980
The Ohio State University

My first day at The Ohio State University was exhilarating.

The Oval — a football-sized grassy area laden with more than a dozen crisscrossing sidewalks — was bustling with pedestrian diversity. Students, professors and visitors were attired in shorts and T-shirts, dhotis and colorful silk saris, bell-bottom blue jeans and polyester shirts, hot pants and halter tops, suits and ties, robes and hijabs.

Something important was happening here, and I was thrilled to be a part of it. Yet I was scared because I had never dreamed of attending graduate school. I worried I wasn't smart enough.

My fears subsided after I met one of the fellows who would be joining me in the Kiplinger Program — Norma Steele, a gregarious, unpretentious and sometimes irreverent woman from Pittsburgh who loved to laugh and banter. She had worked as a newspaper reporter and, I would soon learn, didn't take guff from anyone. We forged a platonic bond that turned into a lifelong friendship.

There were nine fellows — five women and four men — in the year-long "Kippy Program," which granted its graduates a master's degree. All of us were experienced journalists looking for an educational adventure and maybe a boost in our careers. Our Kippy professor was a gleeful, intelligent man named Henry Schulte, who had worked as a reporter and editor for several major southern newspapers.

We took mostly graduate-level courses in different disciplines and met several times a week as a group to talk about issues facing society and journalists. Schulte moderated the discussions, which were often lively and sometimes cheeky.

On one occasion I was giving a presentation and all eyes were glued on me. Norma was sitting across from me at the large table. When I raised my eyes from my notes and looked at her, she was grinning and giving me the finger. We both burst into laughter. Everyone stared, wondering what happened. It was very unprofessional, of course. Schulte admonished us, but he didn't hold a grudge. Newspaper people are like that.

I took courses in money and banking, administrative law, mass media theory, quantitative research methods, civil liberties and the courts, and criminology. We flew to Washington, D.C., sat in on a U.S. Supreme Court hearing, and visited the Chinese and Russian embassies. I also taught an introductory course on reporting, which was challenging but enjoyable. I discovered that I liked teaching.

In 1980, the future of print journalism looked good.

Newspapers had played a vital role in advancing the ideals of the Age of Enlightenment after the 17th century, promoting democracy and the idea that the opinions of ordinary people were important. Newspapers reported on corruption in government and sometimes challenged traditional beliefs, including the idea that a god ordained rulers. Newspapers helped promote reason, logic, science and individual liberty. They provided news and information that enabled people and organizations to achieve their goals. They were, at the same time, a source of change and control, helping individuals and groups to adjust to a changing world.

But, unbeknownst to us Kippies in 1980, print journalism was beginning its great decline, in the private business sector as well as in higher education. From 1980 to 2024, the number of daily newspapers in the United States declined forty-two percent, from about 1,750 to 1,000. Newspaper sales and revenues fell two-thirds, from $61 billion to $21 billion (adjusted for inflation). And circulation dropped from 62 million to 25 million.

The growth of the internet caused most of the problems.

Many online news sources were free and available through social media. The news in a printed newspaper was old news by the time it reached the doorstep. Craig's List, an online classified advertising site that was free to users, killed newspaper classified advertising, which generated about a third of a newspaper's revenue. And the costs of printing and distributing hard copy newspapers were going up.

Journalism programs also were cutting back or shutting down, including the one at Ohio State. About a decade after we graduated, the dean of the College of Social and Behavioral Sciences announced that journalism was no longer central to the mission of the college. The journalism and professional mass communication programs would be downsized and merged with communication studies and a unit called Academic Technology Services and University Systems.

The Kippy Program eventually lost its master's degree and was reduced to offering short training sessions for journalists. In 2019, the program moved to the E. W. Scripps School of Journalism at Ohio University, where it currently continues to offer short courses for journalists.

Enrollments in journalism plummeted after 1980, going from 72,000 to 15,000. In contrast, the number of students majoring in public relations (later called strategic communication) was growing. Only 3,500 public relations people were working in the field in 1980; in 2024, there were 114,000.

These changes didn't mean the number of sources for news and information were declining. On the contrary, increasing structural and technological complexity in industries and organizations was growing the demand for specialized news and information. The internet exploded with websites, blogs and newsletters serving these needs.

These changes were decentralizing control over information, which fans of the Enlightenment view as a good thing. But there was a downside. Newspapers, which once were the sole source of information for people after the 18th century, now had thousands of online and broadcast competitors, many of which didn't follow the professional standards of objectivity, truth and accuracy. Commentaries and one-sided news reports became more popular with audiences, who preferred content that reinforced their own personal, social and political biases.

Nothing wrong with opinion-laden reporting.

But many of the websites began spreading false and misleading information. Some cable news networks also filled their airtime with guests and journalists who had axes to grind and who lacked in-depth knowledge of social problems. Decentralized power was now coupled with increased lack of professionalism and accountability. Anyone could be a journalist.

* * * * *

The year at OSU flew by.

Most of the Kippies went back to their newspaper jobs. I stayed on at Ohio State and enrolled in the master's program in sociology and criminology. One of the classes I had taken the previous semester piqued my interest in social scientific research.

My master's thesis examined the impact of exposure to mass media content on fear of crime. My data consisted of three telephone surveys of voters in the Columbus area and an original survey of OSU students. I found no relationship between exposure to crime content and fear.

To explain this lack of effect, I drew on the work of social psychologist Fritz Heider, who argued, like sociologist William H. Whyte, Jr., that people seek stability in their social and physical environments. I argued that crime news reports have little effect, because people often look for ways to explain away their own fear or victimization. For example, if people think an area is crime-ridden, they avoid going into it, which tamps down any fear presented in news reports. One major exception to this rule, though, is random crimes, such as a serial killer who isn't picky about his victims. News reports of these kinds of crimes generate fear that cannot be easily dismissed.

Years later, University of Minnesota sociologist George A. Donohue, who was a member of my Ph.D. committee, would reinforce these ideas in one of his classes.

"Do people prefer freedom or security?" he asked.

We students, sensing a setup, were quick to choose "security," much to Donohue's delight.

After watching people in action in social institutions for more than five decades, I believe Heider, Whyte and Donohue were right.

* * * * *

I graduated from the sociology/criminology OSU program in 1983 and moved to Scottsdale, Arizona, where my father, Hector, was living in retirement with my stepmother.

Within a month I landed a decent job as a senior marketing research analyst for Winona MRB Associates, a national marketing research company. I analyzed data collected through surveys and wrote up the results for a national clientele that included Ford Motor Company, Honeywell, 3M, United Healthcare, and Burger King. The results were used to create and revise advertising and marketing campaigns for the companies.

I learned a lot about how to analyze data at Winona during my four years there, but the corporate world was not my cup of joe. I had little control over my work and clients often ignored our research findings. The owner of the business also seemed to have more empathy for his pocketbook than his employees.

I missed teaching and wanted to learn more about research, and, to do it right, I needed a Ph.D. So, I enrolled in the University of Minnesota's program in mass communication in January 1987. Mona secured a good job as a market researcher at IDS/American Express, a financial management company headquartered in Minneapolis. Two years later, I filed a freedom-of-information lawsuit against the Minneapolis Police.

Chapter 15
SUING THE MINNEAPOLIS POLICE

March 1989
University of Minnesota

I was organizing my lecture notes when one of my students enters the classroom just before class and tells me the Minneapolis Police Department refused to give her access to the complaints filed against police officers.

"Yeah," says another. "And they weren't very nice about it."

The students were enrolled in a public affairs reporting course I was teaching at the University of Minnesota in the spring quarter of 1989. I had just started my third year in the Ph.D. program in mass communication.

My Ph.D. advisor was Phillip J. Tichenor, a tall, soft-spoken, modest man who grew up on a farm in Wisconsin. Some of his brothers were still farmers. Phil took the academic route. He worked as a correspondent before earning a Ph.D. from Stanford University. His advisor was Wilbur Schramm, who founded some of the first Ph.D. programs in communication in the nation.

At Minnesota, Phil was part of a research team that also included sociologist George A. Donohue and methodologist Clarice N. Olien. They called themselves "The Minnesota Team" and were famous, at least in the academic world, for creating the knowledge gap hypothesis. This theory held that as the flow of information into a social system increases, people high in education gain that knowledge at a faster pace than those low in education. Gaps in knowledge can produce social, political and economic inequalities that adversely affect democratic processes — an anti-Enlightenment outcome.

I had a lot of teachers before Phil, but none of them could compete in terms of saying things that would stick in my head — like the time during my first semester when I naively said a society that allows freedom of expression doesn't control information.

"Oh," he said, gently correcting me, "when you give people the freedom to speak, that's a form of social control. It makes them feel powerful and cools down the revolutionary potential in them."

This idea reinforced the free-speech philosophy in a book I had recently read, titled *The Tolerant Society*. Author Lee C. Bollinger argued that society should tolerate hateful, false, and anti-democratic speech, because tolerance strengthens and fortifies a society. Censoring extremists just makes them more angry, but allowing them to speak, as Phil pointed out, cools them down. Bollinger went on to become president of the University of Michigan and Columbia University.

As part of the requirements for my journalism class, I had asked the students to come up with a group investigative project. At the time, several community leaders had accused the Minneapolis Police Department of using excessive force on minorities. The story attracted coverage in local news media, including the main newspaper in town, the *Minneapolis Star Tribune*.

Community leaders also alleged that police discriminated against minorities who filed complaints of misconduct or unlawful behavior against individual police officers. The leaders accused police of validating a higher proportion of complaints filed by whites versus nonwhites.

Our class didn't have the resources to assess whether police had used excessive force, although research in criminology showed that excessive force was a common event in large police departments. However, we could answer two questions: Were police less likely to sustain complaints filed by minorities? And when an investigation finds that police officers have committed criminal acts, are they punished, and, if so, how?

Minnesota state law required police agencies to release information on incident complaints brought against citizens after they are resolved or become inactive. In other words, those complaint records become public data when police finish their investigation.

The students and I assumed the same standards applied to complaints filed against police officers who are accused of violating the law. Why would they differ? No one in America is above the law, right?

However, the police refused to give the students the records.

On March 21, 1989, I wrote a letter to Minneapolis Police Chief John Laux, formally requesting access to the records over a ten-year period. Five weeks later the chief responded and said information about the complainants, the police officers, and the complaints was not public data. But the department would give us access to everything else at a cost of $2,322.50. It wasn't clear what he meant by "everything else."

Police eventually argued that most of the information in the records was confidential because they were "personnel records." They also asserted that police are often wrongly accused of using excessive force or violating the law, so they deserve special protection from public scrutiny.

We argued just the opposite: The records on allegations of "criminal wrongdoing" should be public because the same information for citizens is public. In fact, police should be more accountable, because they are the only nonmilitary institution in our democratic society authorized to use deadly force on citizens. Enlightenment advocates would expect nothing less.

Minnesota state law specifically stated that citizens did not have to pay for public records if they just wanted to inspect them and did not want photocopies. But attorneys for the city insisted that citizens should have to pay the city for the time it took to generate the records — and to redact information in them — because local government could not afford to absorb such costs.

Laux and I were at an impasse. A lawsuit was my only option.

I asked several campus organizations and a national journalism association for assistance in filing a lawsuit. No one responded.

I mentioned the problem to Minnesota media law professor Don Gillmor, who was coauthor of a popular college-level mass communication law book. He suggested I contact Mark Anfinson, the attorney for the Minnesota Newspaper Association, a nonprofit organization that promoted the interests of newspapers in the state.

Anfinson was an energetic thirty-something attorney who said he would put the paperwork together at no charge. I would just have to pay the filing and paperwork costs, which amounted to about $150. He suggested I argue the case pro se, meaning I would represent myself without an attorney.

If I lost the case or if I won and the city appealed, Anfinson said he would then take over and argue the case in the appeals courts.

It was an offer I couldn't refuse.

* * * * *

The lawsuit was filed in October 1989, long after the public affairs reporting course had disbanded. The students worked on individual in-depth projects instead.

As expected, the attorney for the city of Minneapolis argued in court that the records were not public because they were personnel records. I responded that a democracy is predicated upon openness and accountability in government. The judge listened patiently to my idealistic arguments about democratic processes. What I didn't realize was that the judge would make his decision based not on abstract theories about democracy but on how the state open records law was worded.

"Save that stuff for the classroom," the judge could have told me. But he didn't. He was polite and professional. And, fortunate for me and advocates of government accountability, he could find nothing in Minnesota law that restricted release of the records.

The city appealed.

Anfinson took over, arguing the case before the Minnesota Appeals Court, which also ruled in my favor. The city then appealed to the Minnesota Supreme Court, the highest court in the state.

Meanwhile, in late June 1990, the *Toledo Blade* published a series of stories detailing seventeen years of police misconduct that had been hidden in internal affairs police records. The investigation came after

Ohio courts ruled that everything in the records was public data under the state open-records law.

Blade reporters found scores of cases of abuse of authority. Internal affairs investigators had documented many cases of unlawful conduct, including domestic abuse, drunken driving, theft, and assault. But few officers were punished or prosecuted. Critics alleged that police refused to prosecute the officers in court because of fears the cases would tarnish the reputation of the police, hinder efforts to obtain more resources from taxpayers, and lead to expensive lawsuit settlements.

Several months later, Anfinson appeared before the Minnesota Supreme Court. Mona and I and a handful of other citizens were in the audience. But only the attorneys were allowed to speak to the justices.

At one point, a judge asked Anfinson what kinds of information I was seeking. Anfinson responded that the lawsuit was only concerned about obtaining access to information on the complainants, not on the police officers or other information in the records.

That was incorrect.

I wanted access to all the information in the records that accused officers of criminal violations of the law — the same information that was already public data under Minnesota law when citizens were accused of breaking the law.

I felt betrayed but didn't hold a grudge against Anfinson. He had spent a lot of time helping me obtain access to the records. Besides, the court probably would have ruled the same way regardless of how Anfinson answered the question.

On April 19, 1991, nearly two years after my journalism students first asked for the records, the Minnesota Supreme Court ruled that information about the complainants was public data and that the city could not charge fees for inspecting the records. However, most of the information in the complaints — including the names of the officers, the charges, and facts about the case — would not be disclosed. So, we could not duplicate what investigative reporters did in Toledo. But at least we could answer the first question our class set out to answer: Are police more likely to sustain complaints filed by whites than nonwhites?

In July 1991, while I waited for police to release the records, I wrote a commentary for an alternative weekly newspaper in the Twin Cities, suggesting that Minneapolis police, like the Toledo police, had a history of brutality that had been effectively hidden from the public view. In September 1991, I also wrote a commentary for *Minnesota's Journal of Law & Politics*.

When police turned over the data, one of my former top students, Mark Engebretson, and two others began analyzing the internal affairs complaint information. In March 1992, we published our findings in the *Twin Cities Reader*, an alternative weekly newspaper. The story was titled "The Color of Justice: White People Are Almost Twice as Likely to Prevail in a Complaint Against a Minneapolis Police Officer — and Critics Claim Racism Is the Reason." As community leaders had suspected, we found that police were less likely to sustain complaints filed by nonwhites (11%) than whites (19%).

Police Chief Laux wasn't pleased with the findings.

He and I debated the issue on WCCO's *Jim Rogers Show*.

Laux asserted that his officers were not racist.

I said the data did not say they were. Community leaders had made that assertion. The data simply showed that internal affairs officers are more likely to sustain complaints by whites. The cause of that disparity was unknown.

Our radio debate was cordial. But I did drive slower than the speed limit for the next couple of months.

Meanwhile, several weeks after the Minnesota Supreme Court decision, I filed another pro se lawsuit that specifically requested access to criminal complaint records involving police as the accused offender. I excluded administrative complaint records. I focused only on criminal complaints, the kind that are already public when a citizen is the alleged offender.

The trial and appeals courts ruled against me. They held that even criminal allegations of misconduct were personnel data and, thus, not subject to public scrutiny, unless the officer is prosecuted in a court of law. A double standard. Citizens are not granted such protection.

In September 1992, Engebretson and I presented the findings on the differences between white and nonwhite complainants to the Minnesota Human Rights Commission.

Commissioners showed a lot of interest in the data and asked a lot of questions. But no formal action was ever taken by the commission, the police or the city council. A step backward for the Enlightenment project.

* * * * *

So, what explains why the appeals court would allow criminal complaints against citizens to be open to the public but not criminal complaints against police officers?

The courts' rulings seemed to contradict the theories of German sociologist Max Weber, who argued that bureaucracies [such as the courts] discharge their business through an impersonal, objective process. But the courts were favoring the police.

I asked my advisor Phillip J. Tichenor for advice. "Your success in the courts may very well depend upon whether you are able to convince other elites in the system that there is a problem of police misconduct."

Indeed, local news media were not paying attention to the misconduct issue or to the second lawsuit I had filed to get access to criminal complaints. Although I wrote two articles drawing attention to the misconduct issue, those articles appeared in publications with limited readership.

I was a coyote howling in the wilderness.

Another possible reason the appeals court failed to open the criminal records of police officers is that bureaucracies do not embrace democracy. In fact, Weber was very pessimistic about the long-term consequences that bureaucracies would have for individual freedom and autonomy and democratic decision-making. He even suggested that a bureaucracy can be an "iron cage."

Weber's student Robert Michels developed what he called the "iron law of oligarchy," which contends that bureaucracies often start with a commitment to democracy but are compelled, as the organization grows, to centralize power in professional staff.

To retain their power, these leaders often oppose efforts to democratize their organizations through free elections or other means. This produces an oligarchy — a handful of elites who control most of the power. Michels wrote, “Who says organization says oligarchy.”

Michels examined socialist parties in Germany and elsewhere, which were committed to the principles of democracy, and found ample evidence that the organizations themselves didn’t practice what they preached. Sociologist Michel Crozier also observed that bureaucracies are self-destructive and are unable to acknowledge their faults. “A bureaucratic organization is an organization that can not correct its behaviour by learning from its errors.”

* * * * *

I would end up taking a more sanguine view of bureaucracies in my Ph.D. dissertation in 1992 as well as in my research that followed. My basic hypothesis was the more a newspaper exhibits the characteristics of the corporate or bureaucratic form of organization, the more emphasis it would place on product quality and the less emphasis on profits. Large corporate organizations have more capital and resources to cover the news and hire the best reporters. Professionalism is higher at corporate media.

My national probability surveys and content analyses repeatedly supported these hypotheses through the years. Newspapers become more, not less, critical of political and economic elites as they grow and become more “corporatized.” They publish a larger number and proportion of editorials and letters to the editor that are critical of mainstream values, institutions and elites.

One of my surveys showed that mayors and police chiefs in communities served by large corporate newspapers also viewed those newspapers as being more critical of them and their policies. In contrast, mayors and police chiefs in communities served by entrepreneurial, or less bureaucratic, newspapers perceived their newspapers as being more supportive.

This doesn’t mean that newspapers are adversaries of powerful elites. In fact, the more powerful an elite, the greater access that elite has to the news media. Newspapers generally produce content that helps elites achieve their goals, often to the disadvantage of less powerful, alternative groups.

Of course, my research seemed to contradict the theories of William H. Whyte and other writers critical of corporations and bureaucracies, which argued that they suppress individualism in people. The solution to this conundrum lies in the organization's culture. If an organization places a high value on principles like democracy, free speech, truth, honesty, fairness and due process, then it enhances civil liberties and freedom. Newspapers and universities both have the capacity to promote Enlightenment ideals. But this goal can be lost when the culture in the organization does not value such ideals and fails to reward its employees for embracing them.

I did not fully understand these processes when I graduated from the Ph.D. program in mass communication at the University of Minnesota in December 1992. I had a good "book understanding" of how bureaucracies function. However, my practical knowledge was lacking, as my free-speech controversy at the University of Wisconsin–River Falls illustrated.

Chapter 16
THE $64,000 APOLOGY

Summer 1995
Shoreview, Minnesota

The 1995-96 school year offered respite from the free-speech controversy at the University of Wisconsin–River Falls. I accepted a year-long visiting professorship at the University of Minnesota, which meant I didn't have to teach at UW-RF. I also hired a new attorney who had a strong background in First Amendment law.

Mona and I threw a couple of fun dinner parties. I loved to cook, so we invited Hazel Dicken-Garcia, a journalism historian, and Donald Gillmor, the mass media law professor. We talked about Europe, movies, theater, politics, and food.

A decade later Hazel and one of her graduate students, Giovanni Del'Orto, would coauthor a book which found that during the Civil War, newspaper editors were very intolerant when it came to free speech. "[E]ditors consistently supported the larger political system over any professional journalism ideology, the 'common good' over individual rights, and the military 'discretion' over constitutional principles." Their finding joined a growing body of research showing that the press has never been a staunch defender of First Amendment rights during crises.

These studies also supported the corporate structure theory I was developing. Mass media are institutions of social control, but not the way most people think. In a so-called "free society," mainstream news media don't deliberately produce overt propaganda or false content. They rely heavily on powerful elites and government leaders to do that. Reality is framed from their perspective, not so much from the perspective of the working or middle classes. News media play a "system-maintenance role," producing content that generally supports the interests of powerful institutions and elites.

Yet that summer I was becoming increasingly aware of a discrepancy between my theory and the real world. My personal experiences with bureaucracies at the *Midland Daily News*, the Minnesota court system, the Minneapolis Police Department, and now at the University of Wisconsin–River Falls suggested that they put political interests and personal loyalties before truth and justice.

Maybe I was wrong, and sociologists Max Weber, Robert Michels and Michel Crozier were right. Bureaucracies monopolize knowledge, resist change, create iron (anti-democratic) cages, and are unable to learn from and correct their mistakes. Even my new attorney, Marshall Tanick of Minneapolis, seemed to back these sociologists up when he outlined our legal strategy in the summer of 1995.

"If we file a lawsuit in Wisconsin, we'll lose. The state courts will identify strongly with the UW administrative system. Instead, we'll file in federal court. We'll have a chance there. We'll file a federal First Amendment lawsuit."

* * * * *

Tanick and I met for the first time in April 1995.

He was an employment attorney but also an expert in First Amendment law. He had represented several professors in employment disputes. He also represented the student newspaper (*Minnesota Daily*) in several high-profile legal cases that expanded free speech, and he had authored articles about the First Amendment.

I hired him on the spot and immediately informed Jay Willardson, my attorney in Madison. Jay wasn't upset because he acknowledged he didn't have expertise in First Amendment law.

Tanick was a pit bull in a three-piece suit.

Decisive, commanding, perspicacious.

He earned his law degree from Stanford, graduated summa cum laude and was a member of the Order of the Coif, an honor society for

U.S. law school graduates who rank in the top ten percent of their class.

Tanick's mind always seemed to work twice as fast as everyone else's in the room. As such, he was a bit impatient at times with people who couldn't express an idea in ten seconds or less — people like me. But this flaw, if you want to call it that, was nothing more than a blemish. Tanick could see opportunities where others could not. He loved a challenge. And my case certainly offered that, given that the law and the courts readily defer to universities when it comes to tenure decisions.

Tanick told me that filing in federal court meant that financial remedies would be limited.

"We can fight to keep your job. Is that what you want?"

"Yes," I reply. "This isn't about the money. It's about protecting First Amendment rights. All I want is an apology, and I can continue to work at River Falls, if I must."

If Tanick thought I was naive and idealistic, he never told me.

The first thing he did was to file an amended Notice of Claim, which gives the government a chance to settle the dispute before a formal lawsuit is filed. Jay had filed the original notice in April. The revised notice added several more complaints, including a defamation claim against journalism chair Mike Norman as well as the First Amendment claim.

The UW system denied the claims, of course.

* * * * *

My year at Minnesota turned out to be one of my best years of teaching. I attribute that mostly to the students. They were bright.

Minnesota admits only about fifty percent of applicants. The UM students were far more serious about learning and studying. Most read the material assigned for the day and were prepared to discuss it. That made my job much easier.

My favorite class in fall 1995 was an introduction to mass communication course. One-hundred-and-twenty students, but it was like teaching a seminar of ten. I served more as a moderator than a teacher. Once an issue was introduced, students took over. The discussions were lively and intelligent.

On the final day of the course, I was surprised when many stood and clapped. They were the ones who deserved the recognition.

* * * * *

Tanick filed the free-speech lawsuit on Wednesday, September 6, 1995, in Federal District Court in Madison, and named Mike Norman, journalism chair, and the University of Wisconsin Board of Regents as defendants.

The complaint claimed the university refused to renew my contract because I helped students publish a series of articles about student evaluations of faculty and faculty salaries.

"Because of his involvement in those articles," the complaint stated, "he encountered hostility from other members of the faculty, including his colleagues and superiors within the Department of Journalism and other administrators at the university."

I wrote a news release about the lawsuit. Local newspapers, the Student Press Law Center, and *Quill* magazine, which is published by the Society of Professional Journalists, covered the story.

The media coverage upset many UW-RF university officials. Privacy laws limit their ability to comment to the press. I talked freely and openly about the case. It was one of the few advantages I had over the powerful $2 billion-dollar UW System bureaucracy.

A week after the lawsuit was filed, Mike resigned from his position as chair of the journalism department, saying his workload was too heavy. He was stressed, almost as much as me. However, Mike rescinded that decision two days later, after an administrator in the dean's office asked him to reconsider.

* * * * *

In early February 1996, I received a telephone call from William Glaberson, a reporter at the *New York Times.*

"Dr. Demers, I am working on a story about the loss of family-owned newspapers, and I see you have just published a book about corporate newspaper ownership. May I ask you some questions?"

"Hell yeah!" I wanted to shout, but instead responded professionally, "I'd be delighted to help you, Mr. Glaberson."

Most scholars who develop theories about the social world live their lives in relative obscurity. They publish in journals that are read by a small number of scholars in their fields. As such, many good theories and research findings have little or no impact on changing the world, because policymakers aren't aware of them. Some scholars are content to live a low-key professional life. But, to me, making the world a better place is what scholarship is all about.

Glaberson said he had not yet read my book, but he had ordered a copy. The book summarized my research over the past seven years and was titled *The Menace of the Corporate Newspaper: Fact or Fiction?* The publisher was Iowa State University Press.

I spent the next hour or so answering Glaberson's questions and explaining my theory and the results of my research. Not surprisingly, he was a critic of chain or corporate ownership. In fact, I later learned he was an expert on the newspaper industry, having covered it for more than five years.

By the end of our conversation, I could tell I had not persuaded him as to the validity of my theory. But he said he would withhold judgment until he read my book.

A week passed and we chatted by phone again. Glaberson said he had read parts of my book. I spent another fifteen minutes making my case.

"I don't know if I can buy into your theory," he says.

"You don't have to," I respond. "As a journalist, your role is to report all sides of the story."

His story was published February 19, 1996, on page one of the business section. The story quoted critics of chain and corporate newspaper ownership. And it quoted some newspaper executives, who said consolidation "is a symptom of an industry reshaping itself to compete with new competitors like electronic information distributors."

Bigger means economies of scale. But most of the story focused on the adverse impact of chain and corporate ownership.

And what about the empirical evidence from my book?

Not there.

I wasn't even quoted.

Some might argue that Glaberson refused to quote my research because he was biased.

Perhaps.

But as the years passed, I told my graduate students that I believe my research was less a victim of bias than of failed credibility. When activists, scholars or citizens have a point of view that contradicts well-established beliefs, whether right or wrong, it's extremely difficult for their voices to be heard. Knowledge is not self-evident. It also involves discourse about the credibility of sources and information.

Glaberson was an expert on the newspaper industry.

As an expert, he was more difficult to persuade than a layperson. In short, it would take more than one book to get fifteen minutes of fame in the *New York Times,* and I returned to being one of the professors whose research would live on in relative obscurity.

* * * * *

By February 1996, Mona and I had spent more than $12,000 on legal fees, and it was estimated we would spend another $10,000 before the deposition stage. Going to trial would cost about $50,000, and if the case were appealed, Tanick said the figure could easily top $100,000. That was a lot, but the alternative seemed even worse: the end of my career as a professor.

If we won, the best-case scenario was that all attorney fees would be paid by the university with perhaps some compensation for lost time. But all I really wanted, outside of attorney fees, was an apology.

I understood that few court cases go to trial. Most are settled.

But, as I had learned in my courses at Minnesota, was that public bureaucracies rarely apologize. They'd rather spend taxpayers' money.

While attorneys on both sides were preparing their cases, I was applying for jobs at other universities. Washington State University in Pullman, Washington, had a position open. I told Mona about it.

"Why don't you apply?" she asks.

"But Pullman? Where the hell is that? Are you sure you want to move there, Mona?"

"It's south of Spokane."

I applied and got an interview.

Many Murrow faculty had heard about the lawsuit in River Falls. Some were uneasy about interviewing a faculty member who might be a troublemaker. One of those faculty was a public relations expert who a decade later became the director of the Murrow School at WSU and would target me for dismissal.

The interview went well, however, and a month later I was offered a position in the journalism sequence, which consisted of four full-time faculty and several adjuncts. I suspect that I survived the interviewing process because my Ph.D. advisor Phillip J. Tichenor was a highly respected scholar in the field. That gave me some credibility.

* * * * *

In late March 1996, I received a call from Tanick.

"Dave, the attorney for the UW system and I have reached a possible settlement in your case."

I was surprised because I didn't even know a settlement was in the works.

"Is the university going to apologize?" I ask.

"No. Bureaucracies don't apologize. The legal system doesn't operate like that. The courts are a place where money is exchanged for a wrong that is committed. The UW system is offering you a $62,000 cash settlement. In exchange, you'll have to drop the lawsuit and leave your job."

I was disappointed.

"Dave, take the money and declare victory," Tanick says. "The payment will be interpreted by others as a sign that the university wronged you. You can use that to your advantage."

He pointed out that the alternative was a long and drawn-out lawsuit with an ending that couldn't be guaranteed. The settlement, on the other hand, would cover my costs and I could give some to a scholarship fund.

Tanick suggested that we ask the university to increase the settlement to $64,000, to draw attention to the crooked game show from the 1950s, *The $64,000 Question*.

I laughed and consented.

The university accepted the change.

After the settlement, Tanick and I issued a press release to various media. The story was widely covered in local newspapers and professional media in journalism, including SPJ's *Quill* magazine:

JOURNALISM PROFESSOR VINDICATED

> What is a journalism professor entitled to when he is terminated from his position for exercising his freedom of expression?
>
> In the case of David Demers, the answer is $64,000. That's the amount the University of Wisconsin in River Falls is paying Demers to get him to drop a First Amendment lawsuit against the university and journalism chair ...
>
> Demers filed the lawsuit in federal district court in Madison last September. ... Internal administrative memos obtained after the lawsuit was filed also showed that administrators were trying to fire Demers because he had hired an attorney to help him fight for his job and protect his reputation.
>
> "This was an important case because it demonstrates that colleges must respect First Amendment rights," says Demers's attorney, Marshall H. Tanick of Minneapolis. "It is ironic that a journalism department, which supposedly teaches students about the First Amendment, should have to learn such a costly lesson this way."

UW-RF journalism chair Mike Norman was furious.

On May 8, he wrote a letter to the *Quill* editor, accusing her of publishing a one-sided story. Mike was especially angry about Tanick's comment.

"We found it to be offensive to the faculty and students in this department and completely erroneous in its implications of the quality of journalism education students expect and deserve at UW-River Falls."

Mike was right.

The story was one-sided.

Quill published Mike's response.

But Tanick was also right.

The settlement was nearly as good as an apology.

* * * * *

All told, I piled up about $31,000 in attorney fees and court costs. I gave Mona an extra $5,000 for her "pain and suffering."

I gave $9,000 in scholarships to River Falls journalism students. I gave $2,000 in bonuses to Tanick and his assistant attorney. The rest, which amounted to $17,000, I used to pay off my three-year-old Mazda 626.

Tanick's law firm gave several $500 scholarships to UW–RF students.

From a financial standpoint, the lawsuit was a "no-gainer." No amount of money can compensate one for the stress and mental anguish of fighting a bureaucracy.

However, if I had to do it all over again, I wouldn't change a thing.

Did UW–RF officials learn a lesson from my lawsuit?

Hard to say.

But back then I told myself that things would be different at Washington State University. After all, it was four times bigger than UW–RF, and my own bureaucratic theory predicts that larger institutions are more likely to tolerate conflict, disagreements and activist professors.

Part IV

Gauntlet Two

Chapter 17
PURGING THE PALOUSE

September 1998
Washington State University

They came without warning.

Tiny black motes, no bigger than the head of a pin, moving swiftly through the screen of a window in a second-floor bedroom of my townhouse in Pullman, Washington.

It was early September 1998.

I shut the window within seconds.

But it was too late.

Thousands of them blanketed a windowsill, a desk and the surrounding carpet. A fast-moving thunderstorm with fierce winds propelled them into the room.

But what created them?

Although I had lived in Pullman for two years, it took me several minutes to answer my own question.

Field burning.

The specks were ash from burning the stubble in wheat fields.

The controversial farming practice of crop burning in the Northwest was often in the news in the 1990s and early 2000s. On my occasional trips from Pullman to Spokane along U.S. 195, I could see huge plumes of smoke in shades of light to dark gray, rising hundreds of feet into the sky.

But until now I had never personally experienced the effects.

In Washington state, farmers most often torched the stubble in wheat fields after the fall harvest. In 2006, the Washington State Department of Ecology issued more than a thousand burn permits to

Washington farmers, who set ablaze more than 180,000 acres. About one-fifth of those acres were in Whitman County, where Pullman and Washington State University are located.

Farmers burned for three major reasons: to get rid of pesky insects, to reduce field stubble, and to create a natural fertilizer for the soil. Burning was a cheap alternative to pesticides and fertilizers. It also reduced chemical pollution to streams and underground aquifers.

Most environmental groups didn't dispute the merits of burning for farmers. The environmentalists liked the idea of using fewer chemicals on crops, but they were concerned about the effects of smoke on human lungs. For people with respiratory illnesses, those ashen motes were making it harder to breathe.

In fact, during the first month I arrived in Pullman, an asthmatic woman in a nearby Idaho community died a day after her backyard was inundated with smoke from a grass farm stubble burn. She awoke with breathing problems after camping overnight with her children.

In Oregon in 1988, smoke from field burning blanketed Interstate 5, causing a twenty-three-car collision that killed seven people and injured thirty-seven. Oregon banned field burning in 2009.

But farmers in Washington State and Idaho still purge to this day.

And, unbeknownst to me when I started teaching at WSU in 1996, administrators at Washington State University had been doing some purging of their own.

They were firing tenured faculty.

Chapter 18
MURROW: THE ENLIGHTENED JOURNALIST

August 6, 1996
Pullman, Washington

The skies were sunny and the temperature tipped over ninety at the kidney-shaped swimming pool in my apartment complex in Pullman, Washington, where I was reading Joseph E. Persico's 1988 biography *Edward R. Murrow: An American Original.* In two weeks, I would teach my first class at Washington State University.

I had moved into a one-bedroom apartment three days before. The free-speech battle at River Falls was behind me. I was full of hope. The future was bright again.

My spouse, Mona, had encouraged me to apply for the tenure-track position at WSU, but she decided not to make the move. She had a good-paying job at IDS/American Express. Our divorce was heavy-hearted, but we remained friends.

Murrow is WSU's most famous graduate.

He attended Washington State College, as it was called then, from 1926 to 1930. He became a pioneer in radio and television broadcasting and is best known for helping to end in 1954 the pernicious investigatory practices of radical-right extremist Republican Senator Joseph R. McCarthy, who had falsely accused many Americans of being traitors or communists.

I confess I didn't know much about Murrow before I began teaching at WSU. My heroes were print journalists like Watergate sleuths Bob Woodward and Carl Bernstein, muckraker Ida Tarbell (whose stories helped break up John D. Rockefeller's oil trust), socialist Upton Sinclair (author of *The Jungle* and a Pulitzer Prize winner), and investigative journalist Izzy Stone (publisher of *I. F. Stone's Weekly* newsletter).

But I figured if I were going to teach in the Edward R. Murrow School of Communication, I should have some knowledge of its namesake. So, I bought copies of biographies written by Persico (1988) and A. M. Sperber (1986) and read them during the two weeks before my first day of work. To my surprise, Murrow would have a far bigger impact on my thinking than all of the other print heroes combined.

A thirty-something woman and her school-aged boy joined me at the swimming pool. I smiled, wiped sweat from my forehead, and fell back into my book.

Four decades earlier, on March 9, 1954, Murrow was also sweating, but for a different reason. He was in New York City, just minutes away from telling his national television audience of twelve million *See It Now* viewers that U.S. Senator Joseph R. McCarthy was a tyrant, liar and rumormonger.

* * * * *

McCarthy first garnered national attention on February 9, 1950, when he told a Republican women's club in Wheeling, West Virginia, that "the State Department is infested with communists" and that he had a list of two-hundred-and-five of them.

Although McCarthy never produced the names — a pattern of behavior he would repeat often over the next four years when making allegations — the news media gave his speech a lot of attention. He was, after all, a powerful U.S. senator, and powerful people make news.

But Murrow was unimpressed.

For four years he had watched McCarthy level false or misleading allegations against hundreds of U.S. citizens, including some of his colleagues at CBS. On several occasions, Murrow helped save the careers of these colleagues.

Some journalists and politicians had drawn attention to McCarthy's baneful tactics. But the criticism seemed to have no impact on his popularity. In fact, polls showed that McCarthy's ratings had steadily risen since 1951. In January 1954, just two months before Murrow's broadcast, one-half of American adults had a favorable opinion of McCarthy.

Murrow was apprehensive this evening, partly because he knew McCarthy would retaliate, and Murrow was an easy target. Even though he had rejected radical politics all his life, he had associated with many known communists. Some were friends.

Murrow had a lot to lose financially. He owned two homes and earned more than $1 million a year (in today's dollars) at CBS.

A make-up assistant wipes sweat from Murrow's chin and face.

Then the on-air cue.

"Good evening," he says. "Tonight, *See It Now* devotes its entire half hour to a report on Senator Joseph R. McCarthy, told mainly in his own words and pictures."

After a commercial break, Murrow tells his twelve million viewers that *See It Now* would offer McCarthy equal time if "he believes we have done violence to his words or pictures."

A short time later Murrow says McCarthy often "operates as a one-man committee. He has traveled far, interviewed many, terrorized some, accused civilian and military leaders of the past administration of a great conspiracy to turn the country over to communism, investigated and substantially demoralized the present State Department, made varying charges of espionage at Fort Monmouth. The Army says it has been unable to find anything relating to espionage there."

The time remaining in the half-hour slot is filled mainly with film clips of McCarthy making outrageous accusations against mainstream politicians and organizations, none of which has ties to communism. They include Democratic presidential candidate Adlai Stevenson II, a U.S. Army general, the mainstream press, the Voice of America, the American Civil Liberties Union, and the Institute of Pacific Relations.

McCarthy is incriminating himself. That's what Murrow and his *See It Now* co-producer Fred Friendly intended when putting the show together.

As the show comes to a close, Murrow warns that if a politician's rhetoric is dangerous, anyone who doesn't oppose it is complicit.

> [T]he line between investigating and persecuting is a very fine one and the junior senator from Wisconsin has stepped over it repeatedly. ...
>
> We must not confuse dissent with disloyalty. ...
>
> We will not walk in fear, one of another. ...
>
> The actions of the junior senator from Wisconsin have caused alarm and dismay amongst our allies abroad and given considerable comfort to our enemies, and whose fault is that? Not really his. He didn't create this situation of fear; he merely exploited it, and rather successfully.
>
> Cassius was right: "The fault, dear Brutus, is not in our stars but in ourselves. ... Good night, and good luck."

* * * * *

Then, as today, that *See It Now* segment is often heralded as one of the greatest examples of broadcast journalism.

Columnists and writers at the *New York Times, New York Herald Tribune, Variety, Guardian Weekly,* and *I. F. Stone's Weekly* praised Murrow. CBS and its affiliates received more than 75,000 calls, telegrams and letters after the show—the highest number of responses for a TV show to date. By a ten-to-one margin, they supported Murrow.

Well-wishers mobbed Murrow the following day when he left the CBS building, and 1,500 journalists attending the Overseas Press Club at the Waldorf gave him a standing ovation a week later.

"Murrow did not kill off McCarthy or McCarthyism," Joseph Wershba, who worked under Murrow and helped produce the McCarthy segment, said years after the broadcast. "But he helped halt America's incredible slide toward a native brand of fascism."

Although the show on McCarthy remains one of the greatest examples of broadcast journalism, some journalists criticized it for violating the ethic of objectivity, which admonishes journalists to keep personal biases and opinions out of stories, to cover all sides of a story, and to give roughly equal amounts of coverage and space to all sides.

The assumption is that readers and viewers can sift through the information presented and find the truth.

"Is it right in principle for television to take a clear stand on one side of a great issue?" *Newsweek* magazine asked its readers in a cover story soon after the McCarthy show.

"The McCarthy broadcast was not objective reporting," Persico pointed out three decades later. "It was subjective polemicizing. To those who would insist on purist rules governing even a fight with a barroom brawler, Murrow was wrong. But to millions, it had been satisfying to see the bully thrashed at last."

At the time, the *New York Times* reinforced the ethic, declaring that even if McCarthy's charges "are usually proved false," he was still news, because separating innuendo from truth and accusation from guilt "lies with the readers," not the newspaper.

But, Murrow and other critics asked, how can the public discern the truth if sources are lying and journalists are unable to get all of the facts?

A massive amount of research in mass communication over the next five decades eventually revealed that the ethic of objectivity is not objective in any absolute sense. It produces its own bias, which is neither radical nor blatantly aligned with a particular political ideology.

The bias is mainstream.

In other words, it tends to reinforce the status quo, which means support for mainstream values and powerful political and economic elites and their organizations. Objective reporting tends to marginalize radical or unorthodox ideas, as well as the views of disadvantaged groups and working-class Americans, because they have less power.

Murrow "did not possess the cardinal virtues of the journalist, objectivity and balance," Persico writes. "His power lay rather in his subjectivity, in the passionate moral biases, however coolly concealed, that he brought to his work."

Murrow believed the news needed to be interpreted, not just presented. Stenography was not good journalism because most did not have the resources to understand the news.

But Murrow's brand of subjective journalism was not unbounded.

It eschewed speculation and hyperbole, in contrast to many editorials and commentaries. Murrow's journalism was grounded in facts and logic, like academic scholarship. And although Murrow held a liberal perspective on many issues, he did not define his journalism through his personal ideology.

When a reporter from *Look* magazine asked him to explain his motives for going after McCarthy, Murrow replied: "I wouldn't say it was liberalism. ... I think it stems from my feeling about the sacredness of due process of law. I saw in Germany and Czechoslovakia that the law is destroyed first and then, after the law is gone, the freedom of the people is destroyed. The thing about McCarthy that bothers me is his disrespect for the due process of law."

When I read this comment in Persico's book, I realized then that Murrow's most significant contribution to broadcast journalism wasn't the McCarthy broadcast, even though it helped turn the tide against McCarthy; nor was it his courage or integrity, as he had a number of personal and professional lapses during his lifetime; nor was it his sensate coverage of World War II, which made him a household name.

Murrow's most significant contribution to broadcast journalism was his Enlightenment brand of journalism. He embraced democracy, free speech, due process, egalitarianism, transparent government, education, rule of law and civil liberties. These values are reflected in many other stories he covered through the years, such as the "Harvest of Shame" investigative report, a powerful indictment of America's agricultural system, which mistreated migrant workers.

But Murrow's Enlightenment journalism eventually got him into trouble. His bosses at CBS weren't happy when the targets of Murrow's stories — many of whom were enemies of the Enlightenment project — demanded equal time for a rebuttal of his reports. CBS executives cringed and pushed his programming into low-audience time slots. They eventually cut his shows, and Murrow struck back with a speech at a convention that provided the final nails in his professional coffin.

On October 15, 1958, Murrow criticized CBS corporate bean counters in a speech he gave at the Radio-Television News Directors

Association convention in Chicago.

> [I] can find nothing in the Bill of Rights of the Communications Act which says that they [news corporations] must increase their net profits each year, lest the Republic collapse. ... This instrument can teach, it can illuminate; yes, and it can even inspire. But it can do so only to the extent that humans are determined to use it to those ends. Otherwise, it is merely wires and lights in a box.

CBS executives were furious.

Murrow was biting the hand that fed him.

Asked later by a Chicago journalist why he gave that speech, Murrow replied: "I've always been on the side of the heretics against those who burned them, because the heretics so often proved right in the long run. Dead — but right!"

Murrow fell into a depression.

He took a sabbatical and traveled with his family for nearly a year. After he returned, he left CBS for good, accepting an offer from President John F. Kennedy in 1961 to head up the United States Information Agency, the international propaganda arm of the U.S. government.

He held the position at USIA for three years.

Illness forced him to retire in 1964.

Murrow, who had smoked three packs of cigarettes a day for most of his adult life, died of complications from lung cancer in 1965, two days before his 57th birthday.

Most analysts argue that corporate greed played the key role in why Murrow was pushed out of CBS. But a more nuanced interpretation is that the executives failed to see the importance of "Enlightenment journalism." To them, protecting civil liberties was a far less important goal than profits.

* * * * *

After reading the biographies, I wondered whether Murrow's Enlightenment journalism was embodied in the Edward R. Murrow School of Journalism curriculum and the university.

Were journalism students being taught to become advocates of the cause of the Enlightenment — a role that challenged, at least to some degree, the conventional objective model of journalism? Did university administrators and faculty embrace this model as well as civil liberties and freedom of speech in general? Was decision-making at the university more democratic or autocratic?

Chapter 19

A Friendly Culture of Tensions

Two Years Earlier, August 18, 1996
Washington State University

I am unpacking a box of books in my new apartment in Pullman, Washington, when a hear a knock on the door.

"I'm with the Pullman Police Department," a man dressed in a blue uniform says. "A woman died in a condominium across the courtyard last night. We're going door-to-door to see if anyone heard any strange noises last night or saw anything that looked suspicious."

"No, I didn't officer. I just moved in two days ago. What happened? Was she murdered?"

I arrived in Pullman after a three-day, 1,400-mile drive from Minneapolis. I was forty-three and soon to be single. Mona, who had encouraged me to apply for the faculty position at WSU, decided not to move to Pullman. We mutually agreed to divorce. The parting was bittersweet, but we remained friends. I would begin teaching in four days.

The officer hands me a business card and answers my question. "Her death is suspicious, but we don't know exactly what happened. If you have any information that might help our investigation, please call us at the number on this card."

"I will."

To what kind of town had I just moved?

It would take five years to solve the case.

The victim was Dorothy Martin, an 89-year-old widow in extremely good health who lived alone. She was suffocated with a pillow. Her daughter, who had taken out a $500,000 life insurance policy on her, paid Martin's handyperson $10,000 to kill her. He was convicted and sent to prison. The daughter was living in Tucson and committed suicide before police could arrest her.

* * * * *

Despite my macabre introduction to Pullman, I was grateful to have landed the tenure-track job at WSU, which is located about seventy-two miles south of Spokane, two-hundred-fifty miles southeast of Seattle, and eight miles from Moscow, Idaho (pronounced moss-koe, long "o," rather than moss-cow, the Russian capital), which is home to the University of Idaho.

About 25,000 people lived in Pullman, which was founded in 1886. The town was renamed after George Pullman — the inventor of the Pullman sleeping (railroad) car — who is now remembered more for tyrannical treatment of his employees than his business successes.

When business revenues declined in 1894, Pullman cut wages by thirty percent, increased the length of the working day, laid off workers, and refused to cut rent and utility bills for workers who lived in the Illinois town he built to support his factory.

In response, the workers went on strike. National Guard troops eventually quashed it, killing 34 strikers. Adding insult to injury, the remaining strikers were blacklisted.

A short time later, a national commission concluded that Pullman's town was "un-American." In 1898, the city of Chicago then annexed the village.

A small victory for the Enlightenment.

* * * * *

The city of Pullman is built on four hills (the university is on College Hill) and is surrounded by prairie-like rolling hills known as the Palouse (rhymes with "caboose"). The name may have come from a Native American tribe called the Palus, who lived in the area before the white people came.

Geologists believe the hills were created when glaciers ground up rock and wind blew it into the area. The area gets only about 20 inches of rain a year, so deciduous trees survive only near creeks or riverbeds or from yard watering. Conifers, which need less water, survive best on shady slopes or in low-lying areas.

Winters are mild, with moderate amounts of snowfall that usually melt in a day or two. Summers are dry and pleasant, with temperatures mostly in the 78-to-92-degree range.

Before farmers began growing wheat, barley, peas and lentils on the Palouse, various Native American tribes, including the Palus, Cayuse and Walla Walla, lived in or roamed the area. Traveling down to Pullman from Spokane, drivers pass the town of Rosalia, where the Battle of Pine Creek, also known as the Battle of Tohotonimme, was fought.

On May 17, 1858, about nine-hundred Native Americans from various tribes attacked one-hundred-sixty-four United States Army forces under the command of Lt. Col. Edward J. Steptoe. Seven soldiers were killed; about a dozen were injured. Nine to fifty Native Americans, according to varying accounts, were killed. The remaining soldiers escaped during the night.

Nearly four months later, the U.S. Army sent Col. George Wright and his six-hundred troops to suppress "native resistance." Armed with the new Springfield Model 1855 rifle, which could kill at a distance of more than a hundred yards, the troops inflicted heavy casualties on 5,000 warriors in two separate battles.

To further punish the Native Americans, Wright's troops on September 8, 1858, rounded up eight hundred of their horses and shot them dead. The troops also destroyed the Indians' food stores. The Native Americans quit fighting and eventually were forced to live on reservations in the area.

But a century later some of the tribes opened casinos on their lands, extracting a small measure of financial retribution from the mostly white European American gamblers.

* * * * *

Washington State University was founded in 1890 as Washington Agricultural College and School of Science. The university received 190,000 acres from the federal government under the Morrill Acts of 1862 and 1890, which helped establish land-grant universities across the nation. The university changed its name to Washington State College in 1905.

One disadvantage of Pullman is its geographical isolation. The state capital, Olympia, and Seattle are a six-hour drive to the west. The nearest major city is Spokane (population 210,000), which is more than an hour to the north.

Many professors privately concede that geographical isolation has hindered the university's impact on state and national politics.

News story citations back up their claims.

The University of Washington, which is located in Seattle and a one-hour drive from Olympia, was cited in 82,392 stories published from 1990 to 2012 in *The Seattle Times*, the state's largest and most influential newspaper. WSU was mentioned only 8,388 times.

In the early years, Washington State College was known for its programs in agriculture, veterinary medicine, engineering and mining. Like other land-grant institutions, students often referred to WSC as a "cow college"—a pejorative appellation popular with students coming from big cities.

As Washington State and the nation became more industrialized, urbanized and "informationized," the curriculum at WSC became more diversified. In the late 1990s, about three-fifths of 20,000 students majored in business, education, history, communication, social science or one of the humanities. Reflecting this transition, WSC changed its name to Washington State University in 1959.

The typical student admitted to WSU in 2009 had a combined SAT score of 1600 (critical reading + math + writing). This is slightly higher than the national mean of about 1500 for all universities but significantly lower than the 1745 for national research universities. WSU ranked in the bottom fourth (172 out of 226). The University of Idaho edged out WSU by five points.

* * * * *

In the fall of 1996, the Murrow School was composed of about two dozen full-time faculty, three full-time staff, and nine-hundred majors and five-hundred pre-majors. Nearly one in twelve students at WSU was affiliated with the Murrow School. The only program bigger was business, which had three times as many faculty and about two-thousand majors and pre-majors.

Although I didn't know it at the time, the Murrow program was substantially underfunded compared with other programs at WSU as well as with other mass communication programs across the country. The Murrow School's annual budget was twenty-five to fifty percent less than other programs. About half of its revenue was going to other departments and schools in the university, according to two WSU deans I later spoke with. The university was spending an average of $6,500 to educate a student. The Murrow School, according to an accreditation report issued by the Pacific Northwest Newspaper Association, was receiving about $2,700 per student.

To compensate for the lack of funding and faculty, class sizes for some courses in the Murrow School were big. The introduction to mass communication course, for example, packed three-hundred-fifty to six-hundred students into an auditorium per semester.

Like many other programs in the social sciences, the Murrow School faculty could be roughly divided into three groups: *professional faculty*, who taught skill-based courses; *social science faculty*, who had Ph.D. degrees and taught conceptual/theoretical courses that sought to reform, not radicalize, communication processes; and *critical/cultural faculty*, who had Ph.D. degrees and taught courses that tended to be critical of mainstream communication processes and preferred more radical forms of social change. The tension between these three groups was latent, which meant it never resulted in shouting matches or fisticuffs.

There was also tension between the communication studies and mass communication programs. The former had fewer than fifty majors but consumed one-fourth of the School's resources. Their faculty wielded a disproportionate amount of power partly because all were Ph.D.'s and usually voted together on issues.

But the biggest source of tension in the School was a nationwide trend toward de-professionalization of the mass communication programs. Many academic programs, including WSU, were hiring more Ph.D. scholars and fewer faculty with significant professional experience. This trend was legitimated on two assumptions. The first was that mass communication programs with lots of professional faculty were not academically rigorous enough. Students were learning workplace skills but not how to be critical thinkers. The second assumption was that all faculty at universities should be conducting scientific research or engaging in creative scholarship that contributes to a philosophical or theoretical base of knowledge.

In journalism, the de-professionalization trend was characterized as a battle between the "green eye shades" (which referred to green visors that newspaper editors wore to reduce eye strain when editing copy under incandescent lights) and the "chi-squares" (a statistic Ph.D. faculty often used in their research). Professional faculty complained, rightly so, that they were being treated like "second-class citizens." They typically were paid less, had less power, and often didn't have access to tenure. The power gap was sometimes on display at faculty meetings, where Ph.D.'s usually dominated the discussions. Newspaper publishers and editors also did not appreciate the trend, because they often complained that graduating students were not well-prepared to work in their businesses.

I understood the concerns of newspaper publishers and editors but overestimated my ability to appease them.

* * * * *

Three months after I arrived on campus, I attended a conference of newspaper publishers in Seattle. My goal was to improve relations between the Murrow journalism program and the professional community. But the publishers were giving me the cold shoulder.

During a break, I asked Frank Blethen, publisher of the Seattle

Times, if he knew why the publishers were less than eager to interact with me. Blethen didn't hold back.

"Don't you know?" he says. "You've got a Ph.D."

"You're kidding. The publishers here dislike me because I have a Ph.D.? What about the fact that I worked as a newspaper reporter? Doesn't that count?"

"Not really. WSU's decision to hire you as well as another Ph.D. in the journalism school this year instead of a professional sent a bad message to the publishers. Let me give you some background."

During the ten minutes that were left in the break, Blethen tried to summarize three decades of relations between the University of Washington, WSU's big sibling institution in Seattle, and the Pacific Northwest newspaper industry. Publishers were angry because UW had been replacing professional faculty with Ph.D. research professors, many of whom had little or no professional experience. UW was de-professionalizing their mass communication programs. In fact, the administrators were planning to cut the professional programs in advertising, public relations and broadcasting. Print journalism would be saved partly because of staunch support from Blethen and other newspaper publishers attending this conference.

The best programs, in my opinion, had a good balance of both skills and theory. But a year later when I gave a presentation to the publishers and argued that skills and theory courses in journalism were compatible, the response was tepid. I realized then that significant changes would be needed to win back the support of the professional community. But I would not act on it for another decade.

* * * * *

A good balance of skills and theory courses was also the managerial philosophy of the Murrow Director, Alexis (Alex) Tan, who grew up in the Philippines and earned a Ph.D. in mass communication from the University of Wisconsin. Tan's research and teaching focused on communication interventions to reduce and control prejudices.

As an administrator, Tan was kind and helpful. He gave faculty a great deal of freedom and autonomy to do their jobs. Workplace autonomy is one of the best predictors of job satisfaction, according to social scientific research and my own research on newspaper editors. I thrived in such an environment, so it didn't take me long to become one of Tan's strongest supporters.

Tan's management style was a mix of East and West. He avoided public criticism of staff or faculty and was never paternalistic or condescending. He tried to meet the needs of everyone, even though a lack of resources meant not everyone was pleased all the time.

In 1990, Tan and other administrators persuaded Murrow's widow, Janet, and their son, Casey, to allow the school to rename itself the Edward R. Murrow School of Communication. Although Murrow earned a good salary at CBS, he did not accumulate a big fortune. There would be no big donation to fill the Murrow School coffers. Nevertheless, in the world of academia, big names like Murrow have brand value and often make it easier for development fund managers to raise money and resources for academic programs.

Administrators were optimistic that the Murrow name would draw more resources to the university. The Murrow School certainly needed it, because it was being used as a cash cow for the College of Liberal Arts.

* * * * *

Despite the funding shortfalls and the political tensions in the Murrow School, I was happy to be there. I enjoyed my job and worked about sixty to seventy hours a week. I was productive in terms of research, publishing three scholarly books and six refereed journal articles during my first three years at WSU.

As I told one senior faculty member on one occasion, "I love my job so much I don't know if I will ever retire."

He chuckled. "You might change your mind someday."

In 1996, the only fly in the ointment at the Murrow School that I could see, aside from funding, was a case of censorship.

Chapter 20
WSU CENSORS STUDENT JOURNALISTS

November 1, 1996
Washington State University

I was entering my third month of teaching at WSU when one of my students who was passing in the hallway asks whether I had seen today's issue of the *Daily Evergreen*, WSU's student newspaper.

"Not yet. Why?"

"The newspaper is blank," he says, grinning. "The editors say the WSU administration is trying to censor them."

"You're kidding?"

He shakes his head from side to side.

I dart down the hallway and grab a free copy of the issue from a newsstand.

The front page is blank except for the masthead and short commentary. The inside pages are also blank — no text or headlines or pictures — just display advertising.

"This is an issue of protest," the commentary states, adding that the new general manager of student publications — a full-time university employee — "went back on two of the most important promises made before he was hired: That he would not censor this newspaper, and that he would not attempt to take the student out of Student Publications."

The general manager, John Contrilman, had asked the newspaper's advisor, Jeff Hand, another full-time university staff employee, to prevent publication of an article about a search for a new university provost. Contrilman's boss, interim provost Geoffrey Gamble, a linguist who was one of the candidates for the permanent provost position, had complained to Contrilman about the story.

The student journalists refused to obey Contrilman and published the article about the provost search. Contrilman then suspended Hand for three days. "He was being punished for our actions," one of the student editors told the Student Press Law Center in Washington, D.C.

"That marriage to the administration makes him [Contrilman] a tainted gatekeeper," said Evergreen editor-in-chief Isamu Jordan. "As soon as the staff and faculty get involved, it gets tainted with a lot of politics that shouldn't be in the newspaper."

Student journalists were also upset because several months earlier Contrilman killed a column that criticized the quality of food served in the residence halls. The column was supposed to appear in a special issue distributed to first-year students, who were attending summer orientation.

Some faculty thought that publishing a blank issue was puerile. I thought it was refreshing. It demonstrated that students were strongly committed to the principle of a free press.

Contrilman was a former newspaper editor and a professor at WSU's Murrow School. I didn't know him well. I was surprised, though, that he did not seem to recognize the generally accepted "hands-off" norm of advising for student newspapers. But, as I had learned at the University of Wisconsin–River Falls, loyalty to friends and administrators and self-interest often trumps journalistic principles.

In response to the incident, the Board of Student Publications, which oversaw the newspaper and other student publications, created an ad hoc committee to draft new rules for protecting the First Amendment rights of the students. The committee, which included me, drafted strong language to protect students' free-speech rights.

> Students of Washington State University have the undeniable right as guaranteed by the First Amendment of the U.S. Constitution to speak, write and publish their sentiments freely on all subjects and shall be free from censorship, advance review or approval. ... Washington State University shall make no rule, regulation or policy that abridges students' freedom of speech and of the press.

In terms of the censorship controversy, Ed Murrow no doubt would have sided with the students. But one incident surely was not enough to indict the university or the Murrow program.

Murrow faculty were friendly, but some were upset because there were limited resources. To attend an academic conference, most had to spend some of their own money to make up for shortfalls not covered by the university. Some griped to me about the situation. My attitude was different. "Create your own world," I told them. That's what I did.

* * * * *

I was tenured in 1999, three years after I was hired.

In 2000 and 2001, I wrote a book that applied my corporate theories of mass communication in the United States to global mass media. I also created The Center for Global Media Studies, a nonprofit 501(c)3 corporation, to promote research on the origins and effects of global mass media. I enlisted sixteen scholars to serve on the executive board, most of whom were top scholars in the field of mass communication. I sought financial assistance from the dean, but she turned me down. That didn't stop me.

The Center sponsored two international conferences, one in Spokane in 2002 and the other in Seattle in 2004. My plan was to make the center self-supporting. Although it never achieved this goal, it did raise about $60,000 through conference registration fees, membership fees, donations and sales of conference books. I also spent $25,000 of my own money to help fund the Center.

In February 2001, I moved to Spokane, a metropolitan area of 400,000 located seventy-two miles to the north, where I bought a split-level home just south of downtown Spokane. I moved because Spokane had more restaurants and nightlife. At the time, three of the twenty-nine Murrow faculty lived in Spokane.

That summer I also adopted a seventeen-month-old Chinese baby girl. I was forty-seven and single and always wanted a child. China allowed single men over age forty to adopt. The timing was good because I was on sabbatical during the 2001-2002 school year. That allowed me to spend more time with Lee Ann (named after my mother and aunt) during our first year together.

Two years after the adoption, I met a kind woman, Theresa, and we married. She was a good mother to Lee Ann.

The only irritation in my life at that time was a housing development being built behind my new house. Before buying my home, I contacted Spokane County, which sent me a site plan consisting of duplexes and two-story apartment complexes. But a massive three-story building was going up.

This event eventually triggered the resignation of one county official and led to allegations of censorship against the Spokane *Spokesman-Review*, the major daily in town.

Chapter 21
CENSORED IN SPOKANE

Spring 2002
Washington State University

In spring of 2002, my neighbors and I noticed that new construction behind our homes was violating a county-approved site plan.

Instead of one-story duplexes and two-story apartments, a massive three-story one-hundred-unit assisted-living facility longer than a football field was going up. The developer had reneged on a promise not to change the plan and quietly secured approval from Spokane County building officials without going through normal protocol, which would have required another public hearing.

My neighbors and I were angry.

But our neighborhood association refused to sue, because a former president of the group was now the neighborhood liaison for the mayor of Spokane, and "if word got out that the mayor's neighborhood liaison opposed this developer, other developers in town would stop contributing money to the mayor's reelection campaign and she would lose her liaison job," one member of the association later told me.

Once again, loyalty trumps principle.

County officials refused to stop the construction.

So, I decided some media attention to the issue might help. I was repainting the house but sprayed multi-colored fluorescent paint on the back. I made a poster and protested at a major intersection near my house. The local Fox TV affiliate interviewed me and posted a short segment on the evening news.

I then submitted a classified advertisement to the *Spokesman-Review* that criticized county officials who approved the project as well as the developer who violated the private contractual agreement not to change the plan. I figured I'd have no problem getting the newspaper to publish my little classified ad, because the Cowles family, which owned the newspaper, had placed several half-page advertisements on several occasions criticizing City of Spokane officials for their role in what came to be known as the River Park Square Garage scandal.

That case is complicated, but what happened is that the Cowles family, one of the wealthiest families in Spokane, had built a shopping mall in downtown Spokane and asked the city to give it a free parking garage. The Cowles and their consultants said the parking garage would generate enough revenue to pay for itself.

But it didn't. Some local journalists argued that the revenue numbers were deliberately inflated to seal the deal.

The case eventually produced hundreds of news stories, led to investigations by the Internal Revenue Service, the FBI and local independent journalists, and made national news several times. In a confidential report, the IRS accused Elizabeth A. (Betsy) Cowles, an attorney who headed up the Cowles's TV and radio broadcasting operations, of orchestrating a deal designed to benefit her family's business rather than the community.

In the end, the taxpayers were stuck with the tab, which amounted to more than $35 million. No one went to jail.

I thought I'd have no problem placing my classified ad because the Cowles family had placed their own ads criticizing their adversaries in the garage scandal.

I was wrong.

A spokesperson told me that the newspaper doesn't publish political advertisements. So, I wrote a letter to the editor, criticizing the newspaper for being hypocritical — for publishing its own political advertisements defending itself in the River Park Square Parking Garage scandal but for refusing to publish those submitted by citizens.

The newspaper refused to publish my letter to the editor.

What the hell?

Had the editors at the *Spokesman-Review* skipped Journalism 101 in college?

I called S-R publisher (William) Stacey Cowles.

Stacey was the son of the former publisher William H. Cowles III, who had died in 1992 at age 60 while jogging. Control of the newspaper went to Stacey. His sister, Betsy, got the broadcasting operations.

Stacey defended the decision of the newspaper not to publish my letter.

"We don't publish every letter we receive," he tells me.

"But is your decision not to publish my letter based on the fact that you don't have enough space or because you're afraid it will make your newspaper look hypocritical, because you published your own political ads?"

Cowles refuses to answer the question and instead talks about the boundaries of what a newspaper would publish.

"We would never publish a letter from a neo-Nazi in Idaho," he says at one point.

"Why not?" I rejoin. "As the Supreme Court once noted, the best remedy for 'bad speech' isn't censorship, it's more speech. If you published such a letter, you might be surprised at the positive result that could emerge from that." I briefly summarize the story from UW-RF, when students published the advertisement which claimed that the Holocaust never occurred.

Stacey rejects my appeal.

But then something unexpected happened. As news of the rejection spread through email, friends and colleagues began telling me about other people who had similar experiences with the *Spokesman-Review*. Within weeks I had sixteen examples of censorship. Doctors, professors and activists in the community told me that the *Spokesman-Review* had refused to publish their letters and columns. Within months I had posted thirty examples to a website I titled "Censored in Spokane."

Two categories of censored works emerged.

About half of the letters and commentaries came from people who criticized the newspaper or its staff for their role in the garage scandal. The other half had written letters that were pro-environment. The newspaper owned a printing plant near town that was one of the biggest polluters of the Spokane River, according to state officials.

The editorial page editor at the time was a political conservative who was loyal to the Cowles family. Was he deliberately censoring letters to protect the Cowles family?

The editor eventually was reassigned. The editor-in-chief told me the decision was unrelated to my criticisms of the newspaper.

Over the next two years, I wrote a series of articles for *The Local Planet Weekly*, a local alternative newspaper, that drew attention to the censored works as well as the conflict of interest posed in a community when newspaper owners also have other economic investments in the community. The Cowles family owned a substantial number of properties in downtown Spokane.

These commentaries, I confess, didn't have any noticeable impact on the newspaper or its journalists. However, they no doubt marginalized me among newspaper publishers in the Pacific Northwest.

Loyalties run deep.

After the *Spokesman-Review* rejected my "political advertisement," I approached the *Seattle Times*, which agreed to run the advertisement if I removed the name of the developer.

I consented, referring to him only as a "Spokane developer."

I took my case back to the *Spokesman-Review*, which then reversed its earlier decision and agreed to run the same advertisement. To the best of my knowledge, the advertisements had no effect on either the developer or the county.

The developer never commented publicly on the dispute.

The county official who allowed the developer to change the plans without public input was forced to resign. I eventually had a meeting with one of the county commissioners, who suggested that my neighbors and I file a claim with the county. The county paid $5,000 to each of us for the "wrong" that had been committed.

At one point, an anonymous emailer who had visited the "Censored in Spokane" website sent me a message saying, "You must really be a kook." I responded that many other people would agree with him. I noted that it often takes bizarre actions to get media coverage for a worthy cause. I said the county eventually agreed to pay $5,000 for the wrong committed.

The emailer sent back an apologetic response. "Oh, I didn't know about that."

The principle here, like the situation I experienced at the University of Wisconsin–River Falls, is that payment of money often legitimates protests or causes.

I gave $900 of the money from the settlement to the neighborhood association attorney, who had not been paid for his role in the assisted-living controversy. I spent $1,600 on other costs associated with fighting the case (advertisements, gas). I used the remaining $2,500 to buy trees and shrubs, which grew quickly and blocked out most of the view of the building within three years.

Chapter 22
MARQUETTE BOOKS

Summer 2002
Spokane, Washington

In the summer of 2002, more than seventy scholars from England, Scotland, Canada, Taiwan, France, and the United States came to Spokane to present papers that addressed issues and problems associated with global mass media.

I organized the conference, which was sponsored by the Center for Global Media Studies. Several scholars in attendance suggested that the papers be published in a book. During my college years, I started up two news-oriented publications. I also knew a fair amount about printing, as my father was a printer.

So, I created Marquette Books, a limited liability company. I used my own money to start it up, because if the publishing company failed, I didn't want CGMS to be saddled with the debts.

The conference book was titled *Terrorism, Globalization and Mass Communication* and had nineteen chapters. The book sold about three-hundred copies over the next five years. Total costs for publishing and distributing the book were about $5,900. The book generated about $6,500 in revenues, so I was able to give $600 to the center. Not much, but, to me, a considerable success, because higher education libraries across the United States and Canada were the major buyers, and the book was now available for generations to come.

In spring 2003, Boston University mass communication scholars Melvin and Margaret DeFleur asked if I could publish their book *Learning to Hate Americans*. The book was based on surveys that the DeFleurs's foreign graduate students had conducted of more than 1,300 teenagers in twelve countries. The results showed that teenagers believed Americans were extremely violent and criminally inclined, and American women were sexually immoral.

The DeFleurs placed most of the blame for these negative attitudes on U.S. mass media, especially Hollywood, which produces movies that contain many negative images of Americans. The researchers concluded that unless something is done to correct the problem, future generations of foreign teenagers will grow up "learning to hate Americans."

I was surprised when Mel approached me, because my company had "no prestige" in the academic market.

"We don't care about that," he said. "We want to get the book out at soon as possible. The topic is very newsworthy right now. It takes too long for a big publishing house to do that."

I published the book in three months.

That opened the floodgates.

Ralph Berenger, an American who was teaching at the American University in Cairo, was looking for someone to publish his edited book about global media and the 1990-91 Gulf War, titled *Global Media Go to War.* John C. Merrill, one of the most prominent libertarian First Amendment scholars in the United States, also wanted me to publish his book *Media Musings: Interviews with Great Thinkers.*

I worked on these and other books mostly in the summer, when I was not on appointment. None of the books generated much in the way of profits. In fact, during the first five years of operation, Marquette Books lost $16,634. By the year 2008, the losses would total $42,458. I would eventually make up the losses through the publication of contract-for-hire books — mostly memoirs from retired men. But for now, my goal was to publish works that were contributing to the advancement of knowledge and to help other faculty achieve their publishing goals.

What I didn't realize at the time, though, was that some of the Murrow faculty were becoming resentful.

"They are envious," one professor friend tells me after shutting the door to my office.

"I don't believe it," I respond. "Why would they be envious? They are all very accomplished people."

"Faculty can be just as petty and insecure as any other professional group. And they don't like to be upstaged. They are fiercely competitive."

I guess I didn't know people very well. Perhaps it was because of my working-class origins or my Lutheran education, which emphasized the golden rule. My inferiority complex also might have played a role. No matter how successful I was, I still didn't feel equal to many of my colleagues, so I couldn't understand why they would be envious of me.

Over the next decade, Marquette Books published more than fifty scholarly books and another one hundred or so trade and contract-for-hire books. Only the latter and a couple of textbooks generated significant profits.

I ran MB in my spare time and didn't list it under my service contributions, because it was a profit-making company unrelated to my job at the university. But it was gratifying to collaborate with top-notch scholars and to publish books that contributed to the literature on mass communication and sociology. Later, though, WSU administrators would try to fire me because of my role in MB.

* * * * *

In fall 2002, Director Alex Tan assigned me to teach the "Introduction to Mass Communication" course. The former teacher was retiring. By coincidence, I was at the time writing a textbook for such a course. An *Interpretive Introduction to Mass Communication* was part of my revised program of research, which sought to influence students and the public, not just scholars. I signed a contract with Pearson Education in 2000 to author the book.

The first draft was finished. My publisher suggested I use it in my classes, because I could get feedback from the students. Pearson would publish soft-cover copies for use in my class and make the book available to other scholars across the country who also might want to use it. I told Tan I would defer any royalties from the sale of the book to the nonprofit Center for Global Media Studies. But he said that wasn't necessary. WSU rules allowed faculty to earn royalties on the sale of their books in their classes, and several faculty were doing that. To do that, the book had to be published by a reputable publisher, it had to be available to other faculty across the country, and the department chair/director and the dean's office had to approve the request.

I followed the rules and donated the profits to CGMS. Nevertheless, a year or so later a Murrow faculty member filed a complaint, alleging I was violating university and/or state ethics codes. It also alleged that Tan was giving me "release time" for my work at CGMS, meaning that I didn't have to teach as many courses as a regular faculty member. But I never received release time. My work at CGMS was volunteer. I never earned a penny in compensation.

The complainant came from a faculty member who was coming up for tenure. During his third- and fifth-year reviews, I raised some questions about the quality and quantity of his research record. Some tenured faculty later told him about my concerns.

WSU's internal auditor was called in to investigate. On October 8, 2004, he issued a report to Tan, exonerating me. But the university controller told me in a telephone conversation that even though I was not benefiting financially from the books used in my classes, he said there could be a nonfinancial benefit through CGMS, and that was still prohibited under state and university rules. The internal auditor confirmed this in a follow-up memo.

So, I created PDFs of the books and gave them to students free of charge, and royalties from the intro book were used to help fund CGMS, even though university rules allowed me to keep those royalties for my own use.

Most faculty were unaware of these details.

In 2006, they refiled the complaints against me after the dean replaced Alex Tan as director of the program in 2006.

Chapter 23
A Petit Coup D'État

Spring 2006
Washington State University

Murrow Director Alex Tan was never in jeopardy of losing his tenured position at WSU. He was a competent researcher and teacher.

But he could be removed from the administrative director position.

His four-year contract was up for renewal.

Tan had spent more than two decades at the helm of the school. That's no small feat when you consider the conflict and turmoil that characterize administrative life in the academy.

Departmental heads are often ousted and replaced. Research universities like WSU are also more likely than teaching universities to deny tenure to faculty who fail to publish scholarly works. Faculty often compete for resources and recognition. And administrators and faculty are often at loggerheads over the direction of a program or how to spend resources.

Some outsiders see this social conflict as dysfunctional.

"I've never understood why there is so much political turmoil and in-fighting at universities," one employment attorney who had represented faculty in labor disputes once told me. "The stakes seem so small. The battles rarely revolve around things worth fighting about. Why can't faculty just get along?"

"Because universities are structured to encourage conflict," I replied.

The tenure system and the concept of academic freedom explain in part why universities usually have more visible social conflicts than other types of institutions. I qualify that proposition with the word "visible," because interpersonal conflict and complaints are present in virtually all large- and most small-scale organizations.

But in private businesses and non-academic governmental agencies, dissatisfaction with higher-ups is more likely to be expressed behind closed doors or around the water cooler, because employees of these organizations can be easily fired for the things they say and do. They have no First Amendment protection. They are "at-will" employees, which means they can be fired for any reason as long as it doesn't violate anti-discrimination laws.

In contrast, social conflict and criticism are more visible in the public university, because academics and the courts have carved out some free-speech protection for university professors, at least in the classroom and in scholarship. The crucial point here is that this legal protection, along with the fact that rules at most universities contractually provide free-speech protection to faculty and students, means social actors in universities often engage in robust debates, usually without fear of reprisal. And even without constitutional or contractual protection, most university administrators tolerate a lot of flak from faculty, partly because they know that a robust debate can produce better ideas and decisions.

Viewed from this perspective, then, social conflict is a good thing. It can generate solutions to problems and help an organization adapt to change. If there were no conflict, one could expect greater abuse of power. That's how some professors and I see the university.

And the best place to find social conflict at a university is in its power structure. One can hypothesize, in fact, that the more power an administrator or group has, the greater the potential for conflict.

At the top of the pyramid are university presidents or chancellors, who often report that they are under attack from all kinds of groups and people, including faculty, staff, students, donors, policymakers, journalists and the public. Making one decision that positively affects one group may adversely affect another.

Lower-level administrators face similar problems when they make decisions, but, in relative terms, the levels of conflict tend to decline as one moves down the hierarchy.

At the bottom of the power pyramid, professors and students also can find themselves in conflict, often over grades. However, faculty have much less power over a student's life than administrators have over faculty. The interaction between faculty and students is short-lived as each semester comes and goes. In relative terms, faculty-student conflicts rarely escalate into something big, with the notable exception of sex scandals.

In contrast, the potential for conflict is much greater between department chairs or directors and their faculty, because they interact with each other over longer periods of time and because chairs usually evaluate the performance of faculty. A chair or director of a program can make many decisions that positively or adversely affect each faculty member. Because departments usually have limited resources, a gain or benefit for one faculty member often means a loss or detriment for another (a zero-sum outcome).

Larger departments also tend to have more social conflicts because they have more social actors and, thus, more chances for conflict. I have called this phenomenon the "Quadratic Theory of Social Conflict." The amount of conflict increases at a faster pace as organizational size increases. Plot it out: With two people, there is one case of conflict; with three, three; with four, five; with five, ten; with six, fifteen; etc.

The high levels of social conflict in universities makes them ideal laboratories for studying a phenomenon known as coup d'état — or the sudden overthrow of a government (or department head) by a part of the state (or faculty and administrators). Of course, one significant difference between political coups and academic ones is that the latter are nonviolent (at least most of the time, thankfully).

So, I call them petit coups d'état.

* * * * *

The causes of petit coups in academia vary. But they almost always involve a higher-level administrator and some faculty who are unhappy with the decisions of the targeted administrator.

Petit coups are most successful when the supervisor of the administrator under attack is aligned with the unhappy dissidents. That's because all supervisors dislike making decisions that look capricious or undemocratic. This is particularly true for high-profile decisions, such as removing a lower-level administrator from power. The more support bosses can get from the rank-and-file, the better they look.

World history shows that after political coup d'états, many non-elite supporters of an ousted regime can be quickly co-opted into the new regime. Fear motivates, as Italian Niccolo Machiavelli pointed out about five centuries ago. But some elites in the previous regime cannot be trusted, and so they are sometimes executed. Before the twentieth century, the British preferred hanging and the firing squad. The French opted for the guillotine.

Fortunately, universities today are less barbaric, although you'd have a tough time convincing me they are more civil. When an administrator is removed from office, he or she usually returns to his or her department and resumes teaching and research responsibilities. Appealing these removal decisions is difficult because many administrative positions are limited-term appointments.

To remove faculty who fall out of favor with administrators in power, the preferred form of punishment in modern academe is banishment — in other words, dismiss the nontenured faculty and pressure the tenured ones to leave. As Sophocles wrote in his play *Oedipus the King*:

> OEDIPUS: What is the rite of purification? How shall it be done?
> CREON: By banishing a man ...

To banish non-tenure-track faculty (often called contract employees), you fire them or refuse to renew their work contracts. They are "at-will" employees, which means they don't have a right to due process as do tenure-track professors.

To banish newer faculty who are working to obtain tenure, you give them unsatisfactory performance reviews and then deny them tenure, usually when they reach their third or sixth year. They can appeal the decision, but the faculty member usually loses. Upper-level administrators who consider the appeal usually don't break ranks with lower-level administrative decisions.

To banish tenured faculty, you take away all the privileges you can and give them low performance reviews. The goal is to make their lives miserable. If possible, you enlist the help of your colleagues to turn the faculty member into a pariah — a target of ridicule and rolling eyes.

Sometimes you give the targeted faculty a severance package if they agree to resign. That can be far cheaper than a lawsuit.

If the tenured faculty member still refuses to resign, you fire them and force them to file an administrative appeal, which can take a year or more to adjudicate and will stress them out. Even if they win the appeal, top-level administrators usually have the power to overturn the decision, which then forces the faculty member into filing an expensive lawsuit. Without a job, however, few have the resources to do that.

Attorneys rarely take free-speech cases on a contingency-fee basis, as it is difficult and sometimes impossible in such cases to obtain punitive damages (financial compensation meant to punish the losing party and deter others from committing the same civil offense).

But attorneys will often represent on a contingency-fee basis faculty who claim they were fired because of the color of their skin, their religious beliefs, or their sex or age. Under various laws, these are called "protected categories," and punitive damages are far more common and sometime result in exceptionally large settlements.

Because the courts are often reluctant to interfere with the internal operations of universities, administrators overall enjoy a big advantage over fired faculty in a court of law.

But occasionally a professor prevails.

Administrative purges, like burning fields to wipe out pests, can result in car wrecks.

* * * * *

Murrow Director Alex Tan had support from most faculty when his contract came up for renewal in the spring of 2006.

However, faculty did not have final say on the matter.

The dean of the College of Liberal Arts, Erich Lear, oversaw the selection process and made a recommendation to the provost and president, who in turn made the final decision. In most cases, upper-level administrators rubber-stamp a dean's choice. But on occasion, the higher-ups will take control and call the shots.

Lear met with faculty on several occasions to discuss procedure.

The details of those meetings are confidential.

But I can tell you that two faculty were confused by the process. At least one wanted to change his or her vote. Lear wouldn't allow it.

As the final stages of the appointment process were ending, Tan emailed to the Murrow faculty a copy of an article published in *The Chronicle of Higher Education*, the most prestigious general circulation (weekly) newspaper serving universities.

It was titled, "Mob Rule."

Chapter 24
WORKPLACE MOBBING

April 2006
Washington State University

"In departmental disputes," writes *Chronicle of Higher Education* reporter John Gravois, "professors can act just like animals."

Gravois explains that some bird species, when threatened by predators, will fly toward the threat rather than away. The birds swoop down and harass the predator. Birds "mob" to teach younger birds whom to fear and to drive the predator away.

> Sometimes, especially in winter, Kenneth Westhues can hear a flock of crows tormenting a great horned owl outside his study in Waterloo, Ontario. It is a fitting soundtrack for his work. Mr. Westhues has made a career out of the study of mobbing. Since the late 1990s, he has written or edited five volumes on the topic. However, the mobbers that most captivate him are not sparrows, fieldfares, or jackdaws. They are modern-day college professors.

Westhues, a professor of sociology at the University of Waterloo, told Gravois that universities are ideal places for workplace mobbing, because it is one of the few ways to force tenured faculty out of their jobs. Although no two mobbings are identical, Westhues identified five stages: (1) *increasing isolation*, where the mobbing faculty ignore and often roll their eyes when the targeted faculty speak; (2) *petty harassment*, where the faculty member's administrative requests are delayed or misplaced or when classes or meetings get scheduled at odd times; (3) *critical incident*, in which the faculty member is accused of plagiarism or of making racially or sexually insensitive remarks or is accused of spending university money improperly; (4) *adjudication*, where the allegations are either legitimized or dismissed by a university official or committee; and (5) *resignation*, where the targeted faculty member, even if he or she wins, often leaves office.

Many people who are victims of workplace mobbing often suffer from post-traumatic stress disorders. Some mobbed workers commit suicide. In the summer of 2020, this included Michael Adams, a conservative criminology professor at the University of North Carolina Wilmington who shot himself in the head after sending out a controversial tweet about the COVID-19 crackdown: "I almost felt like a free man who was not living in the slave state of North Carolina." He added, "Massa [Governor Roy] Cooper, let my people go!"

More than 60,000 people signed a petition asking the university to fire him for his tweet. Adams previously had published two books criticizing political correctness on campus. The university tried to fire him once before, but he sued and the courts ruled that his speech was private rather than job-related. He was granted tenure and back pay.

This time around the university backed down again and paid him $500,000 to retire. He accepted the offer, but the stress of these legal battles apparently was more powerful than his free-speech victories.

In rare cases, the victims of mobbers also have attacked their mobbers, sometimes killing them. Professors with foreign accents and those who frequently file grievances and "make noise" are often victims of mobbing.

But, interestingly, the targeted professors usually are not underachievers. The "most common single trait of mobbing targets," Westhues told Gravois, "is that they excel."

> To calculate the odds of your being mobbed, count the ways you show your workmates up: fame, publications, teaching scores, connections, eloquence, wit, writing skills, athletic ability, computer skills, salary, family money, age, class, pedigree, looks, house, clothes, spouse, children, sex appeal. Any one of these will do.

Westhues blames part of the problem on the lack of rigorous legal rules and principles. Most of the professors and staff members sitting in judgment are unschooled in legal processes. Although universities are supposed to be places where the "law of reason" reigns supreme, Westhues writes that often is not the case.

> Academic knives are more polished and keen than those made of steel, and they are thrown with such grace that targets sometimes barely know they have been stabbed in the back until their campus lives are lost.

And how do professors who are mobbed survive?

Principles, Westhues says. Principles sustain them through difficult times.

* * * * *

I never asked Tan why he distributed that article about mobbing. Did he think he was being targeted? Or was he thinking of me? The university had not formally accused me of wrongdoing at this point, but storm clouds were forming.

Although Tan had support from more than half of the faculty, Dean Lear announced that the Murrow School would search for a new director. The details of how Tan lost the reappointment are protected by privacy rules. My purpose is not to assign blame, but to draw some lessons.

The first is a reminder that, despite the concept of shared governance, decision-making at universities does not depend solely or principally on democratic processes. In fact, university bureaucracies are far more autocratic than democratic. Almost every decision at a lower level can be overturned by upper administration. Obtaining consent from faculty is sometimes desired but not necessary.

This doesn't mean shared governance, or the idea that faculty should play a role in management of the university, is illusory. Faculty usually play a big role in curriculum development. But shared governance does not mean faculty share power equally with administrators on other matters. Power still flows from the top down.

The second lesson, as Machiavelli noted, is that no amount of kindness can appease your enemies. When it comes to holding on to power, love is less important than fear.

Tan was a kind man. He was, in my opinion, just as kind to those who helped oust him from power as he was to people who supported him. But that didn't matter when it came time to cast a ballot. Machiavelli elaborates:

> From this arises the question whether it is better to be loved more than feared, or feared more than loved. ... [O]ne ought to be both feared and loved, but as it is difficult for the two to go together, it is much safer to be feared than loved. ... [M]en have less scruple in offending one who makes himself loved than one who makes himself feared; for love is held by a chain of obligation, which, men being selfish, is broken whenever it serves their purpose; but fear is maintained by a dread of punishment which never fails.

To his credit, Tan took his ousting with dignity. The university offered him another administrative post, which he accepted. Offering an alternative position is a common practice that administrators use to reduce conflict after a petit coup.

Shortly after these events, I had a chance meeting with Erica Weintraub Austin, a Murrow faculty member, and suggested she run for the position of interim director of the Murrow School.

She smiled and said nothing.

Was she flattered or had she already been offered the position?

I didn't know.

* * * * *

The first task after a petit coup is to select an interim director.

Two people ran for the office: Austin and a professor in the communication studies sequence who was a vocal critic of Tan.

The voting was secret ballot.

Austin was the only woman in the communication program with full professor status. Her father was Stanley Weintraub, a Pennsylvania State University historian who had written biographies and histories of the American Revolution and both world wars and was an expert on George Bernard Shaw, who once commented:

> The reasonable man adapts himself to the world; the unreasonable one persists in trying to adapt the world to himself. Therefore, all progress depends on the unreasonable man.

Weintraub expected a lot out of Austin. She told me that he once told her that a competent scholar reaches full professor status before turning forty. She didn't disappoint.

Austin was an accomplished mainstream quantitative social scientist, conducting research in health communication. Part of her research focused on children and the effects of alcoholic beverage advertising. She taught in the public relations sequence, which eventually was renamed "strategic communication."

At the time, Austin was coauthor of more than three dozen refereed journal articles and one textbook on public relations. She derived royalties from the sale of her book in her classes, which was permitted under WSU rules. She was one of the most published scholars in the Murrow School, according to a 2005 analysis of faculty productivity I conducted for the school.

Her only shortcoming, some academics would argue, is that she had few sole-authored articles and no theoretically based books. Research universities typically place more value on sole-authored refereed publications.

Austin's opponent for the director's position was a speech communication professor who hadn't published any refereed publications in many years. He was an intelligent man; a good teacher; well liked by students and most Ph.D. faculty. He was working on a book but didn't have a publisher. I offered to publish it for him if he couldn't find a publisher. He never published the book, to the best of my knowledge.

He also told me that he was not a big supporter of democracy. Plato was like that. He believed that ordinary people did not have the intelligence to rule effectively. An educated elite should be in charge. The number of people who admire Plato today no doubt has soared.

Dean Lear collected the votes and announced that Austin had won, but he refused to release the final tally. Only a couple of faculty, myself included, openly criticized the dean for refusing to release the results.

Plato won this time.

And he won again shortly thereafter when WSU began searching for a new president.

Chapter 25
WHEN THE ENDS JUSTIFY THE MEANS

Summer/Fall 2006
Washington State University

In the summer of 2006, WSU President Lane Rawlins announced he was retiring. Free speech on campus had taken a couple of hits during his reign.

In one case, administrators tried to punish an elementary education student who wrote "diversity is perversity" in the margins of a book. In another, administrators tried to disrupt a theater student's play that was deliberately designed to be "offensive or inflammatory to all audiences." Shockingly, administrators trained students to deliberately disrupt the play while it was in progress. In both instances, administrators backed down after the Foundation for Individual Rights in Education admonished their actions, but the university never formally apologized to the students.

The WSU Board of Regents and top administrators began a formal search for Rawlins's replacement in fall 2006. Presidential searches are quite involved and, normally, relatively democratic, at least in terms of appearances. A professional search firm is hired to identify and screen some candidates. Then they are brought to campus, where they spend several days interviewing with various administrators, faculty, students, alumni, and citizens.

Of course, this is a time when administrators love to talk about the importance of "process" in making decisions. Committees are a must. Everyone's opinion must be considered. The process must be as democratic as possible.

Well, that's the talk.

But the walk often strays from the path. Sometimes the ends become more important than the means.

A little background.

The WSU campus is in an area of the nation that has often been associated with racist groups and organizations. Although the number of people in these groups is quite small, no one disputes the fact that the Inland Northwest, which includes eastern areas of Washington State and northern areas of Idaho, is politically conservative, especially outside of the city of Spokane.

In the 1920s, Christian pastors tried to encourage their parishioners to create chapters of the Ku Klux Klan in Pullman and Colfax. Until recently, nearby Coeur d'Alene, Idaho, was home to the largest neo-Fascist Aryan group in the nation. In the 1960s, the first African American to be admitted into a fraternity at WSU charged that some white members of the fraternity harassed him.

In May 1970, some WSU students went on strike to protest racism on campus. The students drew up a list of demands, and even though few of the demands were realized, the university strengthened minority studies programs, put more effort into recruiting minorities, and established a series of racism workshops. In early 2005, two varsity basketball players were accused of making racist gestures and animal calls toward three Asian American female students working at a campus counseling center. After several investigations, the university concluded the accusations were not serious enough to warrant a full investigation. The incident ignited a storm of protest across campus and accusations of a cover-up. At least one administrator lost his job.

On April 2, 2005, the Washington State Democratic Central Committee approved a resolution which alleged that twenty incidents of racial harassment on campus had been inadequately addressed in the last ten years. At its meeting in late June 2005, the Washington State Human Rights Commission was informed that an investigation of racism was underway. African Americans made up only 2.4 percent of the WSU student body and 1.4 percent of the faculty.

During the sixteen years that I worked at WSU, I never personally witnessed any incidents of racism on campus. To me, the biggest problem at WSU wasn't racism, it was trying to convince professors and students of color to come to WSU. After all, why would anyone want to attend or work at a university where resources and cultural activities for people of color were limited?

On Wednesday, December 13, 2006, long before the search process for a new president was completed, the WSU Board of Regents voted to give the job to Elson S. Floyd, who was president of the University of Missouri.

Floyd never even interviewed on campus.

The decision came after two days of closed-door sessions with top-level administrators and board members and took almost everyone by surprise.

"It's not how we do any other hires in the university," Ken Struckmeyer, a former Faculty Senate chairperson who later became an ombudsman at the university, told the *Spokesman-Review*. One communication professor sent an e-mail to many faculty and administrators on campus, strongly criticizing the regents for scuttling the search process and usurping the interests of faculty and others.

Administrators ignored the complaint and told the news media that the regents had to move quickly, because candidates don't want others to know that they are interviewing for another job. Even the chairperson of the Faculty Senate supported the decision.

Two days later, though, Gary Crooks, a columnist for the *Spokesman-Review*, pointed out that searches for the last three presidents hired at WSU and Eastern Washington University were all conducted in public. "The rationale for this speedy, secretive hire [of Floyd] is that no leaders worth having would subject themselves to a public process," Crooks wrote. "Do you buy it?"

Crooks's column and the news story announcing the choice of Floyd never mentioned the alleged racial problems at WSU, nor did any administrator link the regents' decision with that issue.

But the issue of racism on campus faded very quickly after Floyd came to campus.

Why?

Because he was African American.

The regents had made a brilliant move to tamp down concerns about racism on campus, even though democracy, one of the most important Enlightenment ideals, was sacrificed to do that.

Chapter 26
A Restructuring and a Warning

Fall Semester 2006
Washington State University

One of the first things interim Murrow School Director Erica Austin did after her promotion was to conduct one-on-one meetings with faculty to discuss issues and concerns.

A great idea.

She and I met for about twenty minutes.

But we apparently had different agendas.

I told her the school would benefit if it appointed one of the non-tenured professional faculty members to the position of associate director of undergraduate studies. I recommended a nationally recognized newspaper editor with many contacts in the Pacific Northwest. I said some of the professional faculty feel like second-class citizens, and the appointment would help assuage this concern.

Austin had something else on her mind.

"You know, the faculty have concerns about Marquette Books."

By that time, my book publishing company had published seven scholarly books. I wrote one of the books, which was titled *Dictionary of Mass Communication & Media Research: A Guide for Students, Scholars & Professionals*. The book received complimentary reviews *from Journalism & Mass Communication Quarterly*, a scholarly journal, and from *Midwest Review of Books*, which reviews books for libraries. The book was published in 2005 and in spring of 2006 had been selected as the second most important scholarly contribution in our School during the school year. That angered some faculty, one faculty member told me.

Austin was fidgeting in her chair, waiting for my reply to her question about Marquette Books.

"Those issues were settled years ago," I replied. "The university attorneys and controller investigated and found no wrongdoing. Go look at the records."

She didn't respond or ask any more questions.

I assumed the issue was settled.

* * * * *

Meanwhile, the Murrow School was bustling with activity in the fall semester of 2006. More than a half-dozen committees had been formed to correct perceived problems in the curriculum and structure of the program. One of the Murrow committees was tasked with restructuring the program.

"Here we go again," one faculty member who had been around for a couple of decades told me. "We're going to restructure the program for the umpteenth time, and no doubt we'll do that again in several more years."

She was right.

In just the decade that I had been there, the faculty had restructured various aspects of the program and, in some cases, reverted back to a previous structure. Each administrator and faculty member had his or her own idea of how to construct the ideal program, and most of us felt entitled to do that.

I was no exception.

I had two big suggestions.

First, I wanted the School to pursue national accreditation for the mass communication programs, including print journalism. That would elevate the stature of the programs.

Second, I suggested removing the communication studies sequence (formerly known as speech communication) from the School. As I noted earlier, that program had few majors and too many professors. It was an inefficient use of resources.

In addition, at most universities, mass communication programs and communication studies are housed in different departments, because they have different goals and serve different real-world constituencies.

I raised the accreditation issue at faculty meetings on several occasions through the years. My colleagues rejected the idea.

"They are worried about their graduate program," one non-tenure track faculty member explained. "They don't want the undergraduate program to take resources away from their precious graduate program."

As I expected, my plan to separate the communication studies program from the mass communication programs was also not well-received by the seven communication studies faculty. They knew that if their unit were converted into a stand-alone department, the number of faculty would have to be radically cut.

Austin initially refused to appoint me to the structure committee. I think she and others were worried I would be out of step with the other faculty members of the committee. Of course, that was likely. But why appoint a committee if everyone has the same opinion?

Austin capitulated and appointed me to the committee.

But that time, the committee had already met twice. The meeting time conflicted with my daughter's school schedule, so I joined the meetings via telephone for most of the semester.

For nearly two months, faculty on the committee talked about ways to structure the School. From my perspective, the big problem was that the committee members weren't focusing enough on how to raise more donations and grants for the School.

At a meeting in December 2006, one of the communication studies professors made a disparaging remark about the Murrow School's professional advisory board, which was composed of about thirty working mass communication professionals who provided advice about the curriculum.

"We aren't going to let them tell us what to do," the faculty member said.

I had heard enough. It was time to formally propose a plan to re-professionalize and improve the quality of the undergraduate mass communication programs — a plan that would make fundraising and servicing the needs of the professional community key components.

* * * * *

Meanwhile, in late December 2006, Austin sent an email informing faculty that they should not cancel their classes.

Canceling classes is not unusual. Some faculty do it for legitimate reasons, such as compensating students for other class-based activities (e.g., extra library research, attending certain lectures and events). Some do it for illegitimate reasons, such as skipping out of a semester early.

Although the email was sent to all faculty, Austin's order was clearly directed at me. It was no secret that I canceled the last two days of laboratory classes in my Com 101 courses. I had it written right into my syllabus. I did it for pedagogical reasons: to deter students in my large-lecture Com 101 classes from missing exams. I had been doing it for several years. Former Murrow Director Alex Tan was aware of the practice.

One of the biggest problems in a large lecture course is trying to get students to take the exams on time. To deter absences, I only allowed students to make up exams during final exam week. Faculty at WSU are not required to give final exams, so I used the final exam session for make-up exams. Because students are anxious to leave the university at the end of the semester, this was an effective deterrent. The vast majority of students, more than ninety percent, took every exam at the scheduled time.

The faculty manual did not prohibit faculty from canceling classes for pedagogical reasons. I emailed Austin and asked her if she could identify the rule or regulation that prohibited my pedagogical decision. She didn't respond.

So, I emailed Vice Provost Francis McSweeney and asked her if faculty were prohibited from canceling classes for pedagogical reasons. She said there was no rule, but if faculty were canceling a lot of classes that would be of "grave concern."

No argument there.

I sent an email to Austin, passing along the information I learned from McSweeney. I suggested she send an email to Murrow faculty, correcting her previous comments. I said I would be willing to defend my policies before a university grievance committee.

Austin didn't respond, nor did she send a follow-up email to faculty.

A day later I decided that even if faculty had the authority to cancel classes for pedagogical reasons, it was best to change my Com 101 syllabus and hold classes during the week before final exams. I knew now that Austin was targeting me. I assigned my teaching assistants to review material for students and allow them to check their grades during the last week.

I needed to pick and choose my battles more carefully.

My 7-Step Plan to improve the quality of the Murrow School, however, was a worthy battle. I would reach retirement age in less than eight years. It was now or never.

Chapter 27
My 7-Step Plan

January 2007
Washington State University

I sent my 7-Step Plan to WSU Provost Robert Bates on January 16, 2007. I would have sent it to President Lane Rawlins, but he was a lame duck. Incoming President Floyd wouldn't arrive until May 2007.

The plan was four pages, full color, half letter in size. The cover had a picture of the new communication building, headline, and attribution:

> A 7-STEP PLAN FOR MAKING THE EDWARD R. MURROW SCHOOL OF COMMUNICATION FINANCIALLY INDEPENDENT AND A $50,000 DONATION TO KICK OFF A FUNDRAISING CAMPAIGN
>
> -Prepared by Marquette Books LLC, Spokane, Washington

In the cover letter on the second page, I said Marquette Books would donate $50,000 to the university if it implemented the seven steps. The purpose of my donation was to jump-start a formal fundraising campaign for the Murrow School to re-professionalize the mass communication programs.

The third page included a brief history of mass communication programs and the conflict between the scholars and professionals about what makes up a high-quality program. The fourth page contained a small picture of the Murrow Center building and outlined the seven steps, which are condensed below.

1. Separate the mass communication program from the communication studies program ... to send a very strong message to the professional/business community that WSU is committed to enhancing its undergraduate program in mass communication;
2. Hire a director of the Edward R. Murrow School of Communication who has a strong professional background ... to improve its relations with the professional community;
3. Create an Edward R. Murrow Center for Media Research that conducts joint research projects with the professional community;
4. Give real-world professionals an active (rather than the current passive) role in the development of the curriculum in the School
5. Give professional faculty a more active role in the development of the undergraduate curriculum for mass communication students;
6. Seek national accreditation for the mass communication programs. ... [to] enhance the quality and visibility of the School at WSU;
7. Hire more professional faculty with substantial work experience.

I composed a press release announcing the details of the plan and sent it to three dozen news media and university officials. I was hoping to get some support from the professional community.

Seattle Times Publisher Frank Blethen responded: "Very ambitious. And, yes, thankfully, you are not one to follow the most trodden path. ... I understand the issue but am not versed on the particulars. Under the current WSU president (Lane Rawlins), we have lost all our connection with the school. Hope to reconnect with the new 'pres.' I will keep this top of mind. Journalism does matter."

Blethen and other professionals had complained for years that the mass communication programs at the University of Washington and Washington State University were losing touch with the real world, but, interestingly, not one professional organization or journalist openly supported the 7-Step Plan or any elements of it.

A month passed with no response from the provost's office.

In late February, Dean Erich Lear said he'd given the plan to Austin.

At a faculty meeting, Austin announced that "communication studies was central to the mission of the Murrow School." Some faculty wanted to vote down my plan right there. But Austin said the plan had not been submitted to the School for formal review, so there was no reason to vote.

Several more weeks passed and still no response from the provost. Only two faculty expressed some support for the plan, but neither would go public with their opinions.

After nearly two months of no response from WSU, I decided to sweeten the pot. I increased the donation to $100,000.

I composed a new letter on March 29 and sent it to incoming president Elson Floyd. He responded immediately and said he would like to meet to discuss the plan, but that he would be "very busy" that summer. I said fall semester would be fine.

At the Murrow Symposium in April 2007, Provost Bates personally told me that he never received the plan, even though postal records showed the university had signed for the package. He said, though, that he was aware of the plan.

He then asked, in a disapproving tone of voice, "Why did you circumvent the Murrow administration and submit the plan directly to me?"

"Because I had no other choice," I replied, anticipating the question. "The Murrow School administration has refused to acknowledge the value of national accreditation as well as the other ideas in my plan for improving the undergraduate program."

As a rule, bureaucracies don't take kindly to employees who circumvent the hierarchical power structure, even when there is no other option. I knew this, but sometimes one has to take risks.

* * * * *

Meanwhile, unbeknownst to me, resentment was stirring in the department over another issue, one that thank goodness did not involve me. But I did insert my big fat free-speech mouth into the controversy.

After the election of Austin for director of the Murrow School, Dean Lear appointed the faculty member who lost the election to the part-time position of "associate director" in the Murrow School and gave him a $10,000 raise.

That prompted one of the other current "associate directors" to ask for a $10,000 raise, but the dean refused. Until now, associate directors were paid with time off from classes, meaning they were given one less class to teach per semester. Several faculty were also angry because they felt faculty should have been given the chance to apply for the position given to the losing candidate.

Lear said the appointment was designed to bring the factions together. Obviously, not everyone agreed.

In late February 2007, someone wrote an anonymous memo criticizing Lear's decision to appoint the losing candidate without giving other faculty a chance to apply. Austin responded by sending an email to faculty and threatening punishment if they continued to write anonymous letters.

"I want to assure you that I will not tolerate harassment of our faculty and staff. ... I want you to know that I will not let incidents like this go unaddressed."

Of course, no overly idealistic and reckless advocate of the First Amendment like me could allow a comment like that go unanswered. I emailed: "If you, acting on behalf of the university, punish the individual for expressing those opinions, regardless of whether they are true or not, you and the university will be violating the First Amendment and the author's academic freedom."

Dean Lear then emailed, taking issue with my admonition: "We have an obligation to protect those we supervise. We would, if the action of the message's author is inappropriate, operate within the university's disciplinary processes. These sometimes elicit legal action outside of the university, but we need to be brave enough to call things to question."

Frances McSweeney, vice provost for faculty affairs, then backed up Lear. She said she wasn't advocating punishment for the faculty member who wrote the memo, but "if the comments are serious enough, as Erich [Lear] says, we do have a disciplinary process."

I responded: "The university can discipline faculty for unethical action and behavior but not for expressing a point of view on a political issue, even if that view contains errors or falsehoods. The 1940 Statement on Academic Freedom from the American Association of University Professors and the U.S. Supreme Court have made that very clear."

Actually, there was a good chance I was wrong on the latter point, at least in terms of how the courts were interpreting free speech in 2007. Unbeknownst to me, ten months before our spirited email exchange, the U.S. Supreme Court issued a ruling that appeared to support the administrators' arguments.

In *Garcetti v. Ceballos*, the conservative majority of the court ruled 5–4 that public employees generally do not deserve free-speech protection when speaking in their official roles — even when they report wrongdoing among governmental officials. The case involved an assistant district attorney in Los Angeles, Richard Ceballos, who was disciplined after he discovered police had given false information to obtain a search warrant.

The five conservative Supreme Court judges who penned the majority opinion essentially said it is better for the government to control employees than to root out misconduct or corrupt public employees. But because of the long-standing principle of academic freedom, the majority opinion left the door open on the issue of whether professors have more free-speech protection than other government employees. "We need not ... decide whether the analysis we conduct today would apply in the same manner to a case involving speech related to scholarship or teaching."

Prior to *Garcetti*, the courts had relied on what came to be known as the Pickering balancing test. This involved balancing the interests of a public employer with employees' right to free speech through these three questions: (1) Did the employee's speech address a matter or matters of public interest and concern? (2) Was the employee's speech a significant or motivating factor in the employer's decision to punish or terminate the employee? (3) Did the interests of the individual commenting on matters of public concern outweigh the public employer's interest in "promoting the efficiency of public service?"

To prevail, an employee had to convince the court that the answers to all three questions were "yes." *Garcetti* basically mooted the first two questions and assumed that all speech from employees was contrary to the efficiency of public service.

The *Garcetti* decision eventually would figure prominently in my own case against WSU administrators. But the exchange of emails between WSU administrators and me clearly demonstrated that administrators were more concerned about social order than in protecting freedom of speech.

The author of the mysterious letter that criticized Dean Lear never revealed his or her identity. I'm sure some Murrow faculty thought I wrote it, but I didn't. I asked two faculty whether they had written it, but both denied authorship.

I emailed Dean Lear at one point to explain that some faculty saw his appointment of the losing dean candidate as a political payoff.

Lear denied the charge.

I think he was sincere.

He saw it as a way of trying to calm a conflicted situation, but things don't always turn out the way you predict.

* * * * *

In February 2007, I submitted my annual review for the 2006 calendar year to Austin. Other Murrow faculty did the same.

Annual reviews affect merit raise increases, promotion and tenure.

The review contains three major areas: one for research and scholarship, one for teaching and one for service (to the community, university and profession).

Because WSU is a Ph.D.-granting institution, scholarship is just as important as teaching. Each represents forty percent of the performance review. Service is a distant third (20%).

When Alex Tan was the director of the Murrow School, he reviewed the material and rated faculty in terms of their performance. Austin, however, opted for a different procedure, one that created a four-member faculty committee that would review faculty and make recommendations to Austin. The committee would be composed of faculty from various ranks.

This was an ill-conceived plan, for four reasons, as I noted in an email to Austin. First, faculty of lower ranks should not be allowed to rate faculty of higher ranks. This violated university rules on tenure. Second, because the faculty review committee was a unit that did not have formal authority under WSU's faculty manual, giving some faculty the authority to see the performance records of other faculty could violate privacy laws on the release of personnel records. Third, giving some faculty the authority to evaluate other faculty likely would generate a lot of resentment and conflict among faculty, especially if members of the committee had an ax to grind against a colleague. Fourth, the faculty review committee approach might also encourage the Murrow director to displace responsibility for the ratings. The director could even play the role of Pontius Pilate and blame the committee for any errors that might crop up later.

Austin ignored my objections.

The plan was implemented.

At least two of the four faculty on the committee did not like my 7-Step Plan or the idea of removing communication studies from the Murrow program.

During the previous decade, I had received an average annual rating of 4.8 on a 5-point scale, with 5 representing extraordinary performance. I received a perfect 5.0 rating in two of those years.

In 2005, I was also one of the most productive scholars in the Murrow School. On a weighted average, I had published the equivalent of more than five social scientific articles per year since obtaining my Ph.D. My score was high because I had written more refereed scholarly books than other faculty, which are given more weight because they take longer to write than journal articles.

In 2006, I completed the first draft of a three-hundred-and-seventy-page theoretically grounded book titled *History and Future of Mass Media.* This was my 10th academic book. I had signed a contract with Hampton Press of Cresskill, N.J., one of the major private publishers in the field of mass communication, to publish the book in late summer.

In spring 2006, the Murrow School also chose my *Dictionary of Mass Communication & Media Research* as the second-most important contribution from the Murrow School faculty during 2005. My teaching evaluations averaged 4.4 on a five-point scale, which was above departmental averages for faculty.

The year 2006 had been one of my best years as a professor.

But it wouldn't matter.

Chapter 28
My Crummy Annual Review

9:34 a.m., March 22, 2007
Washington State University

I could feel my face flush and my heart rate soar as I read my 2006 annual review.

A 2.7 on a 5.0 scale.

How could the new director give me such a low annual review rating?

That was the lowest or second-lowest faculty rating in the entire Edward R. Murrow School of Communication at Washington State University. Anything lower than 3.0 means a faculty member is failing to meet minimum expectations and can be fired for incompetence — even if they, like me, are tenured.

Incompetence?

Okay, I concede I'll never win a Pulitzer or Nobel prize.

But I'm a good teacher and one of the top scholars in the Murrow School.

I am tempted — really tempted — to start calling Erica Austin a bunch of nasty names, like *scheissekopf*. That's German for shithead. I learned that when I was a kid, because I grew up in a small working-class German town in Michigan.

But now I'm a professor, and we professors are expected to control ourselves and our language. Our motto, if we had one, would be "cool and calm complements scholarly and sagacious."

So, I'm trying my best to turn indignation into compassion. Maybe someone gave Austin faulty information.

Yeah, I bet that's it.

Now I'm even feeling a tinge of Lutheran guilt for thinking about calling her names. She's actually a very pleasant person. I even supported her candidacy for director of the Murrow School last summer. The least I can do is read the rest of her review before I become extremely angry.

"The committee and I," Austin writes, "are concerned that ... [Dr. Demers] has had a class policy of cancelling lab sections. ... When asked by [me] to make a change for future semesters, Dr. Demers declined to alter this schedule. Because failure to comply with expectations regarding class contact time may be constructed as 'serious and repeated neglect of duty' as set for in the faculty manual, Dr. Demers' unresponsiveness on this issue is of concern."

Declined to alter this schedule.

Serious and repeated neglect of duty?

Unresponsiveness?

Is she kidding?

Previous WSU administrators have endorsed my class policies, and, as she had asked, I changed my syllabus to conform to her request not to cancel classes during the last week of classes. *Why didn't she look at my syllabus or contact me before issuing this review?*

The average rating in the department was 3.95 on a 5.0 scale. Ninety-five percent of the faculty were rated higher than me. I received a 2.8 rating in terms of research, even though I had completed my *History and Future of Mass Media* book and had secured a reputable publisher.

One tenured Murrow faculty member chuckled when I told him the results. "Gee, I didn't publish anything and I received a 3.0 rating on research," said Joey Reagan, a full professor who was never afraid to criticize administrators on matters related to university governance.

In the review, Austin said she was giving me a low rating on research because I didn't publish any refereed papers. That's true, but I had completed a refereed theoretical book, which usually has a weighted value of three to five times more than a refereed paper. In my formal written response, I informed her that she would be violating university rules if she punished me or other faculty for authoring refereed theoretical books, because university rules place as much or more value on refereed books as on refereed papers.

She did not respond.

Austin's review also criticized me for not performing enough service, even though I served on two departmental committees, reviewed four papers for journals or conferences, chaired three master's committees and was a member of a fourth, and put in the required eight hours minimum per week.

In my response, I accused Austin of penalizing me not because of poor performance, but because I had supported the previous director Alex Tan, proposed the 7-Step Plan, and criticized her policies and other administrators' policies regarding the administration of the school.

I asked her to change my ratings.

She refused.

I contacted one member of the faculty review committee to find out how Austin could have made the error about my canceling classes in Com 101. The committee member wasn't sure, but he said when the committee discussed the issue, one of the other committee members (a friend of Austin) confessed that she had canceled classes during the last week of classes in one spring semester to leave early for a vacation. She wasn't punished.

The faculty review committee member also told me that the committee did not issue any written findings to Austin. The committee's evaluation of faculty was transmitted verbally, he said, which meant there was no record of accountability.

* * * * *

University rules allow faculty to "appeal" the director's decision to the Dean of Liberal Arts.

Although Dean Lear did not defend Austin's review, he refused to change it. I asked him if I could appeal his decision. He said there was no formal appeals process for annual reviews.

What?

Indeed, the faculty manual had no statements about how to correct errors in annual reviews if the Dean refuses to correct them.

At one point, Dean Lear and Austin asked to meet with me. I agreed if they would give me permission to tape-record the meeting.

They refused.

I declined to meet, because without accountability, they could use the meeting to generate more evidence against me.

The only other possible option was the Faculty Status Committee (FSC), which can hear grievances but cannot force administrators to correct errors. FSC only has the power to make recommendations.

I filed a complaint with FSC in May 2007, because I knew that if I needed to file a lawsuit to protect my job, I would have to exhaust all administrative reviews. The committee sat on my complaint for nine months. I contacted the committee chair and he sent me a letter saying the committee had declined to review the case. No reason was given.

So, it ended there.

* * * * *

In late spring 2007, I learned that I was not the only faculty member who was being targeted by Austin and other WSU administrators. Within a year or so, several Murrow faculty were gone. Within three years, more than a half-dozen had left. All of those who left except one had been Tan supporters.

I might have left, too, except that my wife, Theresa, couldn't leave the Spokane area. She had seven more years before being fully vested in her retirement plan at a state-run hospital for the mentally ill where she worked. Another disincentive to leaving was that Lee Ann was doing well in school. She had just turned seven.

I believe Austin and other administrators initially had good intentions when they took control of the Murrow School. They believed some faculty were not very productive or were poor teachers. They wanted to improve the quality of the Murrow School. But their decisions were not bias-free. One tenured faculty member who hadn't published a thing in a decade was never targeted for dismissal, because he was popular among other Ph.D. faculty.

But all purges have risks.

Two faculty eventually filed discrimination complaints, one based on race and the other on age. The race case was dismissed and the university paid a small sum to settle the age case.

I wasn't a protected category because I was a white male.

I was out of options.

Chapter 29
MURROW SCHOOL BECOMES A COLLEGE

Summer 2007
Washington State University

Elson Floyd assumed the presidency of WSU in the summer of 2007, and one of his first acts was to announce that the university would consider turning the Murrow School into a college.

Floyd previously was president of the University of Missouri, which has one of the best undergraduate mass communication programs in the United States. College status for the Murrow program presumably would mean more funding. The Murrow faculty, myself included, were pleased about that.

But Floyd's announcement was another reminder of that power in a university flows down, not up.

For a decade upper-level WSU administrators had been telling the Murrow School that it was too small to become a college — and then, overnight, one individual at the top changed everything. Presumably Floyd knew that converting the school into a college was a way to bring greater visibility to the entire university, because Edward R. Murrow was its most famous graduate.

* * * * *

Meanwhile, I was preparing to move Marquette Books out of my basement and into a commercial location. I hired a retired man to work part-time. During the school year, faculty are allowed to work one full day at a consulting or other non-university business. During the summer, there was no limit on work hours, as long as a faculty member wasn't teaching.

On September 18, 2007, I distributed a news release stating that Marquette Books would be moving into a commercial location two blocks from my home.

Unbeknownst to me, Murrow's interim Director Erica Austin had been meeting with Vice Provost Frances McSweeney, internal auditor Heather Lopez and university attorneys about Marquette Books and about the issue of online quizzes and exams. I don't know the content of those meetings, but I received an email from Lopez on September 20, 2007, asking for more information about the company.

I was surprised, because she was asking the same questions that had been answered nearly four years earlier, when the university controller investigated and found I had been following university rules. I assumed her inquiry was simply routine follow-up. I told her what I had been telling Austin. If I use a Marquette book in my class, I give them free to students. MB is my summer employment. I had one part-time employee to help me out during the rest of the year.

I also emailed Lopez and argued that my 7-Step Plan was the real reason Austin was penalizing me in my annual reviews. She and many other faculty were not pleased with my recommendations.

In November, I submitted an application to take a one-semester sabbatical in spring 2009 to write a book about the lack of impact of social science research on public policy. I informed WSU officials that the book could contain content "critical of WSU." I wanted them to be fully informed before approving the sabbatical.

Austin had reservations about granting the leave.

But the provost's office approved it, because, I learned later, administrators were planning to fire me if I didn't complete the book and obtain a reputable publisher.

* * * * *

On October 24, 2007, I met with President Elson Floyd to talk about the $100,000 donation and the 7-Step Plan.

Since 1978, he had held fifteen different administrative positions at various universities, including the presidential positions at the University of Missouri and Western Michigan University. He earned all his degrees from the University of North Carolina at Chapel Hill: a bachelor's degree in political science and speech, a master's of education, and a Ph.D. in higher and adult education.

His curriculum vitae showed that he never held a full-time teaching position and had no refereed journal publications or books. Some faculty see the lack of scholarship and teaching experience as a flaw. They believe "managerial administrators" are less likely to identify with the concerns and issues of faculty. They might not, for example, see academic freedom and shared governance as being as important as "academic administrators" would see them. But Floyd was too new to the university for anyone, including me, to draw such conclusions.

He cordially escorted me into his spacious university office, which had yet to be adorned with WSU "Go Cougars" paraphernalia. He apologized for that.

Physically, Floyd reminded me of Laurence Fishburne, the actor who is known for his role as Morpheus in the 1999 science fiction film "The Matrix." Fishburne is charismatic on screen; Floyd is equally impressive in real life. News reports did not exaggerate. He was charming and gracious.

The only discomfort I felt during his visit was his shifting gaze. He seemed to focus on every gesture I made as if looking for clues to flaws in my character. Another university administrator later told me he felt the same way when he spoke with Floyd.

But it surely wasn't fair to judge a man after one encounter, and, after all, this was the man who several weeks earlier announced that the university might turn the Murrow School into a college. Actually, that statement was only partially correct. He had already made the decision.

"I am going to turn the Murrow School into a college," he said.

I told him the Murrow faculty and I had been trying to do that for ten years.

I spent most of the half-hour in his office talking about the 7-Step Plan. I'm not sure he was all that interested. But he was interested in the $100,000 donation I offered if the university accepted the plan.

At one point, he interrupted me and radically altered the conversation.

"Why do you get into it with the faculty over there? I think you enjoy taunting them."

I smiled and told him I had a deep commitment to protecting free speech and improving the quality of the Murrow program. I continued with my presentation.

What was interesting about his comment is that it implied that I had power over other faculty — that I had the power to taunt. But I had little power. When it came to implementing the changes I suggested for improving the Murrow programs, I always lost.

Floyd clearly had no clue that mobbing is a top-down phenomenon, not bottom-up. We parted with an awkward handshake and strained smiles.

* * * * *

After the meeting with Floyd, Austin sent an email to faculty saying four deans from mass communication programs at other universities in the United States would visit the campus to make a recommendation about turning the Murrow School into a college.

I emailed Austin and other faculty and told them that it was a done deal. "Floyd already told me that he was going to turn the school into a college."

Austin responded via email to all faculty that the decision had not been made. Formally, she was correct. The Board of Regents would need to approve the action. But I wondered if Floyd had told her what he told me. If so, she never revealed it.

The college proposal did not change my 7-Step Plan, which was oriented toward restructuring and re-professionalizing the mass communication programs.

I personally knew two of the outside deans who would visit WSU.

One of them, Jean Folkerts, had been editor of a scholarly journal where I had published eight of my refereed journal papers. I also interviewed for a job once at her university, where she was the director of the program. "We need someone like you," she said. But I was never offered the position.

The other dean was Tim Gleason of the School of Journalism and Mass Communication at the University of Oregon. He was a First Amendment scholar and a pleasant man. I had met him on several occasions through a friend who was a colleague on the School's faculty.

I contacted the four deans and gave them copies of the 7-Step Plan.

All four of their journalism programs were accredited. None included a communication studies (or speech communication) program.

I didn't know how they would react to the plan, but I knew they would endorse the college-status proposal. That's how it works in the politics of higher education. Committees often are created to endorse and legitimate a decision, not to provide unsolicited advice.

But the visiting deans' committee recommended that communication studies be included in the new college. The committee also informally advised that the new Murrow College should not seek accreditation, even though all four of their programs were accredited.

In the end, the whole process was nothing more than a ritual — a ceremony of actions performed according to a predetermined order. Much ado about nothing.

The Murrow School officially became a college on July 1, 2008.

When the news was announced at a faculty meeting, most faculty were jubilant. One of the communication studies faculty who had strongly supported the College proposal and the ouster of Alex Tan jokingly said: "I suppose we should be careful of what we ask for, because we might just get it."

Little did he realize how prophetic that statement would be for him and his program.

Chapter 30
MORE CENSORSHIP AND QUESTIONS

Fall 2007
Washington State University

When Elson Floyd took over as president of WSU in the summer of 2007, one of the first controversies he encountered was a planned protest from a student group on campus during Islamo-Fascism Awareness Week, October 22–26, 2007.

On October 12, Floyd issued a preemptive strike: He said the university would punish students if they engaged in speech that was hateful or demeaning to other groups on campus.

> Universities must be places where the free exchange of ideas is not just protected, but encouraged. At the same time, we do not want individuals on our campuses to feel threatened because of their ethnicity or their religious beliefs. Sometimes these two principles appear to be in conflict. At those times, we must rely on the good-faith efforts of all members of the university community to assure that the resulting dialog is both constructive and civil. ... I fully understand concerns raised, in this post-9/11 era; however, civility and constructive discourse must always prevail.

Floyd clearly did not understand the First Amendment or American history.

"Civility" is never a term that historians apply to the "founding fathers" when they were hammering out the Constitution and the Bill of Rights. There was a lot of shouting and arguing and name-calling.

The federal courts also had ruled on several occasions that the First

Amendment protects hate speech. Action or behavior that harms someone could be punished, however. In short, you can say just about anything you want — your speech can be unruly, raucous, mean, contemptuous, scornful, insulting, abusive, and even hateful and unconstructive — but the moment you translate that speech into violent or aggressive action, you've crossed the line.

Floyd did not understand the difference between speech and action.

So, I sent an email to one of his assistants, informing her that Floyd's statement was inconsistent with First Amendment law. The assistant did not respond.

As it turned out, the students never conducted the protest, because they were afraid of being punished. Their voices were censored.

WSU administrators also violated the First Amendment in February 2008 when they were rewriting their 2008–2013 strategic plan. Item number six on the list, "Freedom of Expression," stated that students, faculty and administrators should be "civil" when they discuss issues and problems on campus.

I sent an email to the administrators suggesting they eliminate the words that imply students, faculty and staff must be civil. To my surprise, they changed it to, "We are committed to being a community that protects the free exchange of ideas while also *encouraging* dialog that is constructive and civil."

Much better. There's nothing wrong with "encouraging" civil speech. The university just should not require it.

Unfortunately, though, when WSU created its 2014–2019 Strategic Plan (I was no longer working at the university), it reverted to the original wording: "We are committed to the free exchange of ideas in a constructive and civil environment ... ."

* * * * *

On December 20, five days before Christmas, Internal Auditor Heather Lopez called me again and grilled me about Marquette Books.

I spent an hour and a half on the phone with her.

I asked if she had read the internal affairs and comptroller reports issued several years earlier about Marquette Books. She said she had access to them but didn't confirm that she had read them.

I should have tape-recorded the conversation, but I didn't realize she was going to write a formal report.

Of course, I had nothing to fear from a legal or ethical standpoint.

But my experiences at the University of Wisconsin–River Falls showed that administrators can quickly jettison facts and truth when they are angry.

Lopez's phone call did confirm one thing for me: Now I knew without question that there was a concerted effort in the administration to discredit me or my company, probably with the goal of firing me. Question after question was accusatory.

I sent a follow-up email to Lopez two days later to leave a written record of my responses. I also pointed out that Murrow professor Joey Reagan published nothing in 2006 and got a 3.0 ("meeting expectations") rating for research from Austin, whereas I finished writing a 360-page theoretically based textbook (*History and Future of Mass Media*) and got a rating of 2.8.

But that didn't matter.

Lopez had already made up her mind.

I also began to notice that many faculty in the Murrow School were reducing their interactions with me. No one wanted to be associated with a professor who challenged the power structure, even if he was doing it to promote free speech and national accreditation for the mass communication programs.

"They're all cowards," one of my non-WSU friends would often remark. "They're envious of your accomplishments, and you are shaming them. There's no good defense for not seeking national accreditation for the professional programs."

"I find it hard to believe that faculty are motivated by envy," I sincerely responded. "These are smart, competent people. They need not fear each other or me. Each is very accomplished."

But other friends and colleagues would continue to use the "envy theory" to explain what was becoming a campaign against me. Although I almost always discounted it, I didn't have a better explanation. And sociologist Kenneth Westhues's theory of workplace mobbing listed envy as an important cause of mobbing.

To deal with the stress and the thought that I could lose my career (a second time), I spent as much time with Lee Ann as I could.

She made me laugh every day. She was full of life — a constant reminder of what is important in this world. On one occasion, when she was about four, she looked up at a large, bright moon low on the horizon and, comparing it to a light bulb, said, "Who turns off the moon?"

My spouse, Theresa, was also supportive, which meant a lot to me.

"They're angry because they can't control you, Dave," she would say over the next couple of years. "You're like the little boy who tells the crowd that the emperor has no clothes."

That Christmas I also decided to buy a model train to set up around the Christmas tree. When I was a kid, I loved my HO gauge train set. I had no idea what a slippery slope that purchase would become.

I fell into model railroading with a passion, and I would spend many hours over the next couple of years working on my eight-by-eight-foot layout. I also began playing my guitar again and created a homemade CD of classic blues music. The CD included Eric Clapton's "Before You Accuse Me (Take a Look at Yourself)," the Allman Brothers' "One Way Out," B. B. King's "The Thrill Is Gone," and Blues Traveler's "Run-Around."

My family, the train, and the music were far more effective at keeping depression at bay than antidepressant drugs or therapists.

I was no Howard Roark, the overly confident architect in *The Fountainhead*, but I was tougher than I had been at River Falls.

My principles were sustaining me.

* * * * *

In January 2008, I completed my second annual review for Austin.

I again emphasized that I never canceled any classes in 2007, including Com 101. I pointed out that my book on the *History and Future of Mass Media* had been published by Hampton Press in

September 2007. I also submitted draft chapters of another new theoretical book that examined the lack of impact that social scientific research has on public policy. I titled it *The Ivory Tower of Babel: Why the Social Sciences Are Failing to Live Up to Their Promises.* My teaching evaluations again were better than the school average, and I performed more service, working more than ten hours a week.

She gave me a 2.5 overall rating, which was even lower than the 2.7 in 2006. I again received the lowest or second-lowest rating in the school.

She criticized me for allegedly failing to follow university rules on outside work activities. And she falsely accused me again of canceling classes. "The average teaching evaluation scores for his classes were positive, but Dr. Demers repeatedly cancelled classes despite warnings that the level of cancellations was unacceptable."

In my response to her review, I informed her that her facts were wrong—I did not cancel any classes in 2007, not one. I told her again that I had attendance records and quizzes and exams from all my classes. They were time-stamped, which meant I could prove my classes were never canceled.

Austin did not respond.

But on April 6, 2008, before the errors could be resolved, I received a telephone call from Internal Auditor Heather Lopez.

Chapter 31
AN INTERNAL AUDIT AND A NOTICE

Spring 2008
Louisiana State University

I was preparing for an in-person interview for an endowed chair position at Louisiana State University when my phone rang.

"Dr. Demers, this is Heather Lopez from the Washington State University's Internal Audit Office. I'm sorry it has taken so long to get the results of our investigation back to you. I've been very busy."

"No problem."

"I've just finished the report, which contains two conclusions. The first is that you should have submitted an annual report on your involvement in your book company, Marquette Books. The second is that you violated university rules when you refused to comply with a department directive and canceled classes in your introduction to mass communication course in spring 2007."

"You're kidding me," I respond. "I never canceled classes in my communication course in spring 2007; in fact, I never canceled any classes in 2007, and I've got the records to prove it. I'm being targeted because of my 7-Step Plan."

"My job isn't to investigate the politics, Dr. Demers, but to examine the facts."

"But what if your facts are wrong?"

"My investigation is finished."

"Can I appeal your charges?"

"No, there is no appeal process. But you can write a response and we'll include it in the official record. As far as punishment, that's up to Erica Austin, your interim dean. The report will be given to her.

Goodbye."

I was bewildered.

First, I had no idea that I needed to submit an annual report on my involvement with Marquette Books. No one has ever told me I needed to do that, and I didn't even know what that report was supposed to contain.

Second, I had time-stamped evidence showing that I never canceled any classes. Why did Lopez and other administrators not look at that evidence? And why was there no appeal procedure for an internal audit?

In fifteen minutes I would give a presentation on my research to the journalism and mass communication faculty at Louisiana State University. I was not at my best. I was suffering from my dreaded cough. I was never offered the position.

I obtained a copy of Lopez's written report several days after returning from Louisiana. The most disturbing aspect of her investigation was that she never asked me if I had deliberately violated Murrow School director Erica Austin's order not to cancel classes in spring 2007.

Why would someone presumably trained in investigatory techniques make an accusation without first asking the accused if he was guilty of the offense?

This question haunted me for several days until I recalled a conversation I had with an administrator several months earlier, who told me that Lopez's sister, Denise, works for Erica Austin. Denise was a staff member in the Murrow School (soon to become a College).

I liked Denise. We used to joke a lot and talk about our kids.

But what I didn't know at the time was that Denise was the one who got Lopez involved in the investigation of me in the first place. I learned that several months later after I reviewed university documents obtained through a Freedom of Information Act request.

In August 2006, Denise sent an email to the Murrow School office manager and to Austin, informing them that her sister Lopez was the internal auditor at WSU. Later I also learned that Denise had been sent to see if I was holding class. She reported back on one occasion that my class wasn't in session.

That was true because the class was being conducted online. My students were taking an online test that day. The date and time were stamped on them. Austin incorrectly assumed I had canceled classes and erroneously passed that information on to Lopez.

"Wow, the internal auditor clearly had a conflict of interest," one retired state auditor friend of mine in Seattle told me.

A dozen other professors, colleagues and attorneys I spoke with later echoed that same sentiment. Ironically, Lopez overlooked the fact that her sister's role in the investigation compromised her own investigation, at least in terms of appearances.

This is not to suggest that a conspiracy was in the works. I suspect that Lopez didn't even see the potential conflict of interest.

However, the problem, as I would write in many reports to university officials as the months passed, is that Lopez's relationship with Austin may have enhanced the credibility of Austin's false allegations about canceling classes, thus compromising Lopez's ability to objectively investigate the charges. That could explain why Lopez never asked me whether I had canceled classes in Com 101. She was already thoroughly convinced that Austin was correct and credible; after all, her own sister reported to her.

Before I had a chance to respond to Lopez's report, though, I was blind-sided again.

* * * * *

On April 18, 2008, I received a letter from Austin titled "Notice Concerning Serious or Repeated Neglect of Duty." By this time, I had received so much accusatory mail from the university that I was afraid to collect the mail from the box in front of my house. Theresa, my spouse, did that for me. She would open the mail and read it to me. Oddly, that helped me cope with the stress.

The letter falsely claimed that I administered a final exam during the fourteenth week of the semester in one of my classes, rather than during finals week; that I conducted only two and not three class sessions per week in my classes in fall 2007; and that I had failed to file a form about my involvement with Marquette Books.

The last item was correct and part of Lopez's internal audit, but I was waiting for the university to explain why it believed I had to submit the form. I never did get an explanation.

Where the hell is Austin coming up with these false accusations?

No investigative reporter I know would ever accuse an individual of wrongdoing without first giving them a chance to respond.

"It's a madhouse," I said to my wife, quoting a famous line from the movie *Planet of the Apes.*

I followed up with a response, refuting each charge and repeating again that a vice provost for research at WSU told me that Marquette Books did not have to file the report because the business was not connected to the university.

Once again, there was no response from Austin or the university.

On April 24, 2008, I wrote a formal response to Lopez's report, providing details and evidence to contradict all allegations. I also informed Lopez that she had made several other factual errors in her report, and I asked her to correct them. I added that I would file the annual reports on Marquette Books if the rule applied to my company.

I thought about raising the conflict of interest issue with respect to her sister. But, after talking with two attorneys, I decided not to, at least not at that time.

That was my ace in the hole.

* * * * *

Lopez eventually responded to my request about whether I could appeal the conclusion in her report which contended that Marquette Books is subject to the university rules.

She said no.

I followed up with another email that, among other things, asked her whether she would correct the errors in her report.

Again, she said no.

Lopez's refusal to explain why my interpretation of the university rules was incorrect backed me into a corner. If I didn't file the form on Marquette Books, she and the university would probably use that to fire me.

So, I emailed Austin and asked her what I needed to do to complete the documentation for Marquette Books. She faxed the form that I needed to complete. It was cryptic, basically asking how many days a week one would perform outside work activities "over the next year."

That was it? All of the fuss was over one oddly worded form? Why didn't they send me that form earlier?

The answer to that question was obvious.

They hoped I would refuse to complete the form, because then they might have the grounds to fire me.

Okay, maybe I was paranoid.

But paranoids have enemies, too.

I completed the form and sent it back.

Shortly after that, I ran into a Murrow faculty member who also had performed outside work activities. He was a consultant for private industry. He said he didn't file the form, and he said he resented the university's intrusion into his private life. He said Austin had advised him to file the form.

"I think you are being singled out," he said.

The faculty member never did file the form. He was never punished and, as of this writing, was still teaching in the Murrow College.

Although I filed the form, it still wasn't clear whether the university could punish me for my involvement in Marquette Books. I mentioned this to one of my employment attorneys the following week.

"Why don't you just sell the company to your wife?" he asked.

"But wouldn't I still have a vested interest in the company? Theresa and I live in a community property state. And I still would have the problem of the past ownership — they might still punish me for something that happened several years ago."

"Not so," said the attorney. "It's possible to back-date the sale. It's all perfectly legal. People do it all the time. Moreover, you can exclude it from community property. We'll simply draw up a separate agreement and you'll have no financial interest in the company."

So that's what we did.

According to the law, I only owned Marquette Books for several days back in 2002. My wife was the real owner. This is one of the few times the law seemed to work in my favor, although I would have preferred another solution.

On May 3, 2008, I emailed Austin and other university officials, informing them that I was relinquishing all ownership rights to Marquette Books and its related companies.

"Should I send them a copy of the paperwork?" I asked the attorney.

"Only if they ask for it. Why should you be nice to them after the way they have treated you? Besides, you can learn something from this. You'll see how interested they are in prosecuting you for your involvement in Marquette Books."

That wasn't the way a good Lutheran would approach it. He would have sent the paperwork to the other party out of courtesy.

But the attorney had a good point.

The university never asked for the paperwork.

The allegations against Marquette Books turned out to be a paper tiger.

A month later Dean Lear will confirm this at a meeting to discuss the errors in my annual review. "I am satisfied that you are now in compliance with university rules," he said.

But the end of this particular issue wasn't going to stop other administrators from trying to force me out of my job.

I decided it was time to go on the offensive.

On May 6, 2008, I sent a letter to President Floyd asking for access to numerous records and emails surrounding my case. I cited the state's freedom of information law as grounds for granting my request.

The records office on campus responded that it would take several months to assemble the records.

* * * * *

My options for appealing the errors in my annual reviews as well as in the internal audit were running out. As one attorney pointed out, the university hadn't punished me enough to justify filing a full-fledged lawsuit. Yet it was clear that Austin and other administrators would continue to fabricate small things that might eventually build into a big case against me. The mobbing process was well underway.

"Have you tried talking with the university ombudsman?" one WSU administrator suggested.

According to the WSU website, the primary purpose of the ombudsman "is to protect the interests, rights, and privileges of students, staff, and faculty at all levels of university operations and programs."

I wasn't too optimistic about the role that an ombudsman could play. Several years earlier I had conducted some research on newspaper ombudsmen and found that some news organizations created the position in an attempt to show the world that they can evaluate themselves objectively. Research shows, however, that they spend less time criticizing the newspaper than justifying to the public why journalists make the decisions they do. They were essentially public relations employees.

I suspected the same would be true for a university ombudsman — that he or she would identify more with the power structure than the aggrieved faculty member.

But it was worth a shot.

I called WSU ombudsman Ken Struckmeyer in late May or early June 2008. Struckmeyer was the professor who had criticized the process used to hire Elson Floyd.

Struckmeyer suggested I contact the Washington State attorney general's office about filing a conflict-of-interest complaint against the internal auditor. He assumed she worked for the state auditor.

But she didn't.

She was a WSU employee, so the state auditor's office refused to get involved.

Another dead end.

I went back to Struckmeyer and told him what happened. I also told him that Dean Lear and Austin refused to meet with me if I tape-recorded the meeting.

"I wonder why they would refuse to do that," he said.

"Because they're afraid to be accountable," I responded.

Struckmeyer didn't react to that comment.

Instead, he suggested that I ask them whether they would be willing to allow him to sit in at a meeting. He would be a "neutral" observer.

That was a reasonable compromise.

Lear and Austin agreed to meet on June 30, 2008.

At the meeting, I presented a written report listing six major errors in the two annual reviews I received from Austin. I was most concerned about correcting the error that I had canceled classes, because that was the error duplicated in the internal audit.

Lear seemed a bit surprised to learn that I had not canceled classes. He then tried to justify Austin's error by saying that the "general feeling of the faculty" was that my behavior was inappropriate. He went on for another five minutes. I listened, patiently.

"I don't care what the faculty felt," I respond, pointing my finger on the list of errors in my report. "The charge that I canceled classes is false, and I want it corrected. What I don't understand is how such a blatant error could have been made, because I changed my syllabus and instructed the teaching assistants to hold classes during last week."

Austin then admits that she never saw my syllabus.

"We weren't able to find a copy," she says.

"Why didn't you just ask me for a copy?"

She didn't answer that question. "Your student evaluations also suggested that you had canceled classes," she says. "Many students say they like your class because you 'cancel classes on Fridays.'"

"That statement is inaccurate," I respond. "I conduct online quizzes or exams in my classes on some Fridays. The students love that because they don't have to walk over to the classroom. Some think that I'm 'canceling' class. But that's not true. We hold class in cyberspace. Why didn't you just ask me about those comments before accusing me of canceling classes?"

Austin looked shell-shocked. Her face was red.

Struckmeyer then chimed in.

"So, Erich, you will be issuing a correction in Dave's annual review?"

"Yes, we will do that," Lear says.

"And you will send that correction to the internal auditor?"

"Yes," Lear adds.

"And what about adjusting his annual review quantitative rating and level of compensation."

"I don't know that we can do that —"

I cut Lear off.

"I don't care about the compensation or the rating. I just want the record corrected. I'm most concerned about the internal audit. Lopez duplicated the error that I canceled classes. I'll be satisfied if that correction is made to the internal audit."

Lear adds that he is also satisfied that I had addressed his concerns about Marquette Books and was "now in compliance with university rules."

"Well, I guess I didn't need to sell the company to my wife after all," I say, chuckling.

I was so relieved.

I shook hands with Struckmeyer.

When I returned home, I sent an email to numerous administrators who had been involved in this dispute summarizing the results of the meeting.

I pointed out that one lesson to be learned from this is to always give the accused a chance to respond before issuing charges.

But my celebration was premature.

Chapter 32
THE NEVER-ENDING ACCUSATIONS

August 2008
Washington State University

Murrow Director Erica Austin had revised my 2007 annual review and placed it in my mailbox, but I didn't see it until two months later, in early August 2008. I wasn't teaching the summer session and didn't have a good reason to take the seventy-minute drive down to Pullman. After the meeting with the ombudsman, the dean, and Austin, I assumed the dispute with the university had been solved.

Wrong.

The paragraph which stated that I had deliberately violated Austin's directive not to cancel classes was still in there, but now it stated that I had "failed to hold classes."

Holy semantically.

Austin couldn't let it go. Her actions suggested to me that she was one of those people who can never acknowledge that she made a mistake.

Okay, for the record, I didn't fail to hold classes.

Every class session was conducted, as I've said numerous times before. Some were held online. University regulations clearly permit faculty to give quizzes or tests online. In fact, many of the classes taught through WSU statewide were and still are conducted completely online. The College of Business even offered a Master's of Business Administration completely through online courses.

I emailed Austin again and asked her to correct my annual review and strike all references to canceling or not holding classes.

She refused.

What about the agreement we reached at the meeting with Lear and Struckmeyer, where we agreed that I had not canceled classes? Wasn't that a binding contract?

None of this made sense.

Were university administrators hiding something?

* * * * *

In mid-August 2008, I drove down to Pullman to inspect the data I had requested under the state's FOIA laws.

That's when I learned that Internal Auditor Heather Lopez's sister was helping Austin investigate me. I also learned that Austin sent Lopez's sister to see if I was holding my classes; but oddly, the alleged times and dates were never recorded. The university was never able to provide material evidence that I had canceled classes. Sloppy.

A bigger problem was now emerging.

The records showed that Lopez was advising administrators that they could fire me if I failed to finish writing my *Ivory Tower of Babel* book during my spring 2009 sabbatical AND find a publisher. This was plan B for the university. If they couldn't oust me for canceling classes or incompetence, they would fire me for failing to publish my book. I only had about six months to find a publisher who would submit the book to an outside blind review process.

At this point, I had only three options.

One was to make one last appeal to the administration.

The second was to go public with the internal auditor's conflict of interest.

Third, if neither of those strategies worked, then I would have to file a federal First Amendment lawsuit.

I started with the appeal.

* * * * *

On October 14, 2008, I emailed WSU President Elson Floyd, pointing out that my 2006 and 2007 annual reviews still had six errors of commission or omission.

I asked him to direct university administrators to fix them.

Floyd turned the matter over to interim provost Warwick Bayly, who didn't respond for several months. Not sure why it took so long. I was under no illusion that my complaint was a top priority with upper administration. In fact, aside from the few administrators who were directly involved in this dispute (especially those whose reputations might be adversely affected by an outcome favorable to me), few faculty cared.

But administrators are uncomfortable with conflict.

One of their biggest concerns is social order and stability. Interpersonal or social conflicts within an organization can threaten the power of leaders or elites in the organization because the disputes make the leaders look as if they don't have control.

A participant in a dispute perceives the issues to be very important, but their superiors more often than not do not care about the substantive nature of the dispute. They just want the problem to go away. They want order.

This doesn't mean that all conflicts or disputes in an organization are inconsequential or unimportant. One can hypothesize that *the greater the number of individuals affected by an issue in a dispute, the more legitimacy elites will grant to the dispute.* But if the issue doesn't advance the interests of the elites, they are likely to frame it in a way that reduces the potential of others to see a bigger, more substantive issue.

There was no question in my mind that Austin and other administrators were violating my First Amendment rights and were harassing me with no good reason. They knew that if the dispute were framed as a battle over free speech, they would have more difficulty defending themselves. So, they framed the dispute as a case of professorial incompetence and thought they had evidence that I violated university rules or failed to perform my duties as a professor.

Although this frame is easy to peddle among other friends and administrators in an organization, not all administrators are easily co-opted. Some have the capacity to act professionally and render an “objective” decision in a case.

I always felt that way about my graduate school professors Simon Dinitz (criminology) and Phillip J. Tichenor (my Ph.D. advisor) and my former newspaper editor Dick Carson. They knew how to act like senior statespeople.

I had heard good things about the WSU interim provost, but the sociologist in me predicted he would see the dispute as a case of incompetence rather than as a violation of civil liberties. Vice Provost McSweeney and Austin reported directly to him, and no doubt they had already had conversations with him about the case before I would meet with him.

But, again, maybe I was wrong.

Bayly deserved a chance.

Chapter 33
BAYLY'S KANGAROO COURT

February 18, 2009
Washington State University

By all accounts, Warwick Bayly was a man who had his head screwed on right.

He had been a professor of veterinary science at WSU for more than twenty years and had been named the first four-year Robert B. McEachern Distinguished Professor in Equine Medicine in 1995. In 2001, he was promoted to dean of WSU's College of Veterinary Medicine on a near unanimous vote of the faculty in 2001.

"He's enthusiastic, a solid administrator, and has a strong background and experience in both research and academics," one WSU administrator said about Bayly in a WSU news release. "We are certain his leadership of the college will continue to advance WSU's place among other world class institutions. ... We are fortunate he's chosen to guide the nation's finest veterinary program at WSU."

Bayly grew up in Melbourne, Australia, where he earned a veterinary degree. He also earned a master's degree from The Ohio State University. He completed that in 1979, the year before I began work on my two master's degrees at OSU. He earned his doctorate from the University of Liège in Belgium.

Floyd appointed Bayly to the position of interim provost in fall 2007, replacing Robert Bates, the provost who had questioned why I had submitted my 7-Step Plan without going through Murrow channels. Bayly served for one school year and then stepped down when the university gave the permanent position to University of Kentucky history professor Steven Hoch.

Hoch didn't last long.

On September 10, 2008, after two months on the job, Hoch chaired a budget meeting of top-level WSU officials (mostly vice presidents) when Floyd was out of town. The conversation upset many of those at the meeting. There was name-calling and Hoch alleged that one of the vice presidents "physically abused" him with a shove at the end of the meeting.

Three days later, Floyd asked Antoinette M. Ursich, senior assistant attorney general at Washington State University, to investigate.

Six days after that, she issued her report, which concluded that "Provost Hoch set the tone for the meeting, and the tone set was one of hostility towards and disrespect of colleagues" and that even though the vice president made "unprofessional comments," the "physical contact he had with Hoch was defensive, not offensive."

Was the report designed to force Hoch to resign?

I don't know, but a time-honored practice in bureaucracies when an outsider stirs the pot is to appoint an investigator who you know will produce a report that gives you the outcome you want. If the administration wanted to ensure an independent investigation, it should have hired someone outside of the university.

Hoch made it easy on everyone and resigned as provost. He returned to his position as a professor of history and was transferred to WSU's Tri-Cities campus, located about 140 miles to the west.

In September 2008, Bayly once again put on the interim provost's hat. Five more months would pass before Bayly would respond to my concerns about the errors in my annual reviews.

* * * * *

Meanwhile, I decided to play my ace in the hole.

In November 2008, I emailed Floyd and raised the issue of the internal auditor's potential conflict of interest. I said I had no interest in seeing Lopez punished, but that I would like to file a conflict-of-interest complaint against her. I needed guidance on how to do that, because there were no university rules governing how to file such a complaint.

Floyd turned the matter over to attorney Ursich.

Several months passed with no response from either Bayly or Ursich. Early in 2009 I emailed Floyd again, and he again asked both Bayly and Ursich to look into the matter.

Bayly responded that he would be willing to meet over the matter.

I asked if I could tape-record the meeting. He refused. But he would allow ombudsman Ken Struckmeyer to attend the meeting.

That was better than nothing.

* * * * *

"Hello," I say, greeting Bayly's receptionist and doing my best to hide my angst. "I'm here for a meeting with Provost Bayly. I'm a few minutes early."

It's Wednesday, February 18, 2009.

"Yes, please take a seat," she says cordially but plainly not interested in small talk.

The scene reminds me of a time in high school, when I faced "charges" that I had erased a friend's name from absentee lists after collecting them from classroom doors. The only difference this time is that I'm innocent.

Five minutes later WSU Ombudsman Ken Struckmeyer arrives, greets me, and begins a jovial conversation with the receptionist. As we enter the meeting room, Struckmeyer also has friendly greetings with Bayly and Frances McSweeney, the vice provost who had told me a year earlier that there was no rule prohibiting faculty from canceling classes but now is part of the group that was trying to punish me for allegedly doing that.

I was not informed in advance that she would be attending. But her appearance suggests to me that McSweeney is the point person in the upper administration. I wish I had brought a friend, or, better yet, a stenographer.

Too late.

I hand everyone a copy of the list of errors in my two annual reviews and initiate the conversation.

"The reason I asked for this meeting," I say calmly, because I took a beta-blocker before the meeting, "was to correct errors in my annual reviews and the internal audit, particularly the false allegation that I had canceled classes in 2007."

As I talk, I glance at Bayly for his reaction.

For the first minute or so he refuses to look me in the eye. He stares at the documents on the table I had given him. I suspect he probably had already made up his mind on the case. His body language completes the story.

"Listen," he says, interrupting me after a couple of minutes and sitting more upright in his chair. "As I understand it, your interim dean [Erica Austin] already fixed the errors in your annual review. Isn't that correct, Ken?"

Struckmeyer is sitting on my left. He is fidgeting, and his face is turning red.

He hesitates, an action that Bayly quickly interprets as confirmation that the errors had been corrected.

Was Struckmeyer going to betray me?

"Ken," I intervene, "at the meeting on June 30 with Dean [Erich] Lear and Austin, Lear conceded that the accusation that I had canceled classes was false and that Austin would correct the error. But Austin failed to make that correction. You were there. You were the one to ask them to correct that error. Do you remember?"

"Yes, that is correct."

"What?" Bayly interjects. "Ken, are you sure that's what happened?"

"Yes, Lear agreed to correct the error."

Bayly's brow furrows. He apparently had not been fully informed of what happened at the meeting with Lear, Austin, Struckmeyer and me.

But Bayly isn't ready to toss the noose onto the ground.

He tries, on two more occasions, to get Struckmeyer to admit that the error was corrected or that the allegation that I had canceled classes was true. On both occasions, Struckmeyer stood behind my version of the story. That took a lot of courage, because it was clear that Struckmeyer was on good terms with both McSweeney and Bayly.

McSweeney, meanwhile, looks like she had just seen a ghost.

Finally, after all this time the university is going to fess up and correct the errors.

But Bayly switches topics.

"I don't think your performance here has been satisfactory," he says.

"Oh, really," I respond, confidently. "What makes you say that?"

"I've looked at your book [*History and Future of Mass Media*] and I don't see much theory in there." Austin had given me virtually no credit in my 2006 annual review for writing the book.

I am pleased to see Bayly emphasize theory as the primary component of a research program. As a media sociologist, I, too, argue that theory is the most important criterion in scholarship. Fortunately, I had a copy of the book with me, and I push it to Bayly's side of the table.

"My theory of corporate mass media is unique," I say, suppressing my modest Lutheran heritage. "The last five chapters of the book focus heavily on my theoretical model." He ignores the book.

"Well, I haven't read the whole thing, but it didn't look very significant to me."

"Were you aware, Provost Bayly, that in 2004 I ranked first or second on three measures of research productivity and scholarship among tenured faculty in the Murrow School? I have written or edited ten academic books, twenty first-author or sole-authored refereed articles, and more than one-hundred professional publications."

"Well, I hear your teaching isn't very good," he says, looking at McSweeney. "Isn't that true?"

Before McSweeney could respond, I jump in: "No, that's not true. My evaluations are at or above department and university averages. I get good evaluations and I love teaching."

McSweeney acknowledges that my teaching evaluations are good. Her honest response surprises me.

"Let's face it," Bayly says, looking at me. "You really don't care much about your job, do you?"

Was Bayly as smart and talented as people claimed?

McSweeney then chimes in that the administration is concerned that I was giving too many quizzes online. She implies this is inappropriate.

I am caught off guard again.

Was this a new allegation of wrongdoing? No one has ever criticized me for giving too many online quizzes or exams in my classes.

"Fran, do you really want to go there?" I boldly go on the offensive. "Hundreds of professors at the university conduct quizzes online and hold classes online. In fact, a substantial number of credit hours being offered at the university are offered exclusively online. If you indict me for conducting quizzes online, then you'll be indicting the entire university system."

She doesn't respond. She just stares at me. I can feel her seething underneath a staid exterior. Her reputation is now on trial. Her case is falling apart.

But Bayly doesn't see it that way.

"I don't see any merit to your complaint, and I'm not going to change your annual reviews. I'll speak with Dr. Lear and Dr. Austin, and I'll send you my response."

Court was adjourned.

I gave Struckmeyer one of those shoulder-shrugging "I-can't-believe-this-happened" looks. His face had turned another, deeper shade of red. He turns his head away. He told the truth today, but he was not in my corner. As we get up to leave the room, Struckmeyer asks McSweeney if he could meet with her after the meeting.

The following day I mail a copy of my *History and Future of Mass Media* to Bayly with a note attached: "My theory is summarized in seven major propositions on pages three to five in the introduction to the book. Yours to keep."

* * * * *

The next day Struckmeyer emails me with questions about whether my quizzes or exams were conducted during class or at other times. I assumed the questions came from his meeting with McSweeney.

"Always during class," I respond, "except when we had problems with the Internet service. Then I gave the students more time. The reason I conducted the quizzes during class time is that it reduces cheating, and I know all of the students are available at that time."

"And do you have records of this?" Struckmeyer asked.

"Yes. I have hard copies of all of the quizzes. They even have the time and date stamped on them."

It was easy to see where administrators were going with this.

If I had not conducted the quizzes during class time, they could accuse me of canceling classes (or Austin's favorite new phrase, "not holding them"). The administration was trying desperately to cover its fat ass.

Struckmeyer offers to write a report and give it to the administration. I decline, partly because I had talked with a Spokane attorney who'd had some dealings with Struckmeyer.

"He identifies with the power structure at the university," the attorney said.

A year later I met a WSU professor who also said Struckmeyer identified with the administration when she tried to appeal a poor annual review rating. Another WSU professor who heard about my case called me several weeks later and said administrators had also made factual errors in her annual review, and when she told Struckmeyer about the problem, he advised her "to transfer out of the department."

I couldn't say for sure whether Struckmeyer identified with the power structure when it came to my case. He never told me what he was thinking. And, to his credit, he did back up my version of events at the meeting with Austin and Lear on June 30 and in Bayly's "courtroom."

But Struckmeyer's decision to meet with McSweeney right after the meeting with Bayly troubled me. Over the past two years, Struckmeyer had never offered to meet in person with me to hear my side of the case. All our contact, except for his presence at two meetings, was through email and one phone call.

Also, Struckmeyer had the authority to issue his own report directly to the president at any time. He didn't need my permission. And, finally, the administrators had no problem with Struckmeyer sitting in at the meetings — perhaps they felt they could count on his friendship when it came time to take a side in the dispute.

My sixth sense told me that if I gave him permission to issue a report and it had negative comments about me, then the administration could use this against me. I could hear them all saying: "Well, you gave the ombudsman permission to issue the report."

After the meeting in Bayly's office, I rushed back to my office and wrote down everything that took place so I wouldn't forget.

* * * * *

A week or so after the meeting with Bayly, Dean Lear sent an email saying that the administration was no longer focusing on the issue of canceling classes. Instead, the problem now was that I conducted too many online quizzes or exams. I usually gave seven to eleven quizzes and/or exams per semester. Students perform better when the course content is broken up into smaller sections. But Lear implied that I should have spent more time lecturing or on other activities.

This comment seemed to support what McSweeney was saying at the provost meeting. Once again, I am dumbfounded.

"Is this a moving target?" I write in an email to Lear.

"No, it isn't," he replies. He said the university administration has the authority to control the number of quizzes and other decisions affecting content in courses.

But if that was the case, then why did the administration wait so long to raise this issue?

At about the same time I received an email from Struckmeyer, who said he would not share with the administration any of the information I gave him. Then he added:

> I now believe I understand the whole situation and can speak to it in an informed manner and in a neutral position. The question appears to be: Can and should a faculty member give weekly quizzes in class and what is the format that is appropriate to give them? It is good that you have the records of quizzes, grades and grade books. Different departments and colleges would have different expectations on delivery of information and assessment of learning outcomes. I do understand that departments have different expectations. ... An interesting question is who sets the standard?

Holy bat shit. One new charge after another. Will it ever end?

I went online that evening and spent several hours researching state and federal law regarding the authority of university administrations to control the content in a class.

The case law basically suggested that universities can control things like the number of quizzes and books used for some classes, even though in practice most professors in most classes have a great deal of freedom to control the content and structure.

For a while I thought my goose was cooked.

And then I jumped out of the pot: *Don't fight it. Simply grant WSU administrators the authority to control the number of online quizzes and ask them how many would be appropriate.*

"You watch," I told a friend. "I've just backed them into a corner. No administrator wants to get into micromanaging a professor's course in terms of the number of quizzes he or she can give."

I emailed McSweeney, Lear and Austin and asked them how many online quizzes I should give in a class.

Only Austin responded. She said I could give as many as I wanted.

GOTCHA!

"It truly is an ivory tower of babel," I tell one of my best friends, who was a professor at another university and often provided emotional and strategic support.

"I can't believe what is happening at your university," he says. "It's crazy."

"You're a victim of workplace mobbing," another friend says. "You've rocked the boat. You criticized administrators for incompetence, and your plan to improve the university has embarrassed them. The university doesn't appreciate libertarian First Amendment troublemakers like you. In the university, freedom of speech is a top-down value. Those at the top have more of it than those at the bottom."

"The ivory tower of administration has entered the babel zone," another one of my colleagues at WSU said one day, laughing.

But I wasn't laughing for long.

The response from Austin saying that I could conduct as many online quizzes as I wished was very revealing. It showed that there was confusion among administrators.

Bayly was perhaps the most confused and perhaps the most victimized. I almost felt sorry for him.

The dispute apparently had been framed to him as a case of professorial incompetence, not one of administrative error. He accepted the incompetence framing, even though he knew little about my professional and scholarly background. One might blame him in part for conducting a kangaroo court, but most assuredly other administrators had misled him.

McSweeney flip-flopped on the issues. At one point, she told me there were no fixed rules pertaining to the canceling of classes, and then she later turned around and supported efforts to punish me for allegedly canceling (or "not holding") classes. When that approach failed, she appeared to take Lear's position — that it was inappropriate for me to conduct so many quizzes in my classes. But that approach collapsed, too, when Austin told everyone that I could conduct as many online quizzes as I wished.

Very clearly these administrators were not on the same page.

Austin's position is the most puzzling and difficult to explain.

On numerous occasions I offered to present evidence to her and other administrators showing that I did not cancel classes or fail to hold them in 2007, yet she continued to maintain that I was "not holding classes," even in her 2008 annual review of me, which I was about to receive.

* * * * *

In late February 2009 I submitted my 2008 annual review, my third while Austin was director.

I included the first three-fifths of what was to become my book *The Ivory Tower of Babel: Why the Social Sciences Are Failing to Live Up to Their Promises*. The book provided anecdotal and quantitative evidence that the social sciences have relatively little impact on public policy. I cited a number of reasons. One was that public policymakers care far more about their own and constituent interests than scientific evidence that doesn't align with their goals. The second is that social science professors are not rewarded or encouraged to push for public policy that could make the world a better place.

The three previous professors in our department who had gone on sabbatical in recent years to write books never completed them. No one had tried to fire or punish them for that.

But I would not have that option, because the internal auditor had already implied in emails to various university administrators that the university could fire me if I failed to finish the *Ivory Tower* book. I could see them cackling and rubbing their hands together, like a witch around a cauldron boiling a witch hunter.

There was absolutely no question in my mind that Austin would fail to reward me for writing the *Ivory Tower of Babel*. Some of my friends at the time disagreed, saying the university wasn't dumb enough to subject itself again to allegations of violating the First Amendment rights of a professor. After all, they pointed out, my book contained some strong criticism of WSU officials.

My friends were wrong.

Austin gave me a 2.0 rating for the book (3.0 is meeting expectations) and an overall rating of 2.05, the lowest rating I ever received in an annual review. Her review stated that I should have published a refereed journal article. And she criticized my sabbatical book because it was "too interdisciplinary." My response:

> If Dr. Austin or the university didn't want me to write this book,

> then why did they approve the project? The university is sending a mixed message. Moreover, university administrators have been telling faculty for years that they should conduct more interdisciplinary research. Am I now being punished for doing just that?

Austin also criticized me for failing to "publish refereed scholarship in mainstream communication outlets as well." I pointed out that books are an accepted outlet for scholarship under university rules, and I added:

> One of the reasons mainstream social scientists have so little impact on public policy is because they have trouble thinking "outside of the box." Refereed journal articles are important, especially for granting tenure ... , but refereed journal articles alone are not enough to solve social problems, as my book points out. Faculty must break out of the mold and produce some works that help non-academics and policymakers understand and solve social problems, AND administrators need to reward, not punish, faculty who engage in such endeavors (see my book for more details).

Austin also criticized me again for "failing to hold classes," even though two of her superiors (Lear and McSweeney) were no longer accusing me of canceling classes. Instead, they were accusing me of giving too many quizzes or exams in my classes.

My guess is that Austin was unaware of the events that took place during the meeting in Interim Provost Bayly's office. This is one of the weaknesses of bureaucratic systems (but a good thing for people fighting them): the left hand doesn't know what the right is doing.

As I had done in the past, I responded that university rules require three hours of "organized activities" a week for each class, and online quizzes or exams as well as lectures count as an organized activity.

She also criticized me for allegedly giving grades that were too high.

When is this going to stop?

I pointed out that in my media history class, only ten percent of the students received an A- or A grade; thirty percent received a C or D. She apparently failed to look at the grade records I submitted.

To her credit, she corrected this error, raising my teaching score a mere 0.3 percentage points.

But she refused to correct the error on "not holding classes." And she refused to give me service credit for editing and formatting the six open-access scholarly journals, even though now the work I did for Marquette Books could be counted as service because I had filed the requisite form.

At dinner with friends one evening, I asked for their theories on why the university is refusing to correct the error about "not holding classes" in my annual reviews.

"Because they don't see any consequences to their actions," one psychiatrically trained social scientist said. "They have all the power."

Thus, in March 2009, the only option I had left to get the errors corrected was a lawsuit. Well, almost.

* * * * *

Five months had passed since I had asked President Floyd how I could file a conflict-of-interest claim against the internal auditor. He had referred the matter to Ursich, the attorney general on campus.

But no one there responded. Why was it taking so long?

On April 3, I received an email from Floyd. He wanted to mediate the conflict. My first reaction was bewilderment. I had spent more than two years writing endless emails and letters outlining the problem to various administrators. His email reinforced the idea that confusion prevailed in the administration. My second reaction was one of delight. The email was a sign that the university finally recognized that there was some merit to my complaint.

"They don't go to mediation unless they believe they have done something wrong," one attorney told me. I emailed Floyd saying I wasn't eager to spend taxpayer monies on this dispute, but it certainly was much better and less costly than a full-blown lawsuit.

Chapter 34
MEDIATION BLUES

Spring Semester 2009
Washington State University

In early 2009, the university created a search committee to hire a founding dean for the new Murrow College.

I nominated a highly accomplished newspaper editor who worked at the *Portland Oregonian*. He was a member of the national accrediting association for college mass communication programs and had a lot of contacts in the Northwest. Interim Dean Erica Austin also applied for the position.

Neither was invited to interview, however.

One colleague, who asked not to be identified, told me that Austin failed to get the support of some of the Murrow faculty members on the committee. Interestingly, on several occasions, Austin had defended the interests of some of those members. It reminded me of what happened to former Murrow Director Alex Tan: No amount of kindness can pacify your enemies. Austin's attempts to push faculty out of the College also stirred up a lot of controversy. I was at the top of that list.

But I suspect the main reason she failed to reach the final three was that administrators were looking for someone with more fundraising and real-world professional experience. As I noted in my 7-Step Plan, that's the kind of person universities are hiring to head up colleges of mass communication. Austin's strength was her research.

On May 20, 2009, the university announced that Lawrence Pintak, who was director of the Kamal Adham Center for Journalism Training and Research at The American University in Cairo, would become the founding dean of the Murrow College.

Pintak earned an online Ph.D. degree in Muslim studies from the University of Wales. He had written two books about the Middle East and was finishing a third.

Gee, will the university punish him, like it did me, for writing books instead of publishing refereed articles?

According to a university news release, Pintak was a veteran with more than thirty years of experience in journalism on four continents.

I was impressed that the university decided to hire someone with a strong professional background. Many Murrow Ph.D. faculty preferred a traditional scholar and researcher. Pintak's only shortcoming was that he did not have strong ties to mass media professionals in the Pacific Northwest.

* * * * *

Meanwhile, the university hired William Mackey, a Spokane attorney, to mediate our dispute at a rate of $300 an hour.

On paper, Mackey was about as mainstream as you can get when it comes to attorneys. He worked for a large law firm in Spokane, was a former attorney for a local government, and was described by several attorneys I spoke with as a "political conservative." This alarmed me until I spoke with a liberal attorney friend of mine, who gave Mackey high marks for integrity.

On May 23, 2009, Mackey sent me a letter indicating that he would be mediating the dispute, which was scheduled for July 22. The process could begin as soon as the parties signed the "Agreement to Mediate."

The one-page document contained four points.

The first two and the last one were acceptable to me. The first said the mediator would not serve as an attorney for either party and the parties would be responsible for whatever emerges from the mediation. The second point said either party could withdraw from the mediation process at any time. The fourth point said that the mediator could have private meetings with the parties and that the content of those meetings was confidential.

The third point was troubling, however.

It said that "the mediation process is confidential, including pre-session and post-session conversations and exchanges of information," and that none of the information is "subject to disclosure in any judicial or administrative proceeding." It added: "The only exception to this privilege is a written settlement agreement resulting from the mediation process."

What if the university refused to put the agreement in writing? If this settlement were nonpublic, it couldn't help other WSU professors who might be victims of workplace mobbing. In addition, the public has a right to know how its tax money is being spent.

Mackey tried to convince me that the agreement would be made public because WSU was a public institution. But my experience told me that WSU administrators were not to be trusted. I would not sign the agreement unless WSU agreed in advance that the final settlement would be released to the public.

"The public has a right to know the details of this agreement as well as the costs," I told him. "The university must be accountable for the errors it has made."

I tried to summarize the case as best I could, but after five minutes, he interrupted and said, "Why don't you come down to my office and we'll chat."

We met the following Monday.

His office was in a high-rise building in downtown Spokane. He was one of three partners. He led me back to a room with a wall filled with law books.

We briefly mention the weather and talk about some controversial attorneys in town. He had worked in government, and I was curious about his opinion of the attorneys. He defended them, saying they were doing the bidding of their clients.

"But don't attorneys have a responsibility to inform their clients when they are making bad or illegal decisions?" I ask.

He agrees but is adamant that attorneys should not be judged by the actions of their clients.

I know that's how the profession defends itself.

But should attorneys continue to represent clients who violate the law or organizational rules or refuse to follow their advice? Where does one draw the ethical line?

I know how Ayn Rand would have viewed this situation. She would have called these attorneys "second-handers" — people who don't have the capacity to think on their own. Sociologist David Riesman would have called them "other-directed," as individuals who need the affirmation (and especially the money) of others.

Riesman argued in his 1950 book *The Lonely Crowd* that modern capitalism and the growth of the corporate or bureaucratic form of organization were changing the character of American workers, turning them into passive, dependent sycophants. Other-directed people emerged during the Industrial Revolution and act not on the basis of an abstract set of principles but in terms of cues from others in their world, especially peer groups, coworkers, and mass media. Clients could be added to that list, too.

"The other-directed person wants to be loved rather than esteemed," Riesman writes. "While all people want and need to be liked by some of the people some of the time, it is only the modern other-directed types who make this their chief source of direction and chief area of sensitivity." The counterpart to the other-directed was the inner-directed person, who is driven by an inner moral gyroscope and the Protestant ethic, not the opinions of others, per se.

Before I had time to process these thoughts, Mackey and I are deep into a discussion of the case. He then points out that both parties to a mediation must sign a nondisclosure agreement.

"I will promise to keep all aspects of the mediation process nonpublic except for two things," I say. "The final settlement agreement must be made public, and second, my list of demands must be public. Everything else will be nonpublic."

"You know, the university is afraid that you will quote them," he says, looking up from the yellow notepad in his lap.

"But they are public employees. Most things they do are public record. If university administrators feel that the facts and truth are on their side, then what do they have to fear? The problem here, Bill, is a lack of accountability. This case would never have dragged on if administrators had allowed me to tape-record the meetings we had with Ombudsman Ken Struckmeyer. Your job, Bill, is to convince them that it is in their best interest to make the results of this mediation public."

He agrees to do all he can to convince the university to modify the Agreement to Mediate. He tells me that in the two-thousand mediations he had handled over the years, no one has ever refused to sign a mediation agreement. Most parties to a mediation agreement do not want the results to be public, because "they don't want their neighbors to know they just got a huge settlement from a government bureaucracy," he says.

Vindication, not money, was the issue for me.

What I wanted was an apology, my record fixed, a promise that the university would set up an independent appeals process for annual reviews, my legal bills paid, and a commitment to eventually obtain accreditation for the mass communication programs. Of course, it was highly unlikely the university would agree to all of my demands. University attorneys likely would offer a sum of money and ask me to resign.

Since that kind of settlement didn't interest me, I figured I had nothing to lose by taking a position that the final settlement agreement be made public. In fact, if the university refused to sign the agreement, it would look as if it were trying to hide something again. I wrote and posted to my website a news release predicting the university would reject my request to make the settlement agreement public.

I was right for once.

On July 6, Mackey notified me that the mediation session for July 22 was canceled, because the university would not accept my terms for mediation.

Chapter 35
Time to Lawyer Up

Summer 2009
Washington State University

A free-speech lawsuit was now my only option if I wanted to save my job. Many people dislike those who file lawsuits. Plaintiffs and attorneys are often cast as greedy. Some are.

But as my criminology professors pointed out, lawsuits are the civilized way to settle disputes. Compare that to earlier times, when disputes were often settled with a fistfight or a duel.

On July 11, 1804, Vice President Aaron Burr shot and killed former Secretary of State Alexander Hamilton, who called Burr a "profligate, a voluptuary in the extreme." Hamilton's son also had been killed in a duel a few years earlier.

Doug Llewelyn, the court reporter in TV's *People's Court* in the 1980s, had it right when he said at the end of every show: "Don't take the law into your own hands: You take 'em to court."

My Lutheran elementary schoolteachers never taught me how to fight. "Turn the other cheek" was their motto. But they could have added, "And hire a good attorney."

I spent the rest of the summer of 2009 trying to find a good First Amendment attorney. I ran out of options in Spokane. The city was too small. So, I expanded the search to Seattle.

The first four attorneys I contacted had done work with WSU, so they couldn't represent me. Finally, I found one: Judith (Judy) Endejan at Graham & Dunn, a firm that employed more than fifty attorneys, none of whom had a relationship with WSU.

Judy once worked as a newspaper reporter in the Midwest. She understood my idealism. Former journalists rarely stop embracing free-speech ideals and the First Amendment.

She had received a ten out of ten rating by Avvo, a lawyer rating service, and she had received eleven other awards and honors, including "Best Lawyers in America" recognition from Martindale-Hubbell. From the University of Wisconsin she earned a journalism baccalaureate degree and a law degree, graduating summa cum laude, Order of the Coif.

Most importantly, she was an expert in First Amendment law.

I told her I had about $140,000 to pay for legal fees.

"Don't worry," she said. "We'll get back all of your attorney's fees."

That made me feel good, but I realized there are no guarantees when it comes to litigation.

* * * * *

My sabbatical formally ended in summer 2009 and I started teaching again in August. Nothing much had changed in terms of the way people treated me. Many were uncomfortable around me, and I them.

Denise, the sister of the Internal Auditor Heather Lopez, and I were no longer comfortable around each other. Some faculty with whom I had been friends before the dispute deliberately avoided sitting next to me at faculty meetings.

Meanwhile, I met Lawrence Pintak, the new Murrow dean, in person at the first faculty meeting in late August 2009.

Several faculty had suggested creating a "certificate of journalism" program for citizen journalists and Pintak was promoting the idea. He was seeking some grant money to implement the program. I offered my support and sent a follow-up email.

At the second faculty meeting, on September 2, 2009, Pintak presented his restructuring and hiring plan for the Murrow College. He said he would like, eventually, to seek accreditation for the mass communication programs and would like to develop professional master's degree programs.

Hurray!

But many Ph.D. faculty at the meeting were not pleased.

After Pintak finished his presentation, he asked if anyone had questions or comments.

No one responded.

Very awkward moment but expected.

For three years, faculty members had restructured the Murrow program in their own image, and in one-half hour Pintak informed everyone that he planned to tear it down.

Pintak appeared unaware of what he had done.

I wanted to stand up and shout: "Welcome, colleagues, to the ivory tower of babel."

But, for once, I held my plucky tongue.

A short time later faculty were asked to vote on some revised rules, one of which stated that only Ph.D. faculty could be "graduate faculty." In other words, professional faculty who had earned a master's degree but not a Ph.D. would not be allowed to serve as heads of master's committees. If a Ph.D. faculty member could serve as head of Ph.D. committee, why couldn't a master's degree faculty member serve as head of a master's committee.

"Isn't the language of these revised rules elitist?" I said, poking the Ph.D. bears in the room. "Shouldn't we allow professional faculty to chair master's committees and advise graduate students? I don't think professional faculty should be treated as second-class citizens."

Several Ph.D. faculty, including two scholars sympathetic to neo-Marxist egalitarian doctrines, tried to defend the elitist rules.

I figured I would lose another battle. I was used to it.

"But I think Dave has a point here," Pintak said.

That's all it took to win the day.

One elite endorsing a proposal. The other-directed faculty fell into line.

After several minutes of wrangling about the wording of the new policy, faculty voted in favor of allowing professional faculty to chair graduate master's committees, albeit the measure did not pass unanimously. It was the second time in a year that I had prevailed at a faculty meeting. Nothing short of a miracle.

The other incident involved the hiring of a professional faculty member to teach digital journalism in December 2007. I was a member of a five-person search committee that initially voted unanimously in favor of one candidate, who had a strong journalism background but not much experience in digital journalism. The other candidate had a strong digital background but little experience in journalism. I convinced other members of the committee that the digital part is easy to learn, but journalism experience is either there or not.

When the recommendation went before the entire faculty, though, Murrow Director Erica Austin threw her support behind the digital candidate. When the vote was taken, every member on the search committee except me jumped ship and voted for the other candidate. And when that candidate refused to accept the position, the committee members and rest of the faculty jumped back on board with me.

The incident illustrates the power of elites over subordinates and supports the theories of William H. Whyte Jr and David Riesman. Most people, even professors, have a great fear of being isolated from others, especially administrators and those who have power over them.

At any rate, maybe my luck in the Murrow College was changing.

As I left the room, I made eye contact with one of the professional faculty who understood the power struggle being played out.

He smiled. I winked.

* * * * *

I emailed Pintak the following day and thanked him for his support.

At the next faculty meeting, a proposal from Pintak to collapse the seven majors in our program into three (journalism, strategic communication and communication studies) was approved after one of the faculty pointed out that this change wouldn't have much effect on the structure of the Murrow College.

One faculty member turned to me and said: "Here we go again, for the umpteenth time, changing the program."

At another meeting, Pintak informed faculty that all new Ph.D. tenure-track hires would be required to seek grant money from the government or from private foundations to successfully obtain tenure in the Murrow program. The requirement would be written in each contract. Even current faculty would be expected to generate research money for the university to get maximum rewards at annual review time.

This announcement angered one faculty member who was soon to go up for tenure. He pointed out that seeking grants was not part of his contract for obtaining tenure, because he was not a mainstream researcher. Grant-funded research generally focuses narrowly on the needs and problems of specific governmental agencies or private foundations, not on research that raises questions about the legitimacy or effectiveness of political, social and economic institutions. The faculty member was saying that it was unfair to change the rules in the middle of the game.

He was damn right.

But Pintak showed no sympathy.

The marching orders, we all knew, were coming from the provost's office. Shared governance and democracy didn't apply here.

None of this surprised me.

As state governments pulled back their funding of higher education in the 1990s and early 2000s, universities increasingly turned to grants and donations to make up the revenue loss. In mass communication programs, the emphasis on grants also reinforces the trend of transferring power from the professional faculty to the Ph.D. faculty.

But few faculty in the room that day understood the long-term social consequences of emphasizing grant-funded research. It meant a devaluation of research that challenges powerful elites and mainstream ideas, beliefs and institutions — a devaluation of Enlightenment ideals that embrace democracy, due process and free speech. Hence, the call for grant-funded research is an unwitting call for restraining scholarly criticism of the status quo — a form of social control so subtle that even those who do mainstream research usually cannot see the consequences.

Part V

Court Rulings and Secret Reports

CHAPTER 36
DEMERS V. AUSTIN

October 28, 2009
Spokane, Washington

A front page story on this day in the Spokane *Spokesman-Review* informed readers that fall colors on deciduous trees would be muted because of freezing temperatures two weeks earlier.

It was a fitting metaphor for what was to come in my First Amendment lawsuit with Washington State University, which my attorney Judy Endejan filed electronically on this day in U.S. District Court in Spokane. The lawsuit and appeals stemming from it would dampen the Murrow College's collective mood for the next four years.

Our complaint asserted that WSU administrators gave me low ratings in my annual reviews because they resented the contents of my (1) 7-Step Plan, which implied mismanagement of the Murrow program, and my (2) *Ivory Tower of Babel* book, which, among other things, rebuked WSU and other universities for failing to embrace free-speech ideals and reward faculty for writing books and articles that seek to influence policymakers and the general public. The complaint also accused WSU Internal Auditor Heather Lopez of violating auditors' conflict of interest rules because of her sister's involvement in the investigation.

The defendants, through their state-appointed attorney, Kathryn M. Battuello, denied the allegations. They would provide more details about their case a year later, when they filed a motion to have the case thrown out of court. They did not issue a press release, but a university spokesperson told local media that WSU would "vigorously" defend them against the lawsuit. That turned out to be very true.

* * * * *

Brief stories about the filing of the lawsuit appeared in several news media, including the *Seattle Times*, the *Lewiston Tribune*, and the *Moscow-Pullman Daily News*. The WSU *Daily Evergreen* and the *Spokesman-Review*, however, ignored the story.

I wasn't too surprised by the *Spokesman-Review* snub.

After all, I had, through the years, become an unwitting critic of the newspaper's owners and upper management. I had criticized the publisher and opinion editor for censoring citizen commentaries and letters to the editor and for their involvement in the downtown parking garage scandal. The fact that Elizabeth (Betsy) Cowles, who managed the family's broadcasting stations, was a member of the WSU Board of Regents may also have contributed to the snub.

But the *Evergreen* rebuff was puzzling.

Although student journalists most likely identified with the administrative power structure at WSU, even the most biased of editors could not fail to see that a federal lawsuit alleging that a journalism and mass communication college was violating the free-speech rights of one of its faculty was one helluva story.

I asked one of the faculty advisors to the student newspaper why its editors didn't publish a story. The advisor said he did not know, but he agreed the story was newsworthy. It's possible that one of the editors at the paper simply didn't like me. Or more likely that an editor or staffer dropped the ball.

At any rate, to compensate for the shortage of information on campus, I wrote several letters to the editor and posted updates on the lawsuit to the WSU American Association of University Professors website. As the months and years passed, I would occasionally issue news releases, which sometimes generated admonishing phone calls from the defendants' attorney to Judy. They were mad because I was painting them as villains in a free-speech battle.

"Tough shit," I told Judy. "If university officials didn't want me to talk about the case, then they should have settled the dispute before I filed the lawsuit."

Controlling information about the lawsuit was one of the few power advantages I had over the WSU bureaucracy. Personnel and privacy laws prevented them from talking about some aspects of the case.

But those laws didn't apply to me. My only constraint was the truth. Truth is always a defense for libel.

* * * * *

The lawsuit generated little response from WSU students and faculty. This didn't surprise me, because the *Daily Evergreen* never published a story and I never talked about the lawsuit in class.

Of course, Murrow faculty were aware of the lawsuit. I had a few brief conversations with some of them. But none — not even the journalism professors, who have a professional obligation to defend free speech under the Association for Education in Journalism and Mass Communication code of ethics — publicly criticized the administration for trying to suppress free speech on campus. It takes a great deal of courage to defend a principle when you go up against administrators who have the power to give you raises or promotions, even when you have tenure.

I thought campus faculty associated with the American Association of University Professors, which is one of the strongest voices for free speech in higher education, would be more vocal. But they weren't. "I have to be very careful about how I approach all this," one member who was seeking an important position in Faculty Senate told me.

Power over principle.

Social actors in bureaucracies are vulnerable to this proposition.

On one occasion I asked a WSU junior administrator whether he would defend a faculty member who was being falsely accused of violating university rules.

"Are you kidding?" he said, laughing. "I have a family to support."

That administrator eventually became the head of an academic unit at a major university. This is the kind of person who succeeds in bureaucratic systems, not the "unreasonable man" that George Bernard

Shaw talked about.

The WSU Faculty Senate, which presumably had a vested interest in supporting faculty free speech on campus, also ignored the lawsuit. The issue was never discussed. And when I asked the leadership of the Senate whether I could talk to the full Senate, they refused to allow me to speak.

* * * * *

Although WSU faculty, senators and administrators may have been reluctant to speak out on the issues surrounding the lawsuit, this did not apply to observers outside of the university.

"You should drop this lawsuit," one expert on disputes between faculty and universities told me shortly after I filed the free-speech lawsuit. "Your university will destroy you. They are too powerful. They will build a case against you that you can never beat. You can never win. It will cost you hundreds of thousands of dollars and you will end up bankrupt and bitter. I've seen it happen many times before. Life is too short."

"Do you really think anyone cares about your case?" said another attorney familiar with the lawsuit. "Do you really want to work at WSU? You should settle it while you can. Even if you win, you will lose. You will never get your money back. Life is too short."

Life is too short.

I heard that phrase a lot after the lawsuit was filed.

The speakers imply that whatever I'm fighting for is not worth the personal price I will pay, either emotionally or in terms of cost and job security.

I wholeheartedly disagree. Life is too short not to stand up for what you believe in. Complacency breeds regrets.

The only significant support I received with respect to the lawsuit came from friends and colleagues outside of the Murrow College and from nationally based free-speech organizations.

Most of the colleagues were journalists-turned-professors who valued the fight for free speech in society. They included one retired dean.

"This is an incredible situation," he said, "and one that has my deepest sympathy, and a good deal of empathy as well. I hope you win this case quickly and hands down. ... The 'mobbing' behavior is [a] new [concept] to me, but outrageous, and the faculty and other participants should be ashamed."

Chapter 37
THE STATE AUDITOR'S 'SECRET' REPORT

December 4, 2009
Spokane, Washington

Five weeks after my lawsuit was filed, I received another audit report from Provost Bayly, only this time the author was an auditor who worked at the University of Idaho.

No explanation. The report duplicated the errors contained in Heather Lopez's audit. The UI auditor never spoke to me.

Why would they duplicate the audit? And why would the new auditor fail to contact me about the allegations? Auditor codes of ethics required auditors to objectively search for the truth, and that cannot be accomplished without talking to the target of the audit.

I initially didn't pay much attention to the report because we had filed the lawsuit, and another negative report wouldn't change things.

But two months later I got the answers to my questions.

I was reviewing documents obtained from the university through discovery, a process in which litigants must produce documents related to a complaint and present them to each other.

Among the thousands of pages were two letters exchanged between President Elson Floyd and Washington State Auditor Brian Sonntag in Olympia, the state's capital. Sonntag was an elected official.

I called Judy, my attorney.

My heart was pounding, only this time it was a good feeling.

"Washington State Auditor Brian Sonntag investigated Internal Auditor Heather Lopez and concluded that she had a conflict of interest. But President [Elson] Floyd withheld that information. The internal audit is tainted. That's why his administration wanted to settle the case through mediation. And that's why the university hired the outside [Idaho] auditor — to produce another audit that would replace the tainted internal audit."

She was ecstatic, too. Now it all made sense.

The university's case against me had fallen apart when Sonntag concluded that Lopez's audit of me was tainted by the conflict of interest she had with her sister, and Floyd's administration was trying desperately to duct-tape the case against me back together.

Floyd never gave me instructions on how to file a conflict-of-interest complaint against Lopez. But he and his administration obviously were worried about the potential conflict of interest.

On March 2, 2009, Floyd, without my knowledge, asked Washington State Auditor Brian Sonntag to investigate.

> Dear Mr. Sonntag:
>
> I am requesting your assistance in determining whether or not a conflict exists that would impair the independence of the Washington State University (WSU) director of Internal Audit in the performance of her duties. ...
>
> *–Sincerely, Elson S. Floyd, Ph.D., President*

Sonntag investigated and sent his reply to Floyd three weeks later, on March 23, 2009.

> Dear Dr. Floyd:
>
> Thank you for your letter asking us to review whether the independence of the University's Director of Audit was impaired during an investigation. After consulting Government Audit Standards, we concluded that a conflict of interest and impairment to independence did exist based on the facts you provided. ... Specifically, the Audit Director's investigation of her sister's co-worker was based on assertions from the sister. This relationship creates not only a personal impairment for the Director but also for all audit staff members who are under the Director's control and influence. ...
>
> *–Sincerely, Brian Sonntag, Washington State Auditor*

Floyd never gave me a copy of Sonntag's letter, because it undermined the administration's case against me.

Internal Auditor Heather Lopez tried to defend her actions in a letter she wrote to Floyd after receiving the results of Sonntag's investigation (another document obtained through discovery).

But she probably didn't need to.

Floyd never punished her.

Floyd's administration, realizing that it was in trouble, then tried to settle the case through mediation. But that failed when I demanded the settlement be made public.

Then Floyd's administration asked the auditor at the University of Idaho to issue a new audit report to replace the tainted audit. Oddly, the UI auditor never contacted me and just duplicated the errors contained in the original audit.

On March 11, 2010, I issued a news release announcing the new evidence.

WSU's President Fails to Disclose State Auditor's Report; Breach of Ethics Alleged

PULLMAN — Washington State Auditor Brian Sonntag issued a report a year ago which concluded that Washington State University's director of internal audits had violated conflict of interest rules when she accused a WSU communication professor of canceling classes in violation of university rules. But WSU President Elson Floyd, who requested Sonntag's investigation, never informed the accused professor or the public.

"I don't know about criminal law, but withholding evidence that could exonerate a professor is unquestionably a serious breach of ethics and his due process rights," said David Demers, who was the target of the WSU's internal audit. "Floyd and other university officials continued to punish me even though they knew the audit was tainted. ..."

On June 10, 2010, Judy filed a motion to revise our original complaint to include Sonntag's report.

Nearly three years later I emailed Sonntag and asked him, among other things, whether state auditors have a responsibility under auditing codes of ethics to provide information to state employees when they are falsely accused of wrongdoing.

He never responded.

Two months after that I also mailed him an early draft of this book, which included the story about the Sonntag letter and the statement that he (Sonntag) "failed to notify the target (me) of the (his) audit."

He responded on May 28, 2013: "Communicating directly with the head of a government agency (President Floyd) is in line with auditing standards. I think it is a misrepresentation to say we 'failed.' We took this seriously, as we did all of our work, and acted professionally."

I responded: "You are correct: You and your agency acted professionally and legally. Yet, a great injustice has been done."

So, what did Floyd say when he was asked why he refused to give me a copy of Sonntag's investigation? His answer came in late September 2010, when he and five other administrators were deposed over a four-day period on the WSU campus.

Chapter 38
THE DAMNING DEPOSITIONS

Last Week of September, 2010
Washington State University

Washington State University President Elson Floyd enters the room and shakes hands with everyone, including my attorney, Judy, and me. That Floyd charisma is there, at least for a few minutes. But I could tell he's nervous. His smile is strained.

He tells everyone this is his first deposition.

The university's attorney, Kathryn M. Battuello, tells him there's nothing to be nervous about. All you have to do is answer a few questions and be honest. Typically, during the first part of a deposition, the deponent gets to answer easy questions. They tend to get more difficult as the deposition progresses.

Near the end, Floyd admitted that he did not give me a copy of the letter from Washington State Auditor Brian Sonntag which concluded that a conflict of interest tainted Heather Lopez's internal audit of me.

"Why didn't you give Dr. Demers a copy of the report?" Judy asks.

The room fell silent.

Little beads of water appear on Floyd's forehead. He looks down at the table. "Because the state auditor's report was minuscule," he says. "I had more important things to do."

Judy was rapturous.

She slaps her hands on the documents in front of her and declares, "This deposition is over."

Floyd looks shell-shocked. He didn't realize he had incriminated himself.

It didn't matter whether he was telling the truth or lying, the outcome was the same. He deliberately violated the administrative due process rights of a faculty member when he withheld evidence that could have exonerated him. And he showed little concern for free speech issues on campus.

Floyd rises quickly from his seat and shakes my hand but not Judy's. He is so flustered that he forgets to take his sport coat and returns to the room.

Was the handshake snub deliberate or just an oversight?

Hard to say.

But Floyd's response revealed that he did not have a good grasp of due process and free speech Enlightenment ideals.

* * * * *

Judy interviewed four more administrators.

WSU Vice Provost for Faculty Affairs Frances McSweeney continued to argue that I had canceled or not held classes.

But this was a moot point, because three other administrators who also were deposed that week — Provost Warwick Bayly, former Liberal Arts Dean Erich Lear, and Murrow interim Dean Erica Austin — all said that conducting online quizzes or exams during class time was an acceptable university practice.

McSweeney also revealed that the university had a practice of firing tenured faculty. She said the "five to ten tenured faculty" were forced out of their jobs. The lack of specificity on the number fired suggested to me that she was underestimating the number who got the boot. McSweeney said the targeted faculty were offered two options: resign or be fired.

Is that two choices?

Firing a tenured faculty member normally isn't easy. At most universities across the country, tenure means a job for life unless you commit a felony or kiss a graduate student.

But none of the fired WSU faculty was a mugger or a sex fiend. Their crime, according to McSweeney, was low evaluations from their unit heads in at least two annual reviews. WSU had a rule on the books that allowed administrators to fire any faculty, including tenured ones, if they received below average ratings. This is not a common practice in American public universities.

Nobody likes employees who don't do their jobs.

But using annual reviews to fire tenured faculty violates the American Association of University Professors' rules on academic freedom, because it's very easy for administrators to terminate outspoken faculty with this rule. "The Association emphasizes that no procedure for evaluation of faculty should be used to weaken or undermine the principles of academic freedom and tenure. The Association cautions particularly against allowing any general system of evaluation to be used as grounds for dismissal or other disciplinary sanctions."

The assumption behind the AAUP policy is that truth and knowledge can flourish only when professors are fully insulated from undue political, economic and administrative influences.

Of course, the fired WSU faculty could have requested a formal appeal. But apparently none did. They probably feared a public airing of their alleged incompetence. When a powerful bureaucracy labels someone as incompetent, the stigma is hard to shake.

In exchange for resigning, the university gave the canned professors one year's salary, McSweeney said.

Judy also grilled McSweeney about whether I had a right to attend the depositions.

"You've testified here that you feel that Dr. Demers should not be here attending depositions in his litigation and that you view that to be a violation, I guess, of his teaching duties? Is that your — "

"Object to the form of the question," interjects Battuello. "Misstates her testimony."

"No," McSweeney says without hesitation. "Whether he's here or not is up to him. But if he is here, he should be taking leave without pay."

"Okay," Judy says. "So, you do understand that Dr. Demers has alleged constitutional violations in his lawsuit?"

"Yes, I do."

"And you certainly wouldn't want to infringe upon his right to protect or vindicate those constitutional rights, would you?"

"I did not say he shouldn't be here. I'm just saying that we shouldn't be paying him to be here. We don't have to pay him to do this."

"Well, and if perchance Dr. Demers prevails, should the university be paying you for being here?"

"Absolutely, because it's part of my job," she shouted. "You're asking me questions about my knowledge about this — "

"To violate constitutional rights? Is that part of [your job] — "

"Object to the form of the question," Battuello interrupts again.

The deposition ended a few minutes later.

Several weeks later, the university docked my pay $500 for attending the depositions, even though I had originally proposed that we do them over the weekend so I could teach my classes. None of the deposed defendants was docked.

After McSweeney gave her deposition, one observer familiar with the events that had transpired said to me, "The vice provost hates you. She really hates you. This is personal for her. What did you do to her?"

"Nothing," I replied. "I don't even know her. I've only met her on a couple of occasions."

Did the vice provost hate me? I didn't know. But she certainly did not like what I stood for — a professor who challenged the competency of administrators and their policies.

* * * * *

That evening I distributed another news release to several hundred colleagues and news media across the United States.

WSU President Fails to Give State Audit to Accused Professor Because It Was 'Minuscule'

PULLMAN, Washington — Washington State University's president testified under oath Thursday that he never gave a

> professor accused of canceling classes a copy of a state auditor's report that discredited an investigation of the professor because the matter was "minuscule" — he had more important things to do. ...
>
> Three other current and former administrators deposed Thursday conceded that Demers' practice of giving online tests did not violate university rules on class cancellations and one said that a scholarly book he published in 2007 [*History and Future of Mass Media*] satisfactorily meets standards for promotion. ... [bracketed material added]

The news release also pointed out that WSU had been firing tenured faculty after two or more low job performance reviews.

The release generated a flurry of email responses, including one from Gary D. Rhoades, general secretary of the American Association of University Professors and a professor at the University of Arizona. "Dear Dave, very interesting, and as you say, very troubling. I am copying two colleagues .... They will respond to your inquiry as soon as possible."

Two weeks later, Gregory F. Scholtz, associate secretary and director of the Department of Academic Freedom, Tenure, and Governance at AAUP, emailed, "[T]he AAUP does not endorse post-tenure review, which we believe can threaten academic freedom and tenure."

To justify the firing of the WSU faculty, WSU administrators were probably using an awkwardly worded clause in the faculty manual under the heading "Faculty Conduct Subject to University Discipline."

> INCOMPETENCE OR SERIOUS OR REPEATED NEGLECT OF DUTY. Unless the act is serious or puts individuals and/or property at risk, employees will not be disciplined for inadequate work performance or neglect of duty *unless they have been given written notice of the areas in which the work is considered deficient, and an opportunity to improve their performance.* [emphasis added]

Although this section of the WSU Faculty Manual violates AAUP standards, as Scholtz pointed out, the only faculty on campus who seemed concerned about it were the dozen or so members of the local AAUP chapter.

Faculty Senate never investigated or commented on the matter.

And the names of the terminated faculty have never been released.

* * * * *

Not surprisingly, no WSU group or state agency ever followed up on the allegations that President Floyd had violated my administrative due process rights when he refused to provide me with a copy of Sonntag's letter.

That's the way it usually works in large bureaucracies. They are rarely held accountable for violating university rules or laws.

To bring down a powerful figure like a university president, you have to have another powerful elite behind the effort.

WSU's Faculty Senate had that power.

But not one WSU senator openly criticized the president for his unethical behavior, or for the fact that WSU was terminating professors in violation of AAUP standards. No doubt the senate leadership had bought into the story that I was an incompetent professor. Co-optation is easy on campuses in small communities.

But after the depositions, the "incompetence frame" began fraying.

WSU administrators and their attorney changed course. They decided against going to trial, where they would have to fight the case on its merits. Instead, they asked the U.S. District Court judge to declare that WSU faculty do NOT deserve free-speech rights when speaking in their service-related roles.

Monumental mistake.

This not only elevated the "free-speech frame," it clearly cast the defendants and the university administration as free-speech villains and bolstered my original claims that WSU administrators did not respect the free-speech rights of faculty.

"This is a very bizarre legal strategy," I told a colleague. "The administration is cutting off its nose to spite its face."

Over the next two years, the university would continue to give me lower than satisfactory evaluations. And there was nothing I could do about it. The wagons had completed a full circle.

* * * * *

The WSU defendants and I both hired so-called expert witnesses to help their case. I hired Kenneth Westhues, the sociologist mentioned earlier who was an expert on workplace mobbing at universities. After studying the situation, he wrote:

> To judge by her vita, [Murrow Director Erica] Austin is above average in the sense of having more than an average number of refereed articles to her credit. Demers is above average in a different sense: not only having more than an average number of books to his credit, but having transcended, far more than most professors, a narrow academic and professional definition of a professor's role. ... He is an activist ... a reformer ... an organizer ... an entrepreneur ... In sum, Demers is a type of social-science professor who tends to get in steadily deeper trouble, the more success he enjoys in his work.

The defendants hired three expert witness administrators who would testify that my academic record was worthless and that I failed to do my job at WSU. Two of them were administrators from non-communication programs who were unfamiliar with my research program. The third was one of the deans who visited WSU and rubber-stamped the Murrow College proposal created by President Elson Floyd. Her name was Jean Folkerts, whom I considered an amiable colleague at the time.

I felt betrayed when I heard she would be testifying against me, because years earlier she told me she wanted me to work for her when I interviewed for a position in the School of Media and Public Affairs at George Washington University, a program she directed. In addition, as editor of *Journalism & Mass Communication Quarterly* in the

1990s, she had accepted for publication eight refereed manuscripts I had submitted.

To undermine my academic record, she would have to devalue the very journal that she had edited for more than a decade and then explain why she wanted to hire me. What's more, Folkerts's own academic publication record was far weaker than my own. She hadn't published a refereed manuscript in nearly two decades and, after 28 years as an academic, she had published only nine refereed journal articles and three books, two of which were textbooks and the other an edited book. She had never published the more highly valued theoretical monograph.

In contrast, I had worked for 18 years and had 20 sole or first-authored articles or monographs, four theoretical books, six textbooks or edited books, seven book chapters, and more than 100 professional publications. Folkerts charged about $300 an hour for her services. I had to pay half of the cost of her deposition, which alone was more than $12,000. But it was worth it. She was a better expert witness for me than for the defense.

* * * * *

The defendants' attorney, Kathryn M. Battuello, deposed me over two days in Seattle, a short time after the depositions at WSU.

Although Battuello only received a 6.5 out of 10 rating from Avvo, she had an outstanding record when it came to trial-court experience and involvement in community organizations and issues. She earned a bachelor's degree (summa cum laude) from the University of New Mexico in 1980, a J.D. degree from Duke University School of Law in 1983, and a master's of public health degree from the University of Washington in 2002. She worked for ten years as a litigation attorney and spent five years as a managing partner in a law firm that specialized in health-care issues.

Before joining the AG's office, Battuello was a faculty member in the health law concentration track at the University of Washington Law School. She had published articles and presented papers on a variety of topics, including genetic discrimination, medical malpractice, and other issues associated with genetics. She began working for the Washington state AG's office in 2008.

But the most interesting thing about Battuello, to me, was that she and her husband had adopted a Chinese baby girl. We talked briefly about our experiences. Adoption was one thing we shared — to the best of my knowledge, the only thing.

Battuello was merciless during my deposition. She grilled me with the intensity of a flamethrower. Her goal was to impeach me, to discredit my reputation, to catch me in a lie or an unethical act, to show that I was a self-centered bastard who didn't care about teaching, research, the students or the Murrow program.

My goal, in contrast, was to educate her on the truth of what was happening at WSU — the history of free-speech abuses at the university, the long-term structural problems in the Murrow program, the tainted WSU internal audit of me, President Elson Floyd's unethical act of denying me access to the state auditor's conflict of interest investigation, the merits of the 7-Step Plan, the attempts to stifle free speech in the Murrow program, and the "kangaroo court" in Provost Bayly's office.

Of course, my attorney tried to impeach the deposed defendants and their witnesses, too. And we deponents were being advised by legal experts to provide as little information as possible during the deposition. "Don't give the other side any ammunition."

That's the way the game is played. And what about the truth?

Sure, the depositions shed some light.

But, in hindsight, I'm not sure it was worth the $100,000 or so (my estimate) that it cost me and the taxpayers. The lesson I learned from the deposition stage is this: If you need the truth about a particular event or dispute, consider hiring an investigative journalist before an attorney.

At the end of the deposition, Battuello seemed confident she had obtained enough information to cremate me. However, if she and the defendants were so confident that they could put my ashes into an urn, then why didn't they take the case to trial?

Chapter 39
A MOTION TO DISMISS

March 23, 2011
Washington State University

About five months after the depositions, the WSU defendants filed a motion for summary judgment, which meant they did not want to go to trial and were asking U.S. District Court Judge Robert H. Whaley to dismiss my lawsuit.

In their memorandum, they argued that my free-speech claim should be dismissed because I spoke as an employee, not a citizen, and because my plan did not deal with an issue of public concern.

The defendants' legal arguments were predicated in large part on the 2006 U.S. Supreme Court decision in *Garcetti v. Ceballos*, which held that public employees do not have free-speech rights when acting in their official duties.

In dissent, Justice David H. Souter wrote that he hoped the *Garcetti* ruling did not apply to public universities, "whose teachers necessarily speak and write 'pursuant to official duties.'" Conservative Justice Anthony Kennedy's majority opinion seemed to agree: "We need not ... decide whether the analysis we conduct today would apply in the same manner to a case involving speech related to scholarship or teaching."

But over the next four years, federal courts ignored these dicta and on seven separate occasions denied free-speech rights to professors who criticized administrators for hiring too many adjunct faculty, for making comments in support of a student during a disciplinary hearing, and for raising questions about administrative distribution of grant monies.

Not one federal court after 2006 ruled in favor of faculty who spoke in their service-related roles.

The situation was so grave that, by early 2011, the American Association of University Professors was urging faculty "to defend their academic freedom ... not through the courts but through clear university policies."

Faculty at the University of Minnesota, University of Michigan and the University of Delaware did just that.

Two weeks after WSU defendants filed a motion to dismiss my case, the Fourth Circuit Court of Appeals ruled in *Adams v. Trustees of the University of North Carolina–Wilmington* (2011) that a professor who converted to Christianity and wrote a book critical of political correctness on campus had the right to speak without fear of retaliation. The title of his book was *Welcome to the Ivory Tower of Babel: Confessions of a Conservative College Professor.*

But the Adams case did not expand or even deal with the issue of on-the-job service-related free-speech rights for faculty. The court simply said that Adams's speech was protected because it was private speech, unrelated to his job as a criminologist. Therefore, his university could not deny him a promotion based on those writings, even though he had submitted them to the promotion committee.

The *Adams* case did not break new ground. It simply reinforced *Garcetti*, which refused to extend free-speech rights to government employees for on-the-job speech.

Adams represented a two-edged sword for me.

On the one hand, it enhanced my chances of winning if my 7-Step Plan was defined as citizen speech. After all, I had formally submitted it as the publisher of Marquette Books, not as a professor.

If my plan was citizen speech, however, then my case would fail to address a more important question: Do faculty, while participating on administration-generated committees for the university, have a right to criticize administrators and their policies without fear of retaliation?

That question, to me, was far more important. The search for truth and knowledge on campus cannot be complete without such protection.

But the WSU defendants opposed that idea, too.

In their memorandum, they wrote:

> The *Garcetti* court recognized that faculty expression related to academic scholarship or classroom instruction "could" implicate additional constitutional interests that are entitled to protection. ... However, because the speech at issue is unrelated to Demers' academic teaching or scholarship responsibilities, any "academic freedom exception" does not apply. *The teaching and scholarship exception does not apply to speech about internal organizational issues.* [emphasis added]

In other words, the WSU defendants were arguing that academic freedom does not apply to service-related or shared-governance speech, even though the WSU faculty manual specifically states that "it is the policy of Washington State University to support and promote the rights of all individuals to express their view and opinions for or against actions or ideas in which they have an interest, to associate freely with others, and to assemble peacefully. The faculty has the right to dissent and protest."

WSU's legal strategy was undercutting its entire policy on academic freedom.

What kind of craziness was this?

* * * * *

On June 2, 2011, Judge Whaley threw my case out of court.

Citing the *Garcetti* decision, Whaley wrote that "the First Amendment does not prohibit managerial discipline based on an employee's expressions made pursuant to official responsibilities."

These "expressions" included my speech about accreditation, whether the college should emphasize professional training or theoretical research, the restructuring of the college, and my 7-Step Plan. He also ruled that these speech expressions dealt with "internal matters at WSU" and "were not matters of public concern." He added: " Even if the speech addressed matters of public concern, however, it is clear that Plaintiff was not speaking as a citizen when he initially presented the Plan to his fellow faculty members and to the university administration. He was writing and submitting his document as a member of the faculty."

The judge was correct that faculty members are expected to participate in academic, administrative and personnel functions under the university's principle of shared governance. Usually this involves work on various committees.

But if administrators don't like what faculty say on those committees, Whaley was saying that administrators can punish faculty.

What we have here is failure to communicate.

Also, a Catch-22.

If faculty don't participate in those committees, they can be punished. But if they participate and say things that the administration doesn't like, they can be punished.

What Judge Whaley and the WSU defendant administrators and their attorney didn't understand is that shared governance cannot exist without free-speech protection for faculty.

If universities continue to punish faculty for service-related speech and the courts back them up, then the logical conclusion is that shared governance eventually will cease to exist. Public universities will morph into the business form of organization, in which power is highly centralized and free speech is nonexistent.

And my *Ivory Tower of Babel* book? What did the judge say about that?

The book clearly fell into the category of scholarship, and, as such, probably would have garnered First Amendment protection. Judy, though, never submitted a copy of the draft book as evidence to the court. She had told me before that she didn't think it was central to the issues being litigated. Whaley dismissed that element of my lawsuit.

Lastly, in his ruling, Whaley said the defendants were entitled to qualified immunity, which essentially meant I could not recover punitive damages or attorney fees even if the case went to trial. I didn't file the lawsuit to get rich. But I didn't want to go broke, either.

On June 4, 2011, I sent out a news release about Whaley's

decision.

Dick Carson, one of my former editors, reacted to the news: "Maybe I'm missing something here, but it sounds like the judge thinks the administrators can do no wrong under any circumstances and that employees better keep their mouths shut. Is that what the Framers had in mind for the First Amendment?"

This time the *Daily Evergreen*, WSU's student newspaper, did publish a story about the lawsuit. The headline was: "Lawsuit Against WSU Dismissed."

* * * * *

WSU's decision to seek summary judgment rather than to fight the merits of the lawsuit at trial changed everything — for the better!

That's because it fast-tracked the free-speech issue. And university administrators, including President Elson Floyd, apparently didn't understand the consequences of their legal strategy. They had cast themselves as free-speech villains.

Thus, on principle, I had already won. I had argued that WSU administrators do not respect the free-speech rights of faculty, and their legal strategy supported that position. But did Floyd and the four administrative defendants really believe that faculty do not deserve free-speech rights when speaking in their service roles?

I find it hard to believe they would deliberately take such a position.

Another, more plausible theory is that Floyd and four defendants gave or allowed the attorney general's office to have carte blanche over the case. And the AG's office didn't care about free speech. Its goal was to win the case.

There is one helluva lesson here.

When administrators cede control of a legal matter to attorneys or outsiders, they run the risk of losing control over the moral issues and principles in a dispute. Bureaucracies are more susceptible to this problem because the lines of authority and responsibility are not always clear.

Throughout the dispute, my administrative adversaries were often on different pages. They did not communicate clearly with each other. This produced confusion and contradictory responses. And even though every one of those administrators would no doubt support the principle of academic freedom, no one took the responsibility for ensuring that this principle would be protected when it came to framing a legal strategy.

My analysis may be wrong.

But one thing is clearly right: WSU's legal strategy turned out to be its Achilles' heel.

Chapter 40

AN APPEAL AND THE 'SIN' OF COMPLICITY

July 2011
Washington State University

Judy filed a notice of appeal with the Ninth Circuit Court of Appeals shortly after the District Court's decision. The brief will be submitted in seven months.

Meanwhile, I began writing a commentary titled "How Can Democracy Thrive If It Gags Its Own Public Employees?" The *Seattle Times* refused to publish it, but the *Moscow-Pullman Daily News* accommodated. Here are the first six paragraphs:

> Washington State University's Edward R. Murrow College of Communication has major structural and curricular flaws and the College needs to restructure and seek national accreditation for its programs.
>
> That opinion, which I have been expressing for more than a decade as a citizen and as a journalism professor in the Murrow College, is not protected by the First Amendment, according to a U.S. District Court judge in Spokane.
>
> Robert H. Whaley ruled last month that my speech is not protected because (1) the quality of education at the Murrow College is not a matter of public concern and (2) public employees do not have free-speech rights, even if they reveal corruption, wrongdoing or incompetence in government. ...
>
> Is this America?
>
> I find myself asking that question a lot these days, especially when I am lecturing on constitutional law or the history of the First Amendment in my classes. Is America still committed to the

Enlightenment ideals of democracy, free speech, accountability in government, and due process — ideals espoused by John Locke, Voltaire, Benjamin Franklin, Thomas Jefferson and others?

A decade ago I knew the answer. Today I don't. ...

Taking the First Amendment high ground made me feel better, but it did little to improve my image in the Murrow College and the university during the 2011 calendar year. I volunteered for or was a candidate for four department and university committees, including head of the journalism sequence, but was not appointed or elected to any of them. The WSU Faculty Senate administration also refused to allow me to run for a position on the university-wide Graduate Committee, because it said my lawsuit would interfere with my ability to make decisions. That made no sense to me, but why fight that one?

I eventually was appointed to the campus library committee, which I volunteered to chair. This presumably was a position that would keep me marginalized in terms of university politics. But I enjoyed working with and learning from the head librarian at WSU and the members of the committee, one of whom was a vocal critic of President Floyd's policies.

I spent much of my summer editing the six open-access, free journals that Marquette Books was publishing. I also reviewed fourteen scholarly articles for eight different journals in the field of mass communication.

The American Association of University Professors contacted me and said it would be filing an amici curiae brief in support of my lawsuit against the four WSU administrators. The Thomas Jefferson Center for the Protection of Free Expression also joined in.

In August 2011, the four defendants and I tried to mediate a solution to the dispute. Mediation was required under federal rules before a case could be heard before the Ninth Circuit Court of Appeals judges. Mediation failed for reasons that I cannot disclose, because all parties are prohibited from talking about it.

But I wasn't disappointed. More than ever, I wanted the free-speech issue to be adjudicated, win or lose.

The only problem was that I was running out of money.

By this time, I had spent more than $100,000 in legal fees and court costs. I still owed Graham & Dunn $150,000. If I were unable to recover attorney fees from the lawsuit, I might have to file for bankruptcy.

* * * * *

Algora Publishing of New York City sent out for blind review a draft manuscript of my book, *The Ivory Tower of Babel: Why the Social Sciences Are Failing to Live Up to Their Promises.* Fortunately, the review was positive. Administrators were threatening to fire me if I was unable to get the book published. It was published in the fall 2011.

Administrators sometimes sponsor department luncheons or after-hours get-togethers to celebrate when professors publish books. But there would be no campus celebration for this bad-boy professor.

Meanwhile, Judy was preparing the appeals brief. It was filed with the Ninth Circuit Court of Appeals on February 7, 2012.

Although I have always argued that professors have a right to criticize administrators on any topic related to university operations, Judy took the safe approach and, following *Garcetti* and other court rulings, also argued that my speech regarding the 7-Step Plan was protected because it came from Demers the citizen, not Demers the employee.

To be honest, Judy and I both believed that if my 7-Step Plan was classified as job-related speech, I would lose the lawsuit, per *Garcetti.*

The amici curiae brief from the American Association of University Professors and the Thomas Jefferson Center for the Protection of Free Expression employed a broader legal strategy, arguing that "affirming the district court's opinion will diminish open and honest debate in public universities."

The amici brief acknowledged that the 7-Step Plan, unlike my book, did not fit neatly under either the teaching or scholarship exceptions carved out for protection by the federal courts. But the plan still deserves free-speech protection, the brief argued, because "where an employee is hired to explore new and controversial topics, punishment for a researcher's ideas would defeat the purpose of his employment."

But the brief's strongest moral argument for protecting the 7-Step Plan came at the end of a section that explained why the federal district court erred in not extending First Amendment protection to the plan.

> Allowing Washington State University administrators to retaliate against Demers in this case would undermine the very purpose of Demers' job as a professor and a scholar. Challenging the status quo and speaking candidly about the world and the systems in it, as Demers has done here, are precisely the activities that courts have been careful to protect in academic settings even more so than in other settings. This is what allows professors to serve their most essential function — not just to teach students to memorize information, but to teach them how to think for themselves in order to better society.

On March 1, 2012, about a month after the appeals were filed, legal writer Peter Schmidt of the *Chronicle of Higher Education* published a story headlined "LEGAL DISPUTE PITS WASHINGTON STATE U.'S JOURNALISM SCHOOL AGAINST FREE-SPEECH GROUPS."

> Washington State University's college of journalism has found itself at odds with groups that advocate a First Amendment right to academic freedom after persuading a federal district court to adopt a limited view of the speech rights of faculty members at public colleges.
>
> The case is now pending before the U.S. Court of Appeals ... and expected to be heard in the fall. In a friend-of-the-court brief submitted to that court last month, the American Association of University Professors and the Thomas Jefferson Center for the Protection of Free Expression jointly warn the Ninth Circuit that a ruling upholding the district court's logic would set "a dangerous precedent" jeopardizing academic freedom and the sound governance of public higher-education institutions. ...

On April 26, 2012, the WSU defendants filed their response to our initial brief:

> Indisputable facts establish that Demers' 7-Step Plan originated as an internal academic communication made by Demers as an employee of WSU on the structure of an academic department, a matter irrelevant to the public. The plan was not original research or scholarship, nor was it an example of controversial classroom teaching. It cannot serve as the basis for a First Amendment claim...
>
> The 7-Step Plan emanated from an internal power struggle and was motivated by Demers' self-interest ... Demers' alleged protected speech reflects personal and/or personnel related grievances from a disgruntled employee who is engaged in a workplace power struggle between "Com Studies" and "Mass Com" faculty. As such, Demers' speech is not entitled to First Amendment Protection. ... his proposals for restructuring Murrow School are inextricably related to his discharge of faculty responsibilities and are therefore employee speech, not citizen speech.

The defendants also argued that my claims regarding the *Ivory Tower of Babel* book should be dismissed because a copy of the book had not been submitted as evidence to the district court. Oral arguments before a Ninth Circuit Court of Appeals panel of three judges were set for November 7, 2012.

* * * * *

By February 2012, most WSU faculty were aware of my free-speech lawsuit and the administration's argument that faculty do not deserve free-speech rights when speaking in their service-related roles. But why hadn't the WSU Faculty Senate "publicly gone on the record condemning the administration for its anti-free-speech position?"

On April 8, 2012, I emailed and posed that question to Faculty Senate President David Ray Martinson. He responded on April 19:

"After consulting with a number of people, we have determined that it is not appropriate for us to take any position or become involved in a situation where there is a pending lawsuit."

I responded to Martinson the following day.

"I didn't ask you take a position on the lawsuit. I asked you why the Faculty Senate has refused to criticize a university administration which is arguing in court that faculty do not, as employees, deserve the right to criticize the administration (in our service roles). You should know that if the appeals court rules in favor of the administration on this issue, all of you will lose the right to criticize the administration without fear of reprisal. Any protestations on the legal issues after that point will be too late."

He did not respond.

In early May 2012, I wrote a "letter to the editor" to the WSU *Daily Evergreen* student newspaper explaining the anti-free-speech arguments in the university's legal briefs and added:

> I am dumbfounded that WSU administrators and the Board of Regents could make such arguments while claiming they embrace the principle of shared governance, which presumes free-speech protection. I am even more baffled by the lack of response from the Faculty Senate leadership, which is failing to protect faculty interests. Faculty Senate leaders apparently have forgotten philosopher John Stuart Mill's advice: "Bad men need nothing more to compass their ends, than that good men should look on and do nothing."

In fall 2012, I also asked the new Faculty Senate president, Robert E. Rosenman, why the Faculty Senate had not condemned the anti-free-speech position of President Elson Floyd's administration. "It is not the practice of this Faculty Senate Chair to respond to requests for information about our activities, including votes of record, which are publicly available."

I asked Rosenman whether I could give a brief presentation to the senators about the implications of the administration's anti-free-speech position. He refused. When I pointed out that the Faculty Senate is a public body that cannot, under law, refuse one of its own "citizens" a right to speak before it, he backed down — sort of. It would try to fit me into the senate's schedule in four months.

The upshot is that the senate leadership identified more with the administration than with the faculty, at least on free-speech issues. This was not the first time the leadership had been co-opted. In 2006, the senate president supported the WSU regents' decision to hire President Elson Floyd without a formal interview process. Only one faculty member, the ombudsman, publicly criticized the decision.

Co-optation is easy to achieve in most bureaucratic environments, especially those in small, geographically isolated towns. Pullman was a small city, which meant administrators and faculty often bumped into each other at the grocery store, church, restaurants and social events. Sociologists have pointed out for more than a century that small communities tend to inhibit dissent and conflict and reinforce consensus values and the views of elites in the system. Activists are not welcome.

* * * * *

The 2011-2012 school year ended on an upbeat note — sort of.

In late April, the Murrow administration, after giving me five years of below average annual review ratings, gave me a passing grade on all three performance criteria: teaching, service and research (a 3.0 overall rating; the average department rating was 3.8). I was even given credit for my *Ivory Tower of Babel* book.

I got the passing grade even though I was still giving online exams and quizzes in my classes. University administrators obviously were not on the same page when it came to that issue.

I wasn't much impressed with the rating, however.

Eighty percent of the faculty had been given higher scores, some of whom did not even publish anything during the past year.

I had spent more than a decade researching and writing *The Ivory Tower of Babel: Why the Social Sciences Are Failing to Live Up to*

Their Promises. Other faculty who had published books in the previous five years had been given 4.0 or 5.0 ratings for scholarship/research.

But, at this point, I didn't really care much about annual reviews.

I decided to retire early, at the end of the year.

I was fifty-eight.

That decision was sparked in large part by the death of my high school and college buddy, Jerry. He suffered a heart attack. There were a lot more things I wanted to do in life before I joined him. I especially wanted to do more writing that influenced the public policymaking process.

Don't get me wrong. I'm proud of my scholarly articles and books and believe theoretical research is extremely important in the social sciences. But after writing a book about the relative lack of impact that social science research has on public policy and on solving social problems (my *Ivory Tower of Babel* book), it was difficult for me to see scholarly research as being something more than a ritual whose purpose was to boost the egos of the legends-in-our-own-minds tenure club.

In summer 2012, I sent a memo to administrators informing them that I would retire on December 31. They accepted my resignation — with glee, I am quite certain.

But the lawsuit continued.

* * * * *

On November 7, 2012, a three-judge panel of the Ninth Circuit Court of Appeals heard the appeal (see Chapter 1 in this book). The panel didn't set a deadline for issuing its opinion in the case. Court guidelines advised that judicial panels can take anywhere from several months to one-and-a-half years to issue a ruling.

That gave me more time to begin preparations for moving my family to Phoenix, Arizona.

Did I mention that?

I had wanted to move back to Phoenix for more than three decades. I lived and worked there for four years in the 1980s. I loved the warm weather and sunny blue skies. The big advantage of Phoenix is that life can be lived outdoors year-round.

Not that Spokane was a terrible place. The dry, sunny summers are wonderful. The winters are also much milder than in the Midwest, but they are too gray, too wet, and too long for me.

Theresa, Lee Ann and I set the summer of 2014 as the date for the move. This schedule also gave Theresa enough time to complete thirty years of service at Eastern State Hospital, making her eligible for retirement benefits at age fifty-five. And Lee Ann would start ninth grade at a high school in Phoenix.

So, I had about a year and a half to find a home in a Phoenix-area neighborhood served by a high-quality high school. I spent the next nine months working on this book, writing other articles about civil liberties and fixing up our Spokane house to get it ready for sale.

I also applied for an adjunct teaching position in the Walter Cronkite School of Journalism and Mass Communication at Arizona State University. I was grateful when the school offered me a position teaching one mass media law course in fall 2013. Faculty who sue universities are often blacklisted, even when they fight for good causes. It's possible ASU was not aware of my lawsuit. At any rate, that part-time job would help defray the costs of searching for a new home in Phoenix.

I left in early August for the Grand Canyon state. I rented an apartment in Glendale, a suburb in metro Phoenix, and began teaching at ASU in late August.

The Cronkite dean was Christopher Callahan, who earned a master's in public administration from Harvard University. He also served as the vice chair of the Accrediting Council on Education in Journalism and Mass Communications, the group that extends accreditation to journalism and mass communication programs. Of course, the print and broadcast programs at ASU were accredited.

I met with him on one occasion to talk about journalism education and the impact of *Demers v. Austin*. He didn't ask many questions. He seemed unimpressed. I didn't try to convert him to my cause. Sometimes that can backfire. The students in my law class were inquisitive. They reminded me of University of Minnesota students.

Chapter 41
THE ENLIGHTENED APPEALS COURT

September 4, 2013
Washington State University

Ten minutes before my media law class was to begin in the Cronkite School, my smartphone rang. It was Judy Endejan, my attorney.

"Dave, I've got good news and bad."

"Okay, give it to me." I hold my breath.

"We won on principle but lost on money. The court ruled that the First Amendment protects your 7-Step Plan. I know you've said the money wasn't important. Are you okay?"

"I'm fine," I reply, breathing a sigh of relief. "That's wonderful."

When I enter the classroom a few minutes later, I give the students a nutshell version of the Ninth Circuit Court ruling. They clap. I thank them.

Coincidentally, the topic of my lecture and class discussion that day was "The First Amendment: Constitution, Bill of Rights and Freedom of Expression, then and now."

The stars were aligned that day.

Later that evening I composed a news release.

APPEALS COURT RULING BOLSTERS
PROFESSORS' FREE-SPEECH RIGHTS

SEATTLE — A U.S. District Court judge erred when he ruled that a Washington State University professor was not entitled to First Amendment protection when he developed a controversial plan for restructuring and improving a journalism program, the

> Ninth Circuit Court of Appeals ruled Wednesday.
>
> "The decision is a great victory for those who cherish academic freedom, free-speech ideals and shared governance," said David Demers, a former tenured WSU professor who created the plan to improve the quality of education in the Edward R. Murrow School of Communication.
>
> "Professors should be able to criticize administrators and their policies and play an active role in the affairs of the university," added Demers. ... "The decision bolsters the idea that free-speech protection for professors extends beyond their academic research programs and the classroom. It covers our service role, too." ...

Three days later *The State Press*, ASU's student newspaper, published a story about the lawsuit, under the headline "ASU Adjunct Professor's Struggle for First Amendment Rights Triumphs in Court." WSU's student newspaper, *The Daily Evergreen,* never published a story about the appeals court ruling.

* * * * *

Okay, I admit it. I wrongly predicted the outcome of the Ninth Circuit Court ruling.

But not because I thought Chief Judge William A. Fletcher and his two colleagues — Raymond C. Fisher and Gordon J. Quist — were opponents of the Age of Enlightenment. In fact, all three had judicial records that would allow a reasonable person to classify them as defenders of liberty.

My error in judgment stemmed from my belief that I would lose if my speech were classified as job-related rather than originating in my role as a citizen. What I didn't realize is that the dicta in the *Garcetti* decision — the comments from two Supreme Court justices that the decision in *Garcetti* may not apply to university professors at public universities — would become the guiding principle. The Appeals Court explained in its ruling:

> We conclude that *Garcetti* does not — indeed, consistent with the First Amendment, cannot — apply to teaching and academic writing that are performed "pursuant to the official duties" of a teacher and professor. We hold that academic employee speech not covered by *Garcetti* is protected under the First Amendment … .

The court also held that my 7-Step Plan dealt with an issue of public concern, otherwise it would not have been protected. The defendants prevailed on the issue of qualified immunity, which meant they did not have to pay punitive damages that might arise from the case. The opinion also dismissed my *Ivory Tower* book as a matter of concern because it had not been entered into the record. No surprise there.

The University filed petitions for a panel rehearing and for an *en banc* hearing, meaning they wanted all two-dozen-plus judges in the Ninth Circuit to render an opinion in the case. The university argued the Constitution does not protect employee grievances, implying that my 7-Step Plan was a grievance. They argued that none of the other federal courts since *Garcetti* had ever extended free-speech protection to speech arising from "professional duties," or what I prefer to call "service-related speech."

On this point, they were correct. The courts had only protected speech originating in the classroom or in scholarship.

* * * * *

While everyone was waiting for the Appeals Court panel to rule on the *en banc* appeal, I turned my attention to finding ways to remind professors across the country that shared governance or service-related speech, until now, never enjoyed First Amendment protection.

At Arizona State University, I called Thomas Schildgen, the president of the Faculty Senate in early October 2013, and asked if his governing body was interested in sponsoring a panel or colloquium to discuss the implications of *Demers v. Austin* for faculty.

Let's talk over lunch, he said. We met with one of his colleagues at the University Club on ASU's Tempe campus.

Schildgen was very sympathetic to the panel idea, but he didn't believe the "time was right" to get the Senate involved. He did not elaborate, nor did I press him. I was used to having Faculty Senate leaders marginalize free-speech matters.

Schildgen did refer me to two other faculty groups that sponsor meetings, but they never responded. I also tried to get the Cronkite School to sponsor a session. But one faculty member told me that a top administrator in the program believed the *Demers v. Austin* "ruling wasn't very important."

I wanted to ask where the administrator got that idea but didn't.

After all, what difference would that have made?

* * * * *

That evening, I searched other federal free-speech cases to see how the courts had ruled after the 2006 *Garcetti* decision. I found seven other cases where professors before me had fought to protect service-related speech. Everyone lost. It was time to write another news release —only this time, a commentary. I sent it to more than 500 scholars and academic and free-speech organizations. Here's a brief excerpt:

> I am puzzled by the lack of concern among faculty across the country for protecting shared governance, which is only one court decision away from annihilation. ...
>
> [W]hy ... are faculty so reluctant to get into the game?
>
> Some of the reluctance can be explained by fear ... administrative co-optation ... [and] the "iron law of bureaucracy ..."
>
> Whatever the reason for the lack of action, let there be no mistake.
>
> There may never be another chance to save shared governance.
>
> The time to get into the game is now.

My retired Ph.D. advisor Phillip Tichenor responded.

"You're right, Dave. Most faculty tend to identify with their administrations. In Ag and Engineering colleges, it's near one-hundred percent. Liberal Arts faculties are where we would most expect faculty to support shared governance — but even there I fear to predict what a good poll would find about their attitudes. My experience in faculty judicial processes in an arts college leads me to not be too surprised about the lack of support you're experiencing."

In December 2013, I purchased a three-bedroom, two-bath middle-class home in Phoenix, using some of my retirement funds. I had enough to install an in-ground pool in the backyard, something I always wanted.

* * * * *

The appeals court in my case issued a second ruling on January 29, 2014, that replaced the first one. The court denied the defendant's petition for panel and *en banc* rehearings.

In the original ruling, the court held that "teaching and writing on academic matters" by publicly employed teachers could be protected by the First Amendment, because they are governed by *Pickering*, not by *Garcetti*. In the second ruling, Fletcher wrote instead that *Garcetti* does not apply to "speech related to scholarship or teaching" and reaffirmed that "*Garcetti* does not — indeed, consistent with the First Amendment, cannot — apply to teaching and academic writing that are performed 'pursuant to the official duties' of a teacher and professor."

> In Demers's view, the teaching of mass communications had lost a critical connection to the real world of professional communicators. His Plan, if implemented, would restore that connection and would, in his view, greatly improve the education of mass communications students at the Murrow School. It may in some cases be difficult to distinguish between what qualifies as speech "related to scholarship or teaching" within the meaning of *Garcetti*. But this is not such a case. The 7-Step Plan ... *was a*

> *proposal to implement a change at the Murrow School that, if implemented, would have substantially altered the nature of what was taught at the school, as well as the composition of the faculty that would teach it.* [emphasis added]

The WSU defendants and their counsel had argued that the 7-Step Plan was not protected speech under *Garcetti,* because it was not uttered in the classroom or in scholarship or research. They were arguing that the location of the speech — where it was uttered — was crucial.

The Ninth Circuit panel disagreed.

The issue isn't where the speech is uttered. The issue is whether it is "related" to scholarship or teaching.

The second opinion declared that academic employee speech is protected under the First Amendment by Pickering if it is a (1) matter of public concern, and (2) outweighs the interest of the state in promoting efficiency of service. The court ruled that my 7-Step Plan did address a matter of "public concern," because it was broadly distributed and "contained serious suggestions about the future course of an important department of WSU."

Fletcher wrote that my plan did not focus on a personnel issue or an internal dispute, nor did it voice personal complaints. Rather, the plan proposed changes to the direction and focus of the school.

> The manner in which the Plan was distributed reinforces the conclusion that it addressed matters of public concern. ... Here, Demers sent the Plan to the President and Provost of WSU, to members of the Murrow School's Professional Advisory Board, to other faculty members, to alumni, to friends, and to newspapers. He posted the Plan on his website, making it available to the public. ... Demers's Plan contained serious suggestions about the future course of an important department of WSU, at a time when the Murrow School itself was debating some of those very suggestions.

The opinion remanded my case back to the district court to

determine (1) whether WSU had a "sufficient interest in controlling" the circulation of the plan, (2) whether the circulation was a substantial motivating factor in any adverse employment action, and (3) whether the university would have taken the action in the absence of protected speech.

But to recover my attorney's fees, I needed another $50,000 to $100,000 to take the case to trial. That's how much it would cost to bring in some witnesses and pay for other legal costs.

Unfortunately, I was broke. I had paid more than $100,000 to Graham and Dunn and now I owed another $250,000. I was unable to find any free-speech organizations to help with the costs.

Chapter 42
THE BANKRUPTCY AND SETTLEMENT

January 2014
Spokane, Washington

I was forced to file for bankruptcy in January 2014, two weeks before the Appeals Court handed down its second and final decision. I had paid more than $110,000 in legal fees but still owed about $240,000.

Several lawyers predicted this would happen.

I knew the risks.

I won on principle but lost in the pocketbook.

To me, that was fair exchange.

Fortunately, I was able to keep my retirement funds, my Spokane house (as I continued to make payments on it), and my nine-year-old Volvo.

WSU did not appeal the second ruling of the Appeals Court.

Nine months later, on October 28, 2014, WSU and I settled the case out of court. I distributed a news release on November 4, 2014.

> WASHINGTON STATE UNIVERSITY PAYS
> PROFESSOR TO DROP FREE-SPEECH LAWSUIT
>
> Washington State University is paying former journalism professor David Demers $120,000 to drop his five-year-old federal free-speech lawsuit against four WSU administrators.
>
> "I am extremely pleased with the settlement," Demers said. "It sends a strong message to university administrators that those who intend to violate professors' free-speech rights will be held accountable." ...

> All of the settlement funds are being used to pay Demers' legal fees, according to the agreement. ...

Graham & Dunn earned about $210,000 from the case, nearly $2 of every $3 it had billed for its services.

Just before the settlement, one of the partners at Graham & Dunn emailed and thanked me for agreeing to the settlement. He also acknowledged that the bankruptcy must have been difficult.

The law firm gave Judy, my attorney, a small bonus check for her role in the case. That was nice.

I received nothing from the settlement, but that was okay.

I don't know how much the lawsuit cost the university and taxpayers. But it likely was well over $2 million in today's dollars, as scores of different public officials, attorneys and employees were working on the case at various times over its eight-year history.

* * * * *

WSU President Elson Floyd never apologized for hiding the state audit report or for casting the university as a free-speech villain. On June 20, 2015, he died of complications from colon cancer.

Several news stories and editorials praised Floyd for his accomplishments. None, however, pointed out that his administration almost killed shared governance and service-related speech rights for faculty. So, I wrote a "letter to the editor" to the *Seattle Times* drawing attention to this.

The *Times* refused to publish it.

Chapter 43
WSU Censors a Wolf Researcher

November 2018
Washington State University

After the Ninth Circuit Court of Appeals in 2014 handed down the decision in *Demers v. Austin*, I assumed WSU administrators had learned a lesson about the importance of respecting free-speech rights of faculty. After all, their actions likely cost the taxpayers more than $2 million and tarnished the reputations of at least five administrators.

I figured sociologist Michel Crozier had to be wrong when he argued that bureaucracies fail to learn from their mistakes. If they didn't, how could they thrive?

I was wrong again. WSU administrators violated the First Amendment rights of another professor within two years of the *Demers* ruling, and elements of this case were even more sinister than mine.

It began in 2012, just before my Ninth Circuit Appeals Court hearing. The state of Washington hired Robert Wielgus, a nationally recognized wildlife researcher who was an expert on bears and mountain lions, to calculate a population model for Washington state's wolf-recovery plan. Wolves had been reintroduced in 1995 and were thriving, but ranchers were upset about attacks on their cows and sheep, even though they were financially compensated for the losses.

The state was pleased with Wielgus's research, and he, a professor at WSU, was selected to oversee a multimillion-dollar research project. The project would attempt to understand and solve the alleged wolf-predation problem. Wielgus's research found that killing wolves actually led to more cattle and sheep deaths, not fewer, because it destabilized the structure of wolf packs and produced more mating and offspring the following year.

These findings angered the ranchers, because they wanted permission to kill more wolves. The ranchers persuaded Washington state lawmakers in Olympia to cut Wielgus's funding and remove him as head of the wolf program. State lawmakers also secretly threatened to cut funding for WSU's proposed medical school in Spokane — the same medical school that would be named after former president Elson Floyd, the guy who covered up the tainted audit of me.

So, what did WSU administrators do?

They refused to defend Wielgus's free-speech rights and even issued news releases falsely accusing him of wrongdoing. Here's an example of one published in the August 31, 2016, issue of the WSU *Daily Evergreen* newspaper. "WSU released a statement on Wednesday disavowing comments made by a WSU researcher regarding the killings of wolves ... , publicly accusing him of 'inaccurate and inappropriate' statements."

But wolf dung hit the fan when *The Seattle Times* obtained emails which confirmed that WSU administrators were trying to squelch Wielgus to obtain funding for the medical school. "Highly ranked senators have said that the medical school and wolves are linked," Dan Coyne, a lobbyist for WSU, wrote to a colleague in one of those emails. If the controversy isn't resolved, "there won't be a new medical school." His colleague and a WSU official also confirmed that the med school would not be funded.

The controversy attracted the attention of the *New York Times*. Wielgus told the *Times* that university administrators made his life miserable. As they did with me, administrators sent Wielgus dereliction of duty notices. Administrators also falsely accused Wielgus of fiscal misappropriation, illegal use of state resources, illegal political lobbying, and scientific misconduct, according to Change.org.

Wielgus also told the *Times* that at one point Ron Mittelhammer, who was dean of the College of Agriculture, ordered him not to speak in public about wolves without coordinating with the university — a prior restraint action that clearly violated the ruling in *Demers v. Austin.*

Even WSU President Kirk Schulz failed to stop the assault on Wielgus's free-speech rights. At one point, Schulz informed Mittelhammer that he was concerned WSU might be branded with an "anti-ranching sentiment." In an email to Mittelhammer, Schulz said, "I feel that they (ranchers) need an internal champion or person that they can work with."

Wielgus filed a free-speech lawsuit early in 2018. In May 2018, WSU agreed to pay Wielgus $300,000 to drop the lawsuit. As part of the settlement, he resigned from his position at the university. It should have been the other way around. Some administrators should have resigned, but not one was publicly disciplined.

* * * * *

Okay, Crozier won this one.

But bureaucracies, I still assert, can correct their errors. They just need two things.

First, they need to understand a basic proposition of human behavior: *The greater the funding or resources involved, the greater the probability of bad behavior.* Universities are most likely to lose their moral legs when the stakes are high.

Second, to correct bad behavior, *bureaucracies need to dole out consequences*. You don't need a Ph.D. to figure this one out. Talk to a parent familiar with the social science literature on parenting. You make it well-known to your children (or everyone in the organization) that if they engage in illegal or unethical behavior, they will be given a time-out (or jail time, a pink slip, a demotion, or loss of wages and benefits).

If you don't create consequences for bad behavior, you're going to get more bad behavior. And anti-free-speech behavior is the kind that can be easily deterred, because it is highly instrumental in nature, meaning offenders have lots of time to think about the consequences of what they are doing. They aren't doing it in the heat of passion.

To the best of my knowledge, no administrator involved in my dispute was ever given a time-out for bad behavior.

Part VI

Afterword: Impact and Lessons

Chapter 44
IMPACT OF *DEMERS V. AUSTIN*

Present Day
Phoenix, Arizona

From a societal perspective, the single most important consequence of the Ninth Circuit Court of Appeals ruling in *Demers v. Austin* is the constitutional protection it offers for service-related speech and shared governance in nine Western states.

The ruling applies to public universities and colleges, not privately owned institutions. The ruling may also apply to K–12 public schools, as the court didn't distinguish between "teachers" and "professors," but this remains an issue to be resolved.

The key element of the Ninth Circuit ruling is that teaching and scholarship cannot be divorced from the structure of the organization and its resources. If those who do the teaching and scholarship have no say in how academic units are structured and how resources are distributed, then the academic search for and distribution of truth, knowledge and understanding of the world will be compromised.

"Had the Ninth Circuit ruled the other way," writes legal scholar and blogger Kenneth White, a former prosecutor, shortly after the decision was handed down, "then the state could fire professors at will if it didn't like, for instance, the stance that a history professor took about a historical event, or a political science professor took about a political dispute, or any professor took about an issue of academic governance on a committee."

Had the ruling come down in favor of administrators, they would have had the power to eliminate shared governance at their institutions. In fact, that's what happened at Idaho State University in 2011. Then-

President Arthur C. Vailas disbanded the Faculty Senate, even though university rules mandated shared governance. Vailas then tried to enact a university constitution that ignored the principle of shared governance. He eventually was pushed out of his job.

Legal scholars and free-speech attorneys hailed the decision in *Demers v. Austin.*

University of Vermont President Thomas Sullivan and University of Delaware Vice President and General Counsel Lawrence White argued that even when faculty expression is deemed to be unhelpful or provocative, such speech is crucial for generating knowledge and understanding.

Los Angeles attorney and former prosecutor Kenneth White, writing before the *Demers* settlement agreement, said the Ninth Circuit ruling "stands for the position that a professor's interest in free speech in the academic environment is uniquely important and entitled to the highest level of First Amendment protection."

In an article for *Engage* magazine, which is published by the conservative-leaning Federalist Society, Los Angeles First Amendment attorney Arthur Willner wrote: "The Ninth Circuit [in *Demers v. Austin*] ... strongly affirmed the First Amendment free-speech rights of faculty employed at public colleges and universities. The opinion's robust language in support of free speech should be cause for celebration by both faculty and students on campuses ... ."

The Foundation for Individual Rights in Education noted on its website that "we are very pleased that the Ninth Circuit Court of Appeals has set this critically important precedent."

Chicago-Kent College of Law professor Sheldon Nahmod wrote that "this decision overall is sound in its emphasis on the First Amendment protection of a college or university professor's teaching and scholarship."

Robert O'Neil, former president of and professor of law at the University of Virginia, told *Inside Higher Education* via email that the Appeals Court decision in *Demers* added to the view he shares that *Garcetti* should not be applied to higher education. The decision, he wrote, has "a level of certainty and conviction — a slightly sharper edge, if you will — which further narrows adverse inferences from *Garcetti*."

City University of New York School of Law Professor Ruthann Robson wrote that "this is an important opinion recognizing academic freedom under the First Amendment. At a relatively brief twenty-six pages, it is nevertheless closely reasoned both doctrinally and in its application."

Writing for *Law360*, an online subscription service owned by LexisNexis, legal analyst David Urban correctly points out that in the wake of *Demers v. Austin* "administrators possibly can be faced with personal responsibility for violation of civil rights if they are found to have improperly interfered with an instructor's ... speech. ... *Demers* makes faculty academic freedom rights as against their own employers a federal constitutional matter."

Jayne Benz Chipman, an attorney in a California law firm, wrote that "the Ninth Circuit, in *Demers v. Austin*, ... has boldly gone — where other federal circuit courts have heretofore been reluctant to venture — in declaring that applying *Garcetti* to academic speech would conflict with the First Amendment."

Former university administrator Dean O. Smith wrote in his book *Understanding Authority in Higher Education* that "although Demers has not yet prevailed in court on the merits of the case, this [Ninth Circuit Court] decision was a major victory for advocates of the idea that college faculty members have speech rights beyond those offered other public employees."

Michael Porter, an attorney in an Oregon law firm, wrote that "higher education lawyers and administrators have taken comfort in the Supreme Court's 2006 decision in *Garcetti v. Ceballos*. ... The Ninth Circuit [in *Demers v. Austin*] has taken much speech of faculty members outside its [*Garcetti's*] ambit."

Attorneys and law firms that represent universities also recognize that *Demers v. Austin* circumscribes administrators when it comes to punishing faculty for their speech.

Sharon J. Ormond and Lisa R. Allred, two attorneys who work in a California law firm, wrote on the firm's website that "before a public educational agency takes any adverse action against a teacher or faculty member, the agency should carefully consider the basis for the action and whether the action, if related to speech, can withstand constitutional scrutiny."

A legal advisory issued by the Office of General Counsel for the University of California educational system noted that "the *Demers* decision is significant for the University because the court has signaled that academic employees are likely to have greater protection from adverse employment actions based on speech made in the course of their official duties than other public employees enjoy."

The most comprehensive legal analysis of *Demers* to date was panned by Patrick Fackrell, a law student at the University of Idaho, who, as of this writing, works for a law firm in Houston.

> Courts have long recognized the importance of academic freedom. But until *Demers,* academic freedom has received few protections, if any. ... Though *Garcetti* left uncertain whether its threshold official duties inquiry was intended to apply to academic speech in universities, the Ninth Circuit in *Demers* properly resolved that uncertainty and provided a welcome analytical framework for academic speech that protects the future of academic freedom and disinterested research, scholarship, and teaching.

To the best of my knowledge, only one source criticized the ruling in *Demers.*

An unsigned commentary in the April 2014 issue of the *Harvard Law Review*, a legal journal controlled and edited at the time by law students at Harvard University, accused the Ninth Circuit of engaging in judicial activism. The commentary argued that the *Demers* ruling was misguided, because it (1) conflicts "with the trend toward greater deference to government employers in controlling workplace speech" and (2) "infringes upon institutional autonomy and introduces the excessive judicial interference expressly disfavored in Supreme Court tradition."

To support this statement and the argument that regulating service-related speech will not interfere with truth-seeking, the commentary cited a paper by legal scholar David M. Rabban. I carefully examined the article and discovered that Rabban said just the opposite.

"It makes no sense," Rabban writes, "to expect professors to engage in critical inquiry and simultaneously to allow punishment for its exercise," and "individual academic freedom should cover expression within a professor's scholarly expertise and intramural speech on matters of educational policy."

In response to the *Harvard Law Review* article, I wrote and submitted in November 2014 my own commentary to editors.

They refused to publish it.

No reason was given.

* * * * *

The decision in *Demers v. Austin* was not a passing fad.

A decade later, on March 10, 2025, the Ninth Circuit reaffirmed Demers when it ruled that the Truckee Meadows Community College in Reno, Nevada, violated the First Amendment rights of Lars Jensen, a math professor, who criticized the institution for dumbing down math standards.

"Like the pamphlet in *Demers*, Jensen's speech concerned 'what was taught at the school,'" a panel of three judges wrote in the *Jensen v. Brown* (2025, Ninth Circuit) case. "It denounced the co-requisite policy and the resulting effect on standards for students' completion of math courses. Further, like the plaintiff in *Demers*, Jensen rooted his criticism of the curriculum change in concerns over the quality of education students would receive. Because Jensen's speech was focused on the contents of TMCC's math curriculum, it relates to scholarship or teaching" and thus is protected.

Although the *Jensen* and *Demers* decisions technically only apply in the nine-state Western circuit, which includes Nevada and Arizona, several other federal court rulings across the country over the last decade have incorporated *Demers* into their decisions, according to Jensen's attorney, John Nolan, who cited these cases in his appeals brief:

> The Ninth Circuit is one of five circuits (Second, Fourth, Fifth, Sixth, and Ninth) that have unequivocally affirmed the academic protections afforded to professors under the First Amendment, particularly when engaged in core academic functions such as teaching and writing. This consensus has been adopted from the conclusion of Justice Souter in *Garcetti* which recognized the fundamental importance of preserving academic freedom to foster the vibrant exchange of ideas that lies at the heart of a free society.
>
> The Second Circuit in *Heim v. Daniel* [2023] unequivocally established that *Garcetti*'s scope does not extend to speech related to academic scholarship or teaching that addressed matters of public concern. ... The Fourth Circuit following the decision in *Garcetti* held in a public university case involving speech that an exception to *Garcetti* existed [*Adams v. Trustees of the University of North Carolina–Wilmington, 2011*] ... The Fifth Circuit, in *Buchanan v. Alexander* [2019], likewise affirmed that *Garcetti's* application does not extend to First Amendment claims stemming from a university professor's speech and conduct within the classroom. ... The Sixth Circuit, in *Meriwether v. Hartop* [2021], established an academic freedom exception to *Garcetti* [when a professor refused to address a transgendered student by their preferred pronouns]. ... By citing the holding in *Demers*, the Sixth Circuit reaffirmed the fundamental nature of academic speech and its protection under the First Amendment.

Jensen settled his lawsuit with TMCC, the community college, in November 2025. TMCC paid him $300,000 and issued a college-wide statement acknowledging the institution's wrongdoing and apologizing to Jensen. A copy can be found at <https://thisisreno.com/2025/11/tmcc-lawsuit-jensen-retaliation>.

* * * * *

Demers v. Austin also has promoted speech outside of the courtroom. At the University of Oregon, where faculty in spring 2013 voted to unionize, the UO faculty committee supporting the expansion of free-speech rights for faculty cited *Demers v. Austin* to back up its position that faculty deserved First Amendment protection when speaking in their service-related or shared-governance roles.

UO President Mike Gottfredson's administration initially rejected the faculty proposal. He then tried to limit academic freedom to only speech uttered in the classroom or in scholarship. The administrative proposal also tried to require every faculty member to be civil when "discharging his or her duties."

One of Gottfredson's "lieutenants" in the fight against free-speech rights for faculty was Tim Gleason, former dean of the University of Oregon's School of Journalism and Communication and now serving as UO's strategic communications consultant. Gleason was professor of mass media law and ethics and was one of the four deans who rubber-stamped Washington State University President Elson Floyd's proposal to convert the Murrow School into a College. At that time, Gleason also opposed the idea of seeking accreditation for the new Murrow College programs, which was a key element of my 7-Step Plan.

Gleason and another administrator fought against UO faculty free-speech rights for eighteen months before Gottfredson capitulated in May 2014 and signed into effect a policy that provides strong protection for service-related speech. That action came after O'Neil, the former University of Virginia president, told *Inside Higher Education* that administrators and faculty at Oregon "need to make sure the adequate language currently reflects *Demers* [*v. Austin*]."

Several months after Gottfredson signed the pro-speech policy, he resigned (many faculty say he was forced out) from his position as president. The University of Oregon Board of Trustees gave him a $970,000 severance package.

But before he left, Gottfredson appointed Gleason to the position of university Faculty Athletics Representative for the NCAA, which paid more than $100,000 a year for a half-time appointment. The rest of Gleason's pay, about $150,000, came from his job as a professor in the journalism program. The appointment angered some UO faculty who believed that Gleason had worked against their best interests.

Meanwhile, Rick Levy, a law professor at the University of Kansas, also used *Demers* to challenge a controversial Board of Regents proposal that would have allowed administrators "to suspend, dismiss or terminate from employment any faculty or staff member who makes improper use of social media." The policy change was prompted by a controversial tweet from a University of Kansas journalism professor, who criticized the National Rifle Association after the mass shootings in 2013 that killed thirteen people in the Washington, D.C., Navy Yard.

In response to the proposed policy change, Levy wrote a memorandum that, he said, reflected only his views. "Two federal appellate courts have ruled that there is a higher education exception to the *Garcetti* rule. ... In the most recent of these decisions [*Demers v. Austin*], the court declared, '*Garcetti* does not — indeed, consistent with the First Amendment, cannot — apply to teaching and academic writing that are performed pursuant to the official duties of a teacher and professor."

The Regents policy, which was enacted in 2014, says universities can terminate faculty, administrators and staff who post messages on social media, when made pursuant to the employee's official duties, are "contrary to the best interests of the employer." That clause was opposed by the faculty, and the UK Faculty Senate created in April 2015 a procedure for ensuring due process for those accused of violating the policy.

On June 2, 2015, Greg Lukianoff, president and chief executive officer of the Foundation for Individual Rights in Education, urged the Subcommittee on the Constitution and Civil Justice for the U.S. House of Representatives to enact a law that would protect freedom of expression at public colleges and universities in the United States.

A law is needed, he said, because the courts have handed down mixed rulings on the issue of speech on campus. He cited *Demers v. Austin* and other cases to back this up.

"By leaving unanswered the question of whether an academic freedom exception applies to public employee speech doctrine following *Garcetti*, the Supreme Court's decision threatens academic freedom and free speech," he testified. "Congress should statutorily protect academic freedom by making clear that there is an exception to *Garcetti* for academics."

Lukianoff proposed several draft bills. One of them borrowed directly from the language of the Ninth Circuit Court ruling in *Demers*.

To date, though, Congress has failed to act.

Chapter 45
LESSONS OF *DEMERS V. AUSTIN*

Present Day
Phoenix, Arizona

Educators, journalists, politicians, judges and corporate executives aren't doing enough to defend and promote the ideals of the Age of Enlightenment.

That is the single most important lesson of *Demers v. Austin.*

These officials often talk about the importance of freedom of expression, due process, democracy, accountability, objectivity, economic equity and individualism — as these ideals can be used to justify hierarchical power relationships — but they frequently fail to practice what they preach.

This memoir has provided many examples: courts denying the public access to police officers' criminal records and to public information about crimes; university administrations denying due process rights to faculty and refusing to follow democratic procedures in hiring administrators; newspapers censoring stories and refusing to cover stories that conflict with their institutional relationships; Ph.D. faculty denying master's-educated faculty the right to serve as chairs of master's committees; a former dean and mass media law professor helping a university president squelch the free-speech rights of faculty; a university president disbanding a faculty senate; administrators punishing faculty for helping students publish controversial stories; and professors, including journalism and communication faculty, refusing to criticize administrators for violating the free-speech rights of faculty.

The last item in this list highlights the problem of complicity, which enables administrators, executives and managers to engage in immoral or illegal behavior with fewer consequences. John Stuart Mill argued that everyone, not just diplomats or attorneys, has a responsibility to speak up when injustice occurs. "Let not any one pacify his conscience by the delusion that he can do no harm if he takes no part, and forms no opinion. ... He is not a good man who, without a protest, allows wrong to be committed in his name."

Of course, none of us can speak up on every matter in which a wrong is being committed. We don't have enough time and resources to do that. But this exemption does not and should not apply to professionals bound by codes of ethics and statutory laws.

In most states, teachers are required by law to report an alleged case of physical abuse against a student. Police officers have a moral and legal duty to protect citizens and to report wrongdoing in their departments. University presidents have a moral duty to protect the due process and free speech rights of faculty. Health professionals who refuse to report a case of medical malpractice are also complicit, as are business executives who refuse to speak up when their company issues false financial statements to deceive stockholders and the public (e.g., Enron scandal).

In academia, journalism professors are required to promote and protect freedom of speech and the press under a code of ethics created by the Association for Education in Journalism and Mass Communication: "AEJMC members should serve as the voice and support of free expression on their campuses and in their communities whenever that right is threatened."

Yet none of the journalism faculty at either the University of Wisconsin–River Falls or Washington State University spoke up after their administrators deliberately punished faculty for their speech. Four journalism deans who visited the WSU campus also turned a blind eye to the violations of free speech taking place there, and one of them even became an expert witness for the anti-free-speech defense, as I noted earlier.

The lack of commitment to Enlightenment ideals is also evident in declining financial support for the humanities and social sciences, disciplines that historically have played the lead role in protecting democracy and civil liberties from autocratic authority. This includes programs in journalism, sociology, English, history, philosophy, fine arts, political science, economics and in some cases the law. University administrators are investing more in technology and natural science programs because they generate more revenue for their institutions. Nothing wrong with that. But of what value are those financial gains without robust freedoms in terms of speech, the press and other civil liberties?

The lack of support for Enlightenment ideals is even greater in non-academic and non-journalistic settings. Organizational theorists Robert J. Bies and Thomas M. Tripp point out that even though defenders of centralized power in organizations recognize that punishments of underlings "may be harsh or even cruel, they [punishments] are absolutely necessary and essential for creating high-performance organizations. In other words, the survival of the organization demands tyranny!" These executives fail to see that giving underlings more autonomy and authority can lead to greater job satisfaction and generate ideas that can help their organizations adapt to changing conditions.

Counter-Enlightenment movements also represent an existential threat to Enlightenment ideals. These anti-democratic movements picked up steam in the 1980s, when President Ronald Reagan and Congress gave massive tax breaks to the wealthy — an action that has been repeated three more times since then under Republican administrations. Conservatives at that time also placed a high priority on stacking federal and state courts with their own. They blocked President Barack Obama's appointments to the judiciary, including a Supreme Court justice, and approved President Donald Trump's appointments in record numbers. These anti-Enlightenment trends were in full swing again during the January 6, 2021, insurrection and Trump's election in 2024.

In fact, the counter-Enlightenment movement in government today is so strong that it has even normalized unlawful and immoral behavior. Every day, news media are filled with new reports about how Trump and his colleagues and family members are violating laws and financially profiting from the office he holds — actions that clearly violate the Constitution's emoluments clauses.

Like the boy who cried "wolf," conservatives also falsely warned that chaos and violence were just around the corner if the rights of minorities, women and undocumented immigrates were extended. This fallacious law-and-order campaign played a major role in securing votes for Trump in all three election campaigns, especially in 2024.

The bottom line is that Enlightenment ideals are under greater threat today than ever before, and the failure to advance Enlightenment ideals is responsible in large part for the growth of authoritarian politics, in my opinion, because mainstream politics has failed to address and alleviate the financial insecurities facing the working and middle classes.

Five major reasons or conditions help explain why organizational elites, politicians, university administrators, and judges resist extending civil liberties and more power or authority to subordinates or the public: (1) conservatism, (2) political impotence of the social sciences, (3) ideology of American management theory, (4) prescriptive bureaucratic control, and (5) ignorance (insufficient knowledge). I cover these in more depth in an essay available at my website: <https://www.DrDavidDemers.com/enlightenment.html>.

Forty More Lessons

In addition to the lesson that elites are not doing enough to defend and promote the ideals of the Age of Enlightenment, forty more lessons drawn from my experiences as a journalist and professor are presented below. They are grouped under six headings: Bureaucracies, Principles, Activism, Social Control and Social Change, Journalism, and Democracy and The Enlightenment.

Bureaucracies

1. If there are no consequences for bad behavior, bureaucratic actors will continue to engage in that behavior.

2. Never overestimate the moral principles of adversaries when they have something big to gain or lose. Money and economic resources are powerful mechanisms for co-opting bureaucracies as well as individuals.

3. Bureaucracies tend to be more concerned about social order than moral principles. That's partly because social conflict threatens administrators' job security.

4. Public bureaucracies have a great deal of power and, thus, can insulate themselves from public accountability.

5. When administrators cede control of a legal matter to attorneys or outsiders, they risk losing control over the moral issues in a dispute. Bureaucracies are more susceptible to this problem because multiple actors often fail to communicate with each other.

6. Although bureaucracies require cooperation and consensus from their members to achieve their goals, bureaucracies also contain more competition and conflict than their smaller counterparts (entrepreneurial organizations), because social conflict increases at a faster pace as the number of social actors increases.

7. When confronted with inconsistent behavior or illogical actions, bureaucratic elites rarely correct such problems. Even in the face of hard facts, elites in bureaucracies will actively work to marginalize or fire those who draw attention to their shortcomings.

8. Larger bureaucracies, as a rule, tolerate conflict and disagreements more than their smaller counterparts, partly because they have more formal mechanisms (e.g., grievance boards) for controlling such conflict. But even big universities lack proper appeals processes to eliminate such conflict.

9. Elites in bureaucratic organizations often use rules to punish recalcitrant members, but elites often break the rules when it suits their interests. They are able to do this because there are few options, other than a lawsuit, for holding them accountable.

PRINCIPLES

10. Principles fortify you, intellectually and emotionally. They sustain you.

11. Idealism changes the world. Realism maintains it.

12. People in positions of power often fail to embrace Enlightenment ideals, because they don't fully understand them or they value counter-Enlightenment values more.

13. Most people are realists. Make friends with idealists.

14. Loyalty trumps principles, especially when principles and codes of ethics are weak or nonexistent.

15. Complacency breeds regrets. Get off the sidelines when an important principle or idea is on the line.

16. Always give the accused a chance to respond before issuing charges. Your reputation depends upon it.

17. People seek security more than freedom. Money and climbing the social ladder mean more to most people than acting ethically or doing the right thing.

ACTIVISM

18. "Throw stones" at powerful institutions or elites when they hurt people or deny them rights. Do the right thing.

19. When you seek to change the world, expect to be misinterpreted. People are suspicious and often envious of people who have good motives.

20. If you want to fight for your principles, be prepared to lose almost everything except your dignity.

21. Never assume leaders or followers in American organizations embrace civil liberties like freedom of expression, due process, democracy and individualism. Pay attention to their actions, not their words.

22. Never assume your organizational colleagues, friends or even relatives will support you in a dispute over civil liberties or some other issue. Never. Most are more concerned about themselves than the abstract principles you champion.

23. Success is not a necessary condition for learning.

24. As Machiavelli pointed out, no amount of kindness can appease your adversaries. But don't be unkind. Don't turn into your adversary.

25. Remember, elites prefer to control you with fear, not love. Never assume an adversary loves you.

26. People who are actively involved in principled disputes with bureaucracies often see their plight as an important matter to everyone else. Not usually. But if the matter is important to you, that's all that matters.

27. Pick and choose your battles — ones with a principle worth defending.

28. Do not blame others who do not support you in a principled cause. There are many motivations for not joining a cause. But you don't have to praise their behavior, either. Tyrants love complacent people who stand on the sidelines.

29. If you ever find yourself in a jam, hire an attorney as soon as possible. They can help you navigate administrative and legal matters.

Social Control and Social Change

30. Competition and conflict are more likely to produce meaningful social change than cooperation and consensus.

31. Social control and security are almost always more important to administrators than civil liberties and freedom.

32. Institutions that value competition and conflict are better equipped to adapt to a changing world.

Journalism

33. Do not trust news organizations to champion your cause, because they tend to identify with powerful elites and institutions. But be honest with journalists, as they can be more effective than depositions in finding the truth.

34. The perceived credibility of news sources and their ties to community organizations play a powerful role in shaping what and how news is covered.

35. The greater the power of a news source, the greater the probability of getting news coverage and, in general, the more favorable news coverage.

36. Don't wait for news organizations to cover your activism and frame your case. Create and distribute your own messages.

Democracy and The Enlightenment

37. Despite the concept of shared governance, decision-making at universities does not depend solely or principally on democratic processes. University bureaucracies are far more autocratic than democratic.

38. Conservatism represents the biggest threat to liberty and Enlightenment ideals. That's because conservatives value traditionalism over reason and because conservatism reinforces the ideology of American business.

39. People who have a strong need for personal security have less commitment to Enlightenment ideals such as liberty and individual freedom. The need for personal security increases as people get married, have children, go into debt, and climb the social and economic ladders.

40. The Enlightenment is an unfinished project, but the future of it is in doubt in America, even though it was the first nation to embrace the project. There are powerful counter-Enlightenment forces at work in America today.

Aftermath

Twelve years have passed since the Ninth Circuit handed down its landmark decision in *Demers v. Austin.* A lot has changed at UW–RF and WSU and in my life.

UW-RF eliminated its accredited journalism program and replaced it with a department that focuses more on communication studies and marketing communication.

The Murrow College eventually eliminated majors in the communication studies sequence, as I had recommended in my 7-Step

Plan. All seven communication studies faculty eventually took jobs at other universities or left the College, including the professor who ironically commented after the Murrow School was converted into a College, "I suppose we should be careful of what we ask for, because we might just get it." The Murrow School still offers degrees in print and broadcast journalism, advertising and strategic communication (public relations).

The Murrow program is no longer poor. As of this writing, the college employs nearly twice as many full-time faculty as it did when it was a School, and the number of staff is about eight times greater. However, the mass communication programs still are not nationally accredited, which was the single most important recommendation of my 7-Step Plan.

Here's a brief update on my key adversaries:

- UW-RF journalism chair J. Michael Norman retired in 2003 and died in 2021 at age 74.
- UW-RF Chancellor Gary A. Thibodeau retired in 2000.
- WSU President Elson Floyd died of complications from colon cancer in 2015.
- WSU Provost Warwick Bayly stepped down from his administrative position in 2013 and continues to teach in the College of Veterinary Medicine.
- WSU Vice Provost Francis McSweeney retired in 2017.
- WSU Dean Erich Lear died of cancer in 2015.
- WSU Murrow Interim Dean Erica Austin continues to teach in the Murrow program.
- WSU Murrow Dean Lawrence Pintak's contract as dean was not renewed, but he remains on the faculty of the Murrow College.

Alex Tan, my old boss at WSU, retired in 2025.

Judy Endejan, my attorney, opened her own law practice in Mukilteo, Washington, near Seattle, and retired in 2024.

My former editor Dick Carson retired from his position as editorial editor of the *Columbus Dispatch* and now lives in an assisted living facility where he continues to tell lots of stories.

Sue Nichols, my undergraduate mentor, retired and worked as a docent in Toledo. She died in 2022 after a very interesting and happy life.

Phillip J. Tichenor, my Ph.D. advisor who helped create the knowledge gap hypothesis, died in 2025. He was 93.

* * * * *

Lee Ann, Theresa, Homer (our Maltese-mix dog) and I moved to north central Phoenix in the summer of 2014 after I purchased a modest three-bedroom home. I spent the first couple of years fixing it up.

Lee Ann entered high school and was valedictorian of her graduating class of three-hundred-and-four. She qualified for a full-ride scholarship to the University of Arizona, where she earned bachelor's and master's degrees in statistics, sociology, and education. She teaches high school math. I'm very proud of her.

Theresa worked at a mental health facility in Phoenix for five years before moving back to Spokane to be closer to her family. She and Lee Ann are close and continue to see each other. I appreciate the support she gave me through the ordeal at WSU.

On Saturday mornings, I teach a college-level introduction-to-sociology course at Glendale Community College near Phoenix for high school students from families who have limited financial resources. I own and manage two rental properties and continue to write books and commentaries about Age of Enlightenment ideals, especially growing wealth gaps and their deleterious effects on democracy. I took up the guitar last year. "Waiting on the World to Change" by John Mayer is one of my favorite songs.

Appendix A
FOREWORD FROM THE ORIGINAL EDITION
(FIRST THREE PAGES)

By Gary D. Rhoades*

On September 30, 2010, I received an e-mail from Washington State University professor David Demers, who informed me that WSU administrators had forced as many as ten tenured faculty to resign because they allegedly received unsatisfactory performance ratings in two or three post-tenure annual reviews.

The forced terminations came to light during a deposition conducted earlier that day as part of Demers's 2009 free speech lawsuit against WSU (*Demers v. Austin*). At the time, I was general secretary of the American Association of University Professors. I copied two AAUP staff members on the e-mail, who later examined the policy and informed Demers and me that the firings appeared to violate AAUP standards.

Using annual reviews to terminate tenured faculty makes it easier to fire faculty who oppose administrators' policies and actions. In fact, WSU administrators were using their termination policy to build a case to fire Demers, because, according to the lawsuit, they didn't like the 7-Step Plan he had created in 2007 to improve the quality of his academic unit, the Edward R. Murrow School (now a college) of

---

*Gary D. Rhoades served as general secretary of the American Association of University Professors from 2009-2011, when *Demers v. Austin* was filed in federal district court in Spokane, Washington. Rhoades is a professor of educational policy studies and practice at the University of Arizona. This reprint includes only the first

Communication.

Demers's case illustrates that meaningful shared governance in colleges and universities depends upon the First Amendment right of free speech. That is a core analytical point of this compelling social memoir.

Adventures of a Quixotic Professor also probes the systemic forces of bureaucracy and patterns of faculty co-optation and complicity that undermine, violate, and fail to defend the Enlightenment ideal of free speech. Indeed, the *Demers v. Austin* Ninth Circuit Court of Appeals ruling offers a counterpoint to *Garcetti v. Ceballos* (2006), a U.S. Supreme Court decision that deprived public employees of free speech rights on the job. Some public universities in forty-one states still invoke that decision to discipline and/or terminate faculty who have been critical of their administrations.

The *Demers* ruling established that faculty speech related to scholarship or teaching is covered by the First Amendment in public universities and colleges. The ruling also applies to K–12 faculty, but it covers only the nine Western states that make up the Ninth Circuit. The ruling does not protect faculty or teachers who work in private and proprietary educational institutions. The Ninth Circuit declared that professors as academic citizens may speak in the course of their duties about institutional matters openly and without fear of retaliation.

Remarkably, Washington State University invoked *Garcetti v Ceballos* — contrary to the university's own written policy embracing academic freedom and free speech rights — arguing that Demers's speech, articulated in the course of his duties, was not protected by the First Amendment. Even more remarkably, the WSU Faculty Senate did not come to Demers's defense.

Demers's book unabashedly offers an academic morality play embedded in the individualism of the Enlightenment Project, as he calls it, but embodied in the pre-Enlightenment character and idealism of Miguel Cervantes's heroic errant knight, Don Quixote. Demers offers a call to action for individuals to "do the right thing" (with a nod to Spike Lee). By that, he means that individuals should take on universities (and other powerful institutions) that deny them basic rights and thereby do them and academia harm. Throughout and in closing his book, Demers provides analysis and advice to individuals if they take on their universities. The tribulations and costs are high and are clearly laid out and detailed. Ultimately, though, Demers is a hopeful idealist, closing his book with this line: "I still believe one person can make a difference. Quixotic, I know."

As someone who has studied and worked in various ways and venues to support meaningful shared governance and an independent voice for employees in academe, I, for one, am grateful to Demers for his hopeful idealism, and for his commitment and work culminating in the Court of Appeals decision. Indeed, all in academe should be as well, for his successful case defends a fundamental right that is at the core of higher education through meaningful shared governance: debate, challenge, and calling of higher education institutions to their publicly expressed values. ...

Appendix B

RESPONSE FROM OFFICIALS CITED IN THIS BOOK

Response from Warwick Bayly, former WSU Provost

Thank you for the opportunity to review the pre-publication draft of *The 2 Gauntlets* by David Demers. For the record, the "facts" described by Dr Demers and attributed to interactions involving me, differ substantially from my recollections, especially with respect to the events that led to the series of meetings he describes.

Sincerely,
Warwick Bayly
Professor, Equine Medicine
Dep't Vet Clin Sciences
Washington State University
PO Box 646610
Pullman, WA 99164-6610

INDEX

D

E

F

G

H

I

J

K

L

M

N

O

P

Q

R

S

T

U

V

W

Z

Acknowledgments

This memoir is a David-and-Goliath story, but the heroes are my elementary and high school teachers and college professors, who taught me the importance of moral principles, free speech, democracy, civil liberties, and other Age of Enlightenment ideals. I list them on the dedication page.

Many relatives, friends, colleagues, former teachers, students and employers played an active or indirect role in the production of this book. I am most grateful to *Lee Ann*, my daughter, for her love and support; my father, *Hector*, who taught me not to accept authority at face value; *Dick Carson*, who nurtured my early career as a newspaper reporter and edited earlier drafts of this manuscript; *Judy Endejan*, my attorney, for believing that my free-speech case at WSU was worthy of a good fight; *Igor Klyukanov*, a good friend and professor of communication studies at Eastern Washington University, who gave valuable counsel during my ordeal at WSU; the late *Sue Nichols*, my mentor and former undergraduate journalism professor, who infused in me a deep appreciation for the profession of journalism and its ideals; *Mona Pearce*, who stood by me during the controversy at the University of Wisconsin–River Falls and continues to be a good friend; *Patrice Peterson*, who boldly defended me when my colleagues were complicit; *Liz Prouty*, who edited the unabridged edition of this book; *Gary Rhoades*, past general secretary of the American Association of University Professors, for listening to my concerns and for promoting the cause of academic freedom; *Joseph Russomanno*, professor emeritus of Arizona State University, who penned the gracious foreword to this book; Sibel85 at Fiverr, who proofed the final draft; *Theresa Stimson*, who provided unwavering support and good advice during the ordeal at WSU; the late *Phillip J. Tichenor*, my Ph.D.

adviser, an astute observer of social processes; and *Kenneth Westhues*, a professor emeritus of sociology at the University of Waterloo, Canada, who provided constructive feedback about the free-speech dispute at WSU and often predicted well in advance many of the events that unfolded.

I also thank, in alphabetical order, the following people who read or edited portions of the manuscript or provided advice and support during or after the lawsuits: the late Ridge Anderson, Kristina Bialaszewski, Helene Cahill, the late Hazel Dicken-Garcia, the late Simon Dinitz, Karen and Paul Lindholdt, the late Richard Lundman; John Nolan, Trudy Patterson, David Perlmutter, Laura Perry, the late Jan Polek, the late Dan Robison, Kathy Kerchner Roeske, Mike Scantlin, John Schulz, Joseph E. Scott, Galina Sinekopova, Alex Tan, and Carolyn Walker.

I am also indebted to the American Association of University Professors and the Thomas Jefferson Center for the Protection of Free Expression for coauthoring an amici curiae brief submitted to the Ninth Circuit U.S. Court of Appeals 2012 in support of my case; to the Foundation for Individual Rights in Education (TheFIRE.org), which provided news coverage of the lawsuit as well as financial support so that I could attend and present a paper at its convention in Dallas in 2017; to the Frankenmuth James E. Wickson Library, which provided free access to *Frankenmuth News* archives; and to the staff at Kevin Anderson & Associates, who edited portions of this manuscript and offered encouraging words of support.

I also appreciate the thousands of students who took my classes through the years. I hope they learned as much from me as I from them.

ABOUT THE AUTHOR

David Demers worked as a newspaper reporter, market research analyst, and journalism and mass media sociology professor for four decades before embarking on a full-time writing career. He is author or editor of two dozen books, including *The Ivory Tower of Babel: Why the Social Sciences Are Failing to Live Up to Their Promises* (New York: Algora, 2011); *History and Future of Mass Media: An Integrated Perspective* (Cresskill, NJ: Hampton Press, 2007); and *The Menace of the Corporate Newspaper: Fact or Fiction?* (Ames: Iowa State University Press, 1996).

In the 1970s, he earned a bachelor's degree in journalism from Central Michigan University and worked as a newspaper reporter in Michigan, where he earned two statewide awards for investigative reporting. During the early 1980s, he earned master's degrees in journalism and sociology from The Ohio State University and afterward worked as a senior research analyst for a national marketing research company. In 1992, he graduated with a Ph.D. in mass communication from the University of Minnesota.

Demers's research specialties include organizational structure, social systems theory, and mass media law. His research has garnered five national scholarly paper awards. In 2010, the Society for Collegiate Journalists honored Demers with the Louis Ingelhart Freedom of Expression Award, which is given to individuals who contribute to freedom of expression at the risk of personal and/or professional cost.

He is founding editor of *Mass Communication & Society* and also founded and directed the nonprofit Center for Global Media Studies and Marquette Books LLC, a private company that has published more than one-hundred-seventy academic and trade titles. Demers lives in Phoenix with his trustworthy, guileless canine friend, Homer.

www.ingramcontent.com/pod-product-compliance
Lightning Source LLC
LaVergne TN
LVHW100253210926
848480LV00003B/915